MW01712665

KEN DANBY

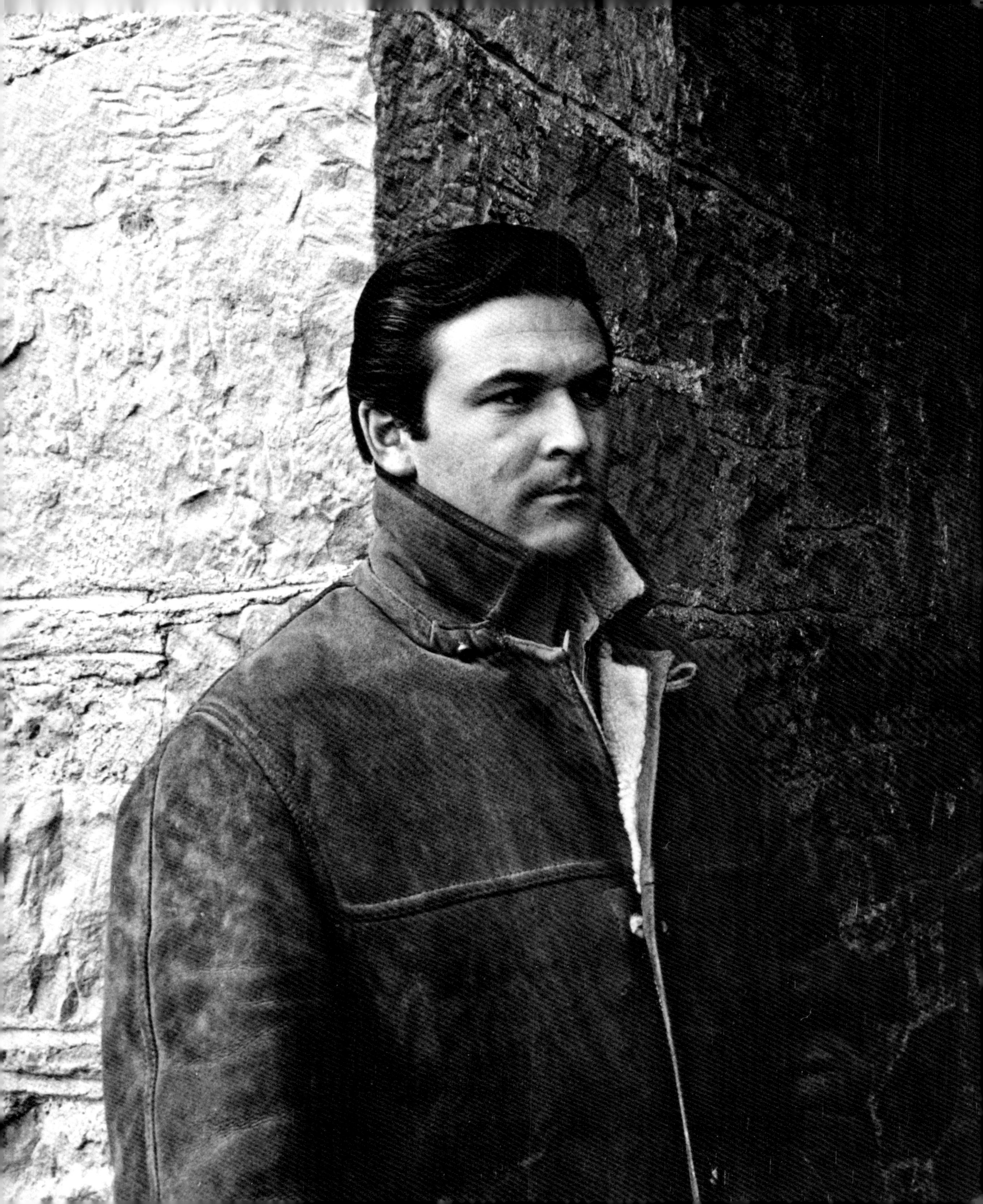

Beyond the Crease

KEN DANBY

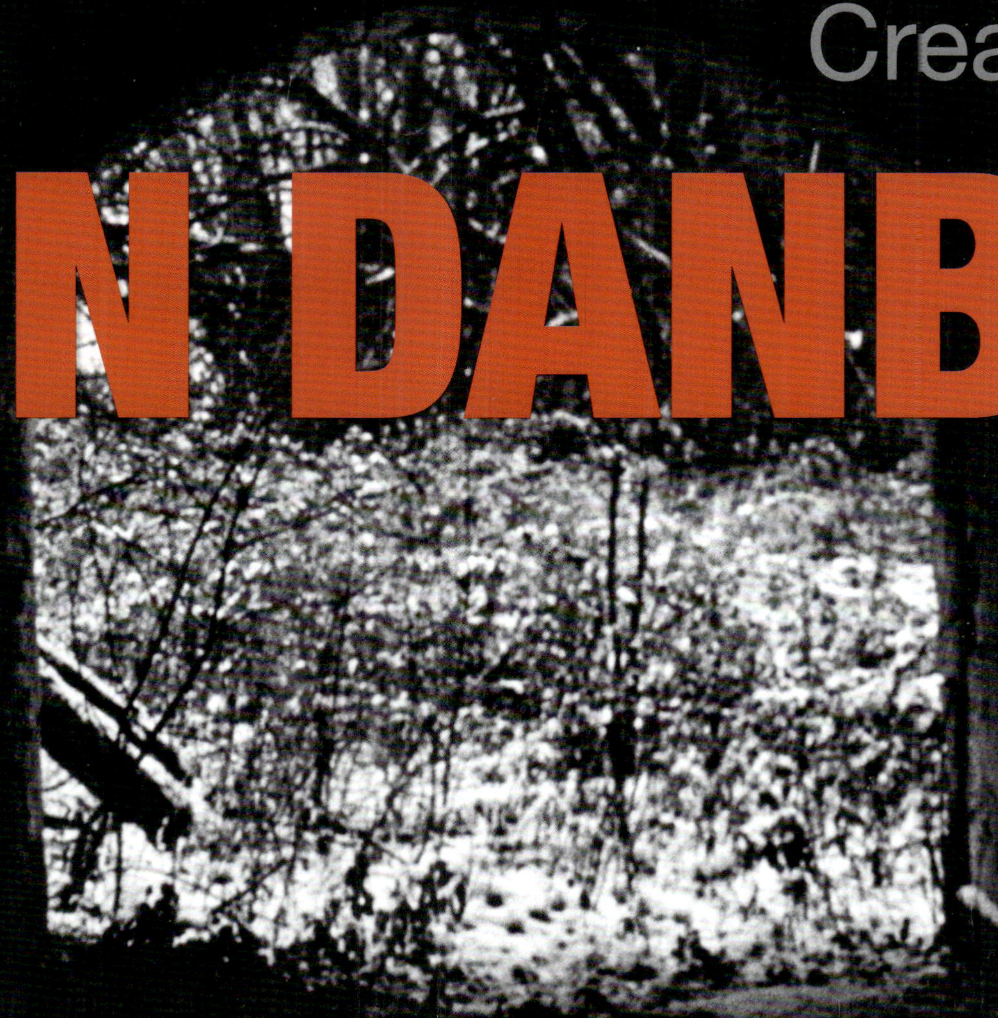

for Walter

overleaf: **Ken at the mill property, shortly after its purchase**, 1968
(photo: John Reeves)

Beyond the Crease

KEN DANBY

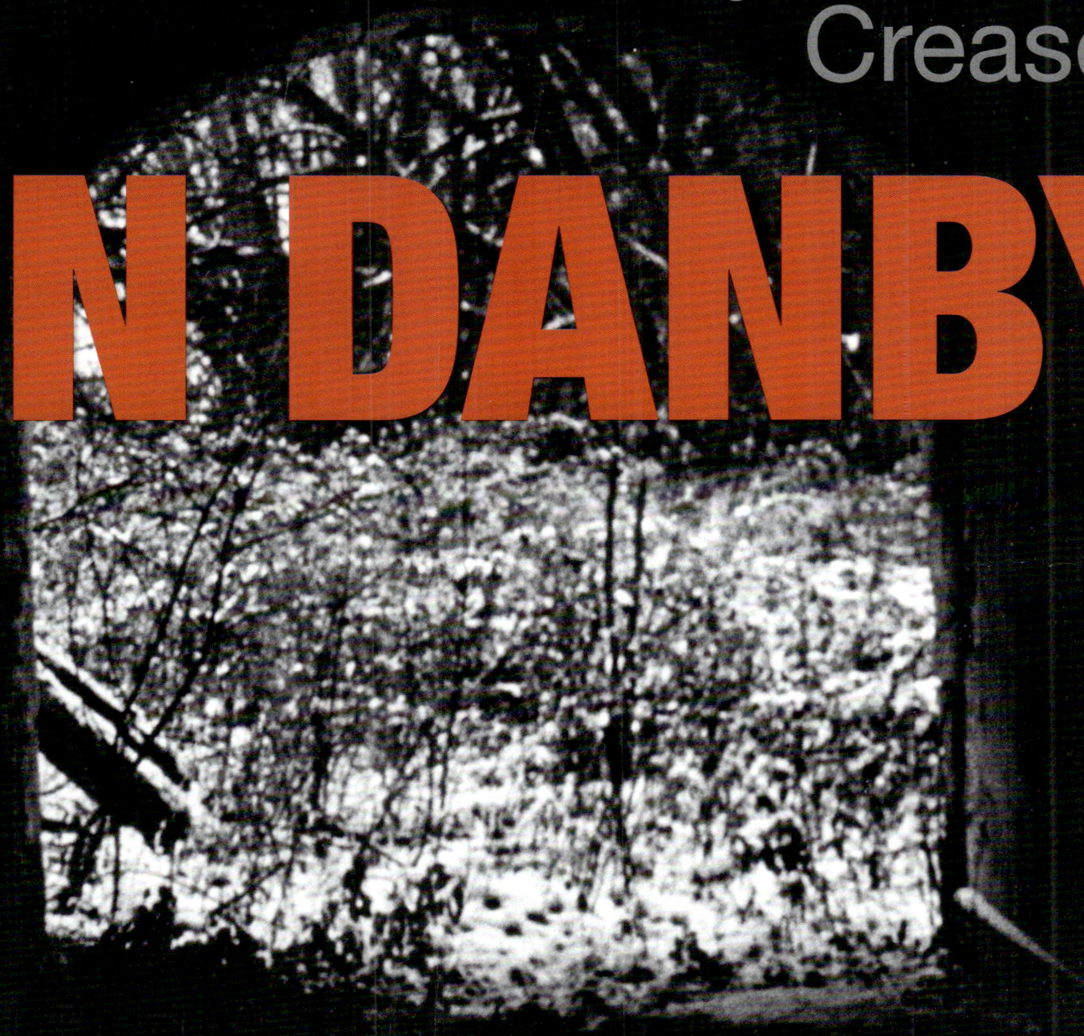

with essays by **Ihor Holubizky** and **Greg McKee**

Goose Lane Editions | Art Gallery of Hamilton

for Walter

overleaf: **Ken at the mill property, shortly after its purchase**, 1968
(photo: John Reeves)

Contents

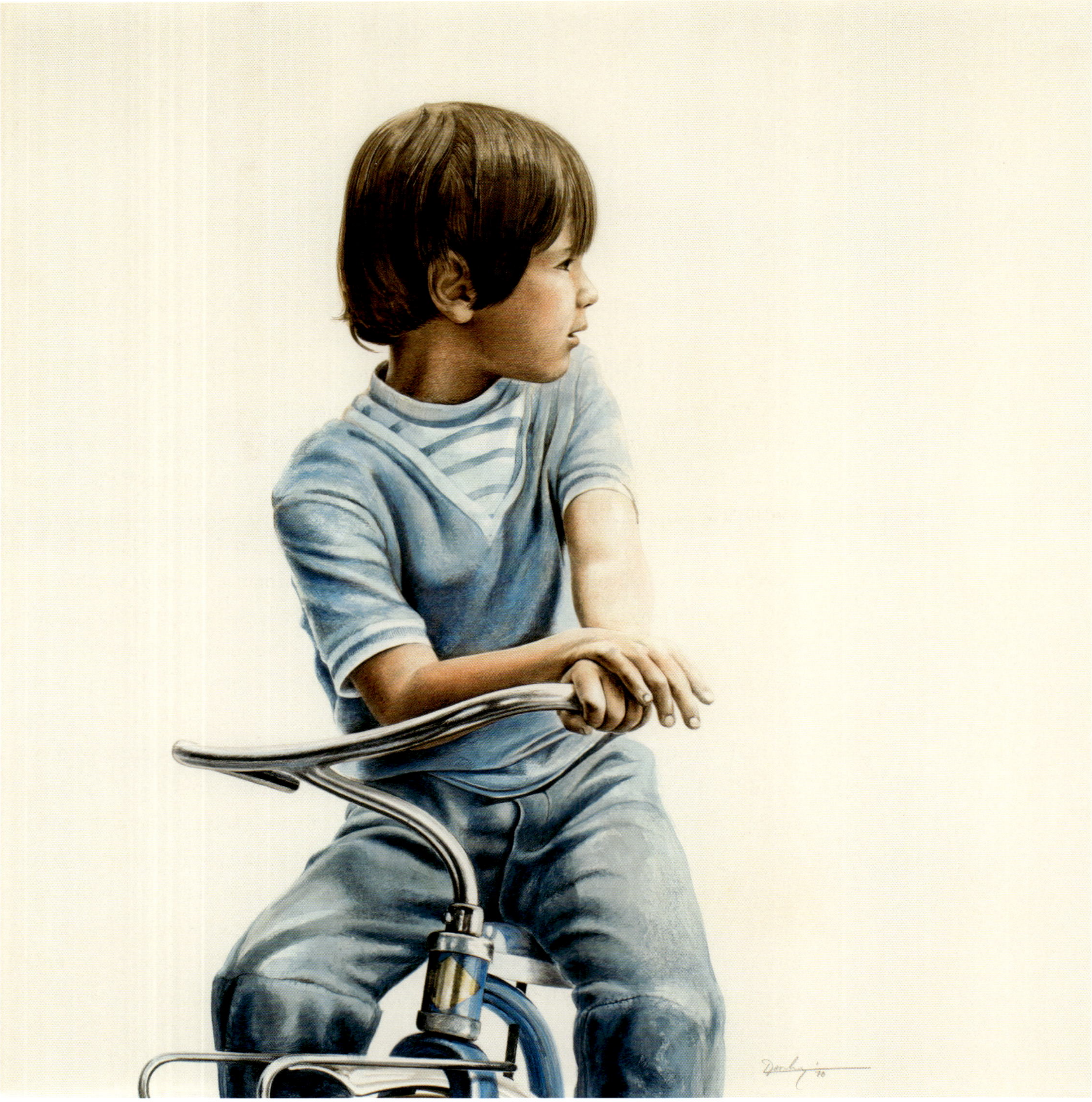

 Sean, 1970

Foreword

I believe that the role of an artist can be related to
that of an explorer and teacher, a teacher of seeing...
— Ken Danby

Ken Danby: Beyond the Crease brings together for the first time more than seventy significant works from private and public collections. The Art Gallery of Hamilton is especially pleased that we can hold this exhibition in tandem with the Guelph Civic Museum and deeply honoured, on the eve of the tenth anniversary of his death, to present and consider a remarkable Canadian artist from our region, who lent visual form to familiar Canadian icons and ideals that may be part of our nostalgic past but continue to inform and resonate.

Danby was born in Sault Ste. Marie, Ontario, and he was a resident of Guelph for forty years. The works in this exhibition connect the early intimate corners of southwestern Ontario to his now famous iconic sports, figurative, and bucolic images of the Canadian landscape — his uncompromising lens forever linked to the energy and ideas of his era. Nourished by his rural Ontario roots, his practice reflects a profound link to the broader Canadian landscape and psyche. A passionate Canadian, Danby began his story in the mid-twentieth century and it unfolded throughout the sixties, seventies, and latter decades, with important links to Toronto's emerging folk music scene of the sixties and seminal moments in Canadian sports. His work and life intersects deliberately with the fervent nationalism expressed in the music of Ian and Sylvia Tyson, Gordon Lightfoot, and American Pete Seeger, as well as the expansion of Canadian hockey in the 1960s, including the seminal 1972 series against the Soviet Union. Whether expressed through his passions for music, sports, or the land, his Canadianness — sense of place and unique lens — is also undoubtedly linked to the country's emerging confidence and nationalism of the period.

The many works comprising this exhibition reflect a broad and diverse creative practice. An accomplished painter, watercolourist, printmaker, and commercial artist, Danby, through his work, reveals the skills of a superior draughtsman and technician. His carefully structured compositions and complex technique are in evidence throughout his body of work; from his rigorous handling of the egg tempera medium to his printmaking process, he masterfully negotiated the descriptive and the evocative with quiet simplicity. While the watercolours invite intimacy and insight into the complex relationship between line, place, and space, the medium, as essayist Walter Benjamin notes, "stand[s] squarely between the two (painting and drawing). The only instance in which colour and line coincide … in which the pencil outlines are visible and the paint is put on transparently" (*Paintings, or Signs and Marks*, 1917). Danby's watercolours often reveal a vigour and immediacy that rank him among this past century's most important Canadian watercolourists.

The driving force behind this project began with my discovery of Ken Danby's manuscript, found carefully wrapped in brown kraft paper in a small cardboard paper box in his studio closet. Now several years following his death, the words provided new insights and perspectives on familiar works often reproduced but rarely seen. The decision to mine the past — from AGO former curator Mario Amaya's 1970-72 companion essays for the exhibitions *Realism(e)s* and *Ken Danby* to Australia's Patrick Hutchings's 1971 lecture, *Some Contemporary Realisms*, and AGH curator Andrew J. Oko's original 1980 interview with Danby, along with fresh interpretations from art historian Dr. Ihor Holubizky and Danby's long time studio manager and master printer, Greg McKee — reminds us of the shifting perspectives that history and the contemporary lens can bring to understanding the past in the present. While Holubizky probes "aesthetic realism" and Danby's ambiguity of perception, McKee invites understanding of the complex process and relationship of printmaking to the artist's practice. Both the exhibition and the publication have been a deeply collaborative effort and we are enormously grateful to the numerous contributions from many individuals and institutions. Our collaboration was strengthened by the support of the Danby family and Estate — Gillian Danby, Kim Smith, Ryan Danby, Noah Danby, and Julie Reid, with special gratitude to Ken's eldest son, filmmaker Sean Danby, the curator of our film component, tirelessly filming and editing new material for this project.

My heartfelt gratitude to all our colleagues and partners; exhibition projects and publications are often the culmination of many, and *Ken Danby: Beyond the Crease* is no exception. Both public and private collections have been generous and supportive with their loans including Canada's Sports Hall of Fame, the City of Sault Ste. Marie, the Confederation Centre Art Gallery, le Musée d'art contemporain de Montréal, the National Gallery of Canada, the National Portrait Gallery, Rennie Collection, Smithsonian Institution, Tim Horton Children's Foundation, and the Vancouver Art Gallery. The thoughtful work of Dr. Ihor Holubizky (McMaster University), Christine Braun, and Greg McKee has lent richness and depth to our understanding of Ken's legacy while the tireless work of AGH exhibition and publication coordinator, Lela Radisevic ensured we accomplished an important project within a challenging timeframe. I would also like to thank our publisher, Goose Lane Editions, for rising to the challenge and being steadfast. Three of our major regional sponsors — Laurie Davidson of RBC, Lou and Sabrina Celli of Grant Thornton, and Paul Sauve of Tim Hortons — joined us in supporting and presenting this project; their ongoing support and funding continues to be crucial to the AGH's exploration and presentation of significant artists from this region.

Shelley Falconer
President & CEO
Art Gallery of Hamilton

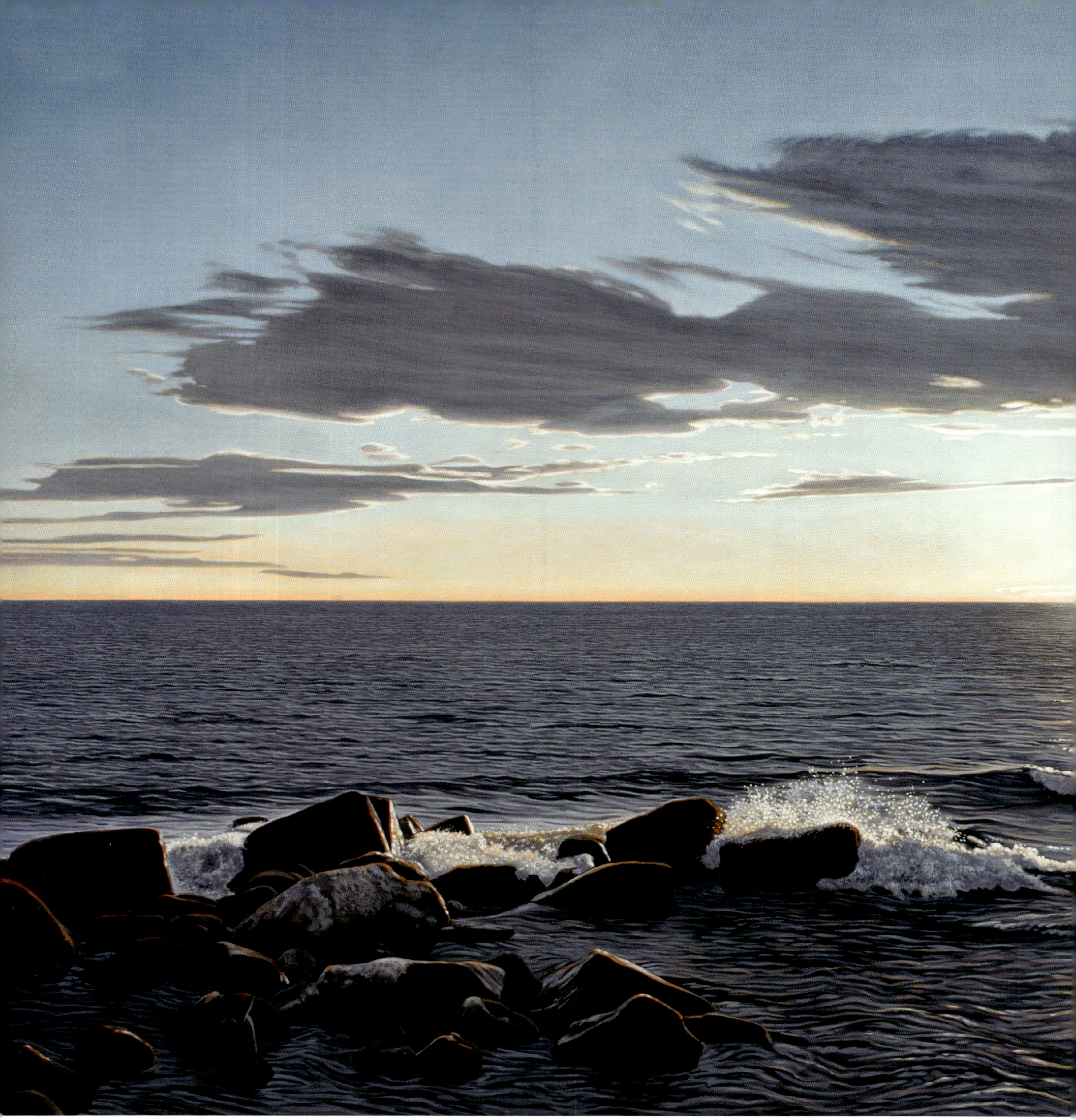

 Lake Superior, 2004

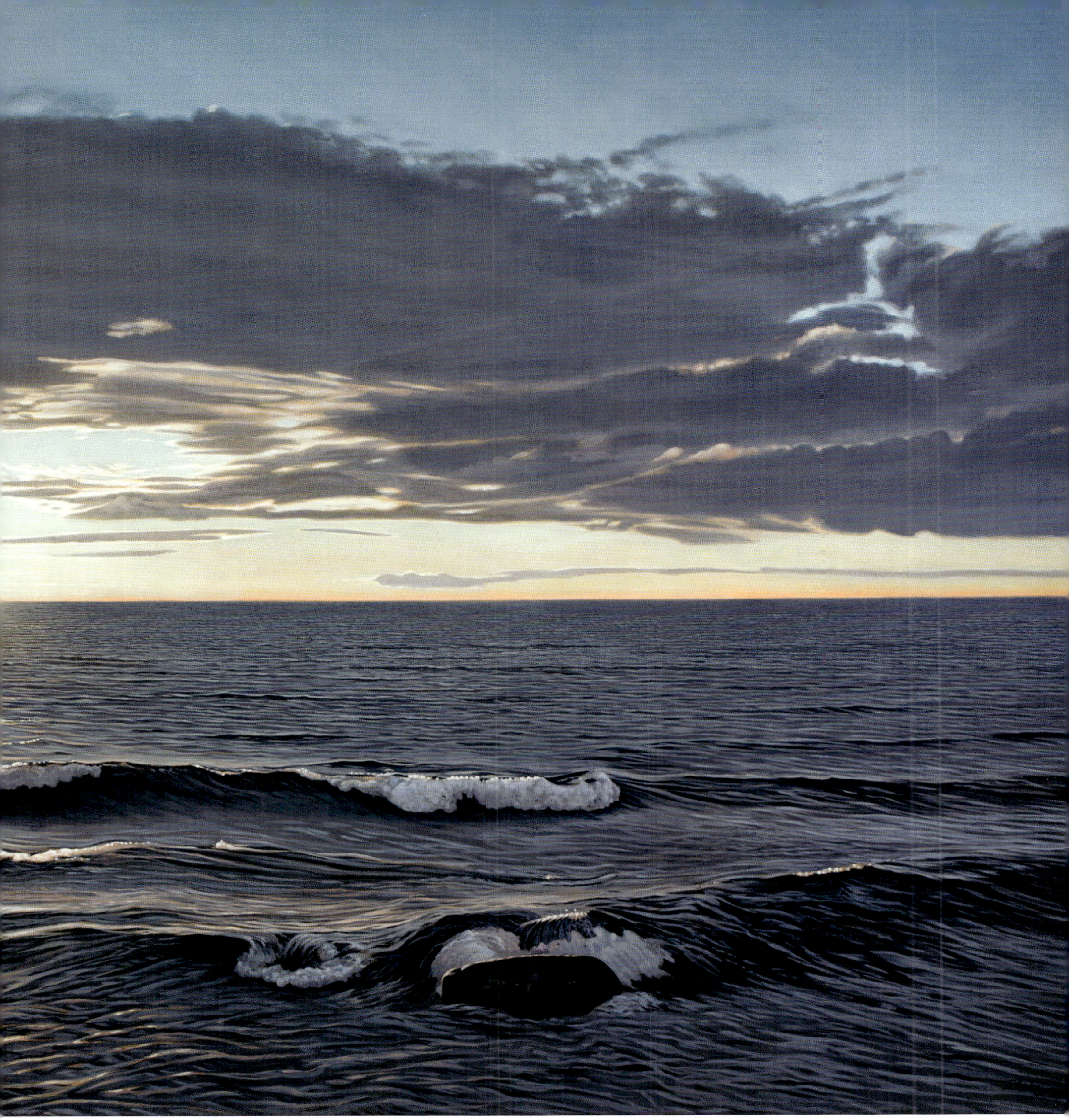

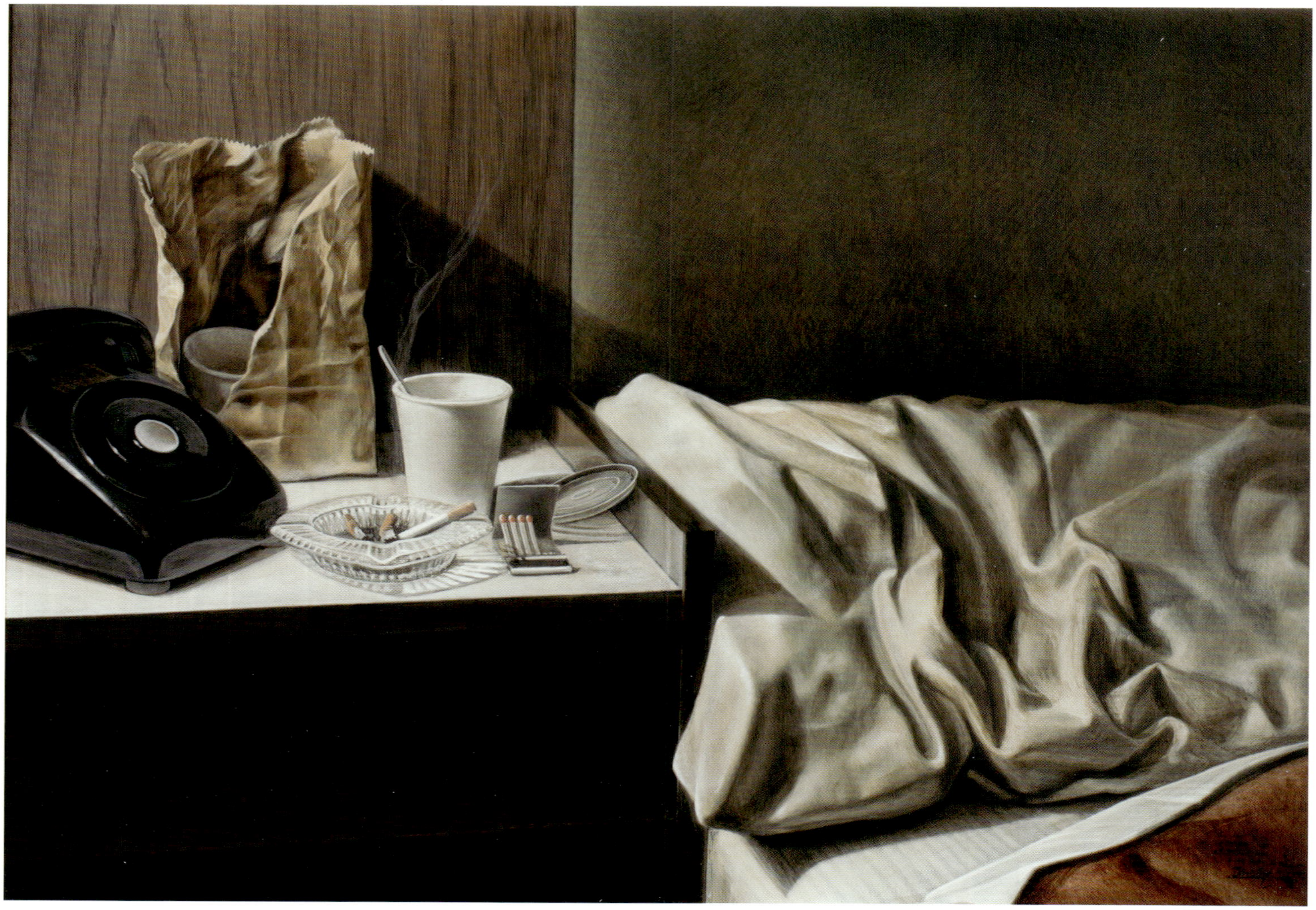

 Motel, 1971

Realism and the Real

A Preface, in Dialogue with Mario Amaya, and with Patrick Hutchings Eavesdropping

Ihor Holubizky

To call Ken Danby a realist is to state the obvious — realism describes what we can see depicted in his work and what we can register of the world around us. But as Mario Amaya, chief curator of the Art Gallery of Ontario from 1969 to 1972, wrote of the thirty-two-year-old Danby in 1972, we are likely to misunderstand his work within the shifting notions of what realism proposes and means to us.

> In the 20th century "realism" (…in its many manifest forms…) has on the whole come to mean an approach to painting recognizable things with more rather than less perceptual objectivity.… There has been much talk recently of a "revival" of realist painting [yet] one cannot "revive" something, but only renew its usefulness by adding to it a new point of view, a new statement, a fresh attitude to established conventions.
>
> This is what Ken Danby has done.[1]

The history of practiced art in the Western world has, without too much debate, moved towards a fidelity of representation — ways of verifying the visible world — although realism refers to a dominant movement from ca. 1840 to 1870-80 in Europe and the United States. American art historian and curator Linda Nochlin differentiates between realism in art and the long philosophical discussion of reality, from Plato onwards, but notes that realism is "closely connected to central philosophical issues" and cites the influential German philosopher Georg Hegel (1770-1831).[2] We can, however, nominate Albrecht Dürer (1471-1528) as a beginning, keeping in mind that it is a century-long journey before arriving at Johannes Vermeer. One is not more real than the other, nor can we say that there is an ever-refining approach to realism; chronologically, Pieter Bruegel the Elder sits between Dürer and Vermeer. Rather, these artists provide evidence that cultural expressions, explorations, and needs change over time. Perhaps the realist vision achieved a high point in the empiricism of John James Audubon's *The Birds of America* in the second and third decades of the nineteenth century, although Audubon is not highly regarded in the pantheon of fine art.[3]

In 1970, Amaya emphasized that "there is no one realist style as such [because] contemporary realism is an attitude of mind which wishes to express the visible world in a variety of ways, as description, as message, as symbol, as metaphor."[4] Earlier still, when examining the phenomenon of pop in art in 1965, and which he termed the "new super-realism," Amaya wrote:

> In dealing with "reality"... the new art throws open another vital question: what exactly is realism in art as compared to reality in life? The nineteenth-century *Salon* painter and academician believed realism to be the development of illusionistic art techniques from the Renaissance onward; the Pre-Raphaelite [Victorian artists] believed it to be truth to nature observed minutely.[5]

The camera has much to do with the shift in how realism can be expressed in the twentieth century. The photograph is an inclusive moment — all that is observable, or a captured happening. American Edward Weston, a member of Group f/64, formed in 1932, stated, "The camera should be used for a recording of life, for rendering the very substance and quintessence of the thing itself, whether it be polished steel or palpitating flesh."[6]

Weston's declaration positions the camera as a tool (to be used), whereas the brush for a painter does not *make* but provides the means for decisions *in the making* of a constructed image before it becomes a reality, distinct from the tweaking of a camera negative in the dark room to adjust the final tones of the photograph as output. Content can neither be added nor taken away; otherwise the photograph is a lie. It is no surprise that the so-called lying photograph is a prime tool for the propagandists and agents provocateurs of the twentieth and early twenty-first centuries. Granted, the commemorative painting in art's history did not need conform to what actually took place, as it was understood that such compositions were produced to ennoble the event and not to serve as a prime historical document.

Danby adjusted his paintings to generate a new and fresh point of view, as Amaya noted. Some early writers and critics described the work as hyper or magic realism, but these are journalistic terms to underscore the newness of something. Danby's work can be characterized by the absence of ambiguity, irony, or contradiction (which are hallmarks of the modern and contemporary age), yet open to interpretations. It is what the subject matter means to a viewer on a personal level. Danby's approach is as much reductivist as it is hyperrealist. *At the Crease*, one of his most recognized paintings, is an apt example. The goalie is in position alone, as the antagonist in a dramatic moment, with no indication of opposing, advancing players, nor of the crowd in the stands. There is, however, attention to detail, such as the accumulation of ice at the posts and sides of the net, and the mended and distressed netting. Such elements do not advance any sense of narrative because there is none. Nonetheless it is observed by Danby and included.[7] So too for *Pancho* and its tour de force droplets of water on the subject's rain slicker.[8]

We can apply and project subjective terms in speaking of such character-subjects: defiant, determined, and pensive. The same can be said of Danby's single figure black-and-white lithographs produced almost annually from 1965 to 1979 — but this is a parlour game of misplaced psychoanalysis.

Without hesitation, we can also say that Ken Danby is responsible for a handful of publically recognized images to which the term *iconic* is ascribed, although that term is relative.[9] Even in their most ambitious moment, artists may aim for something remarkable, but cannot *make the iconic*. When the iconic does happen, it is the result of an external cultural dynamic, which in turn does not conform to any single template. Consider paintings that fed the modern cult of nationalism: American Edward Hopper's *Nighthawks* (1942) and Grant Wood's *American Gothic* (1930). The former evokes mood, texture, and urban alienation, and the latter depicts the determined faces of the American heartland at the beginning of the Depression.[10] Such works activate the popular imagination. This, however, should not be mistaken for some version of a meritocracy — what is high or low, or middlebrow culture. In 1958, the Welsh academic

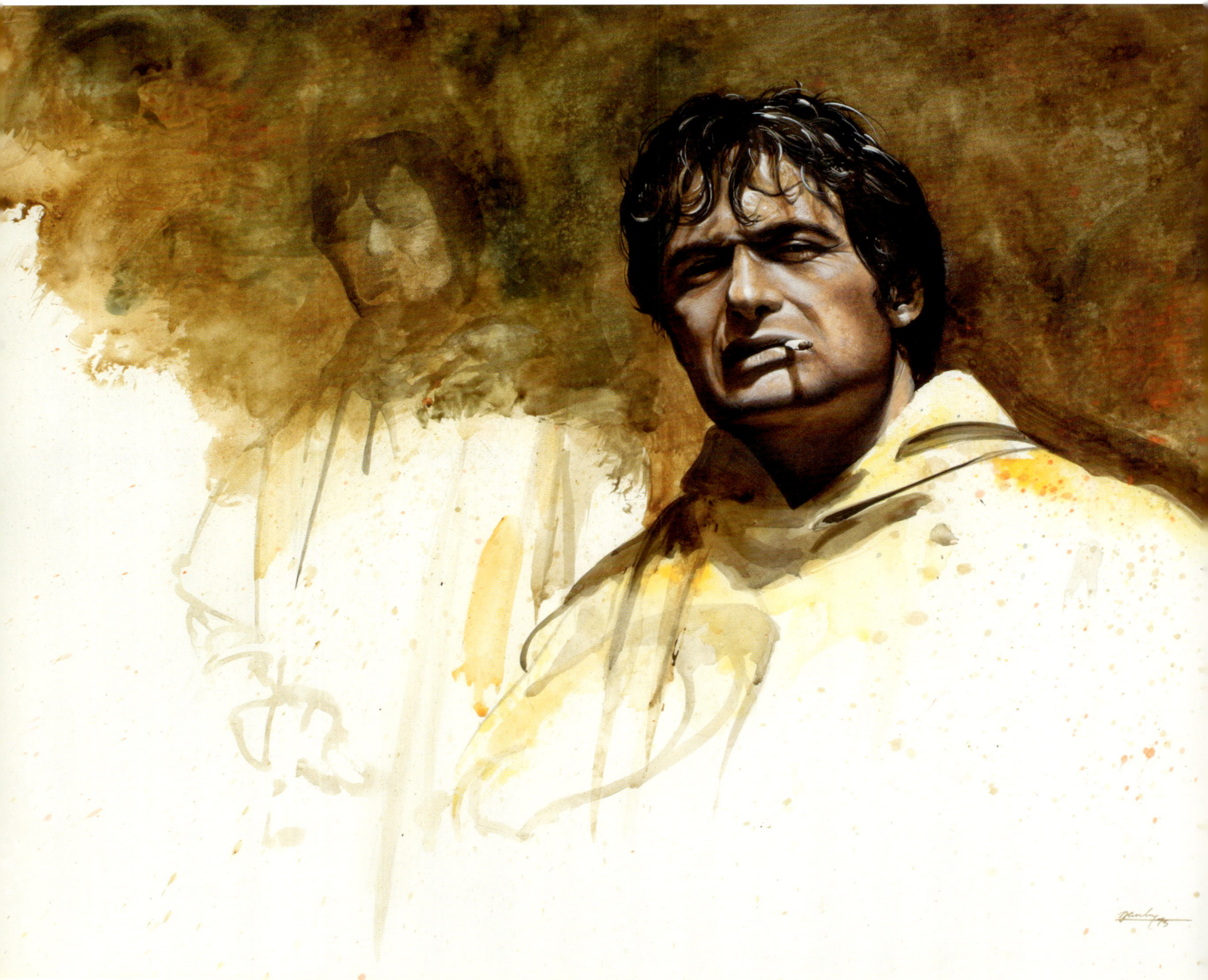

 Study for Pancho, 1973

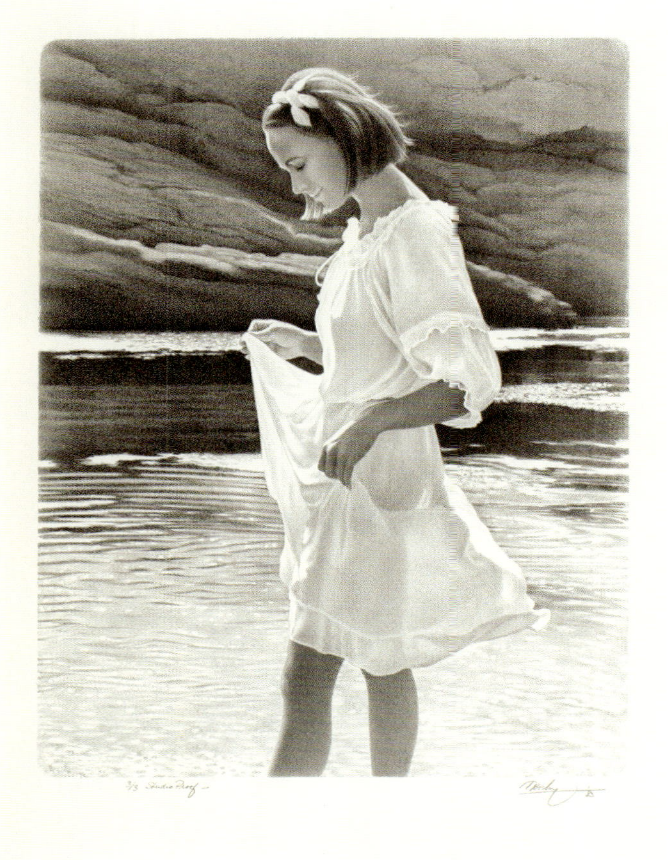

The Suncatcher, 1983

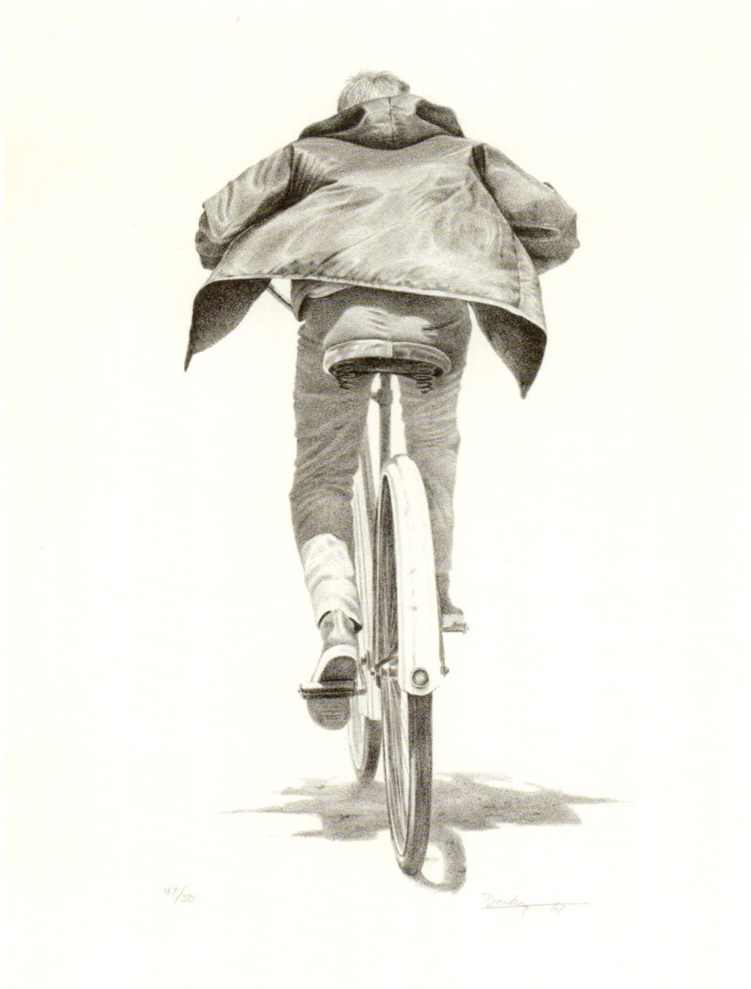

The Cyclist, 1967

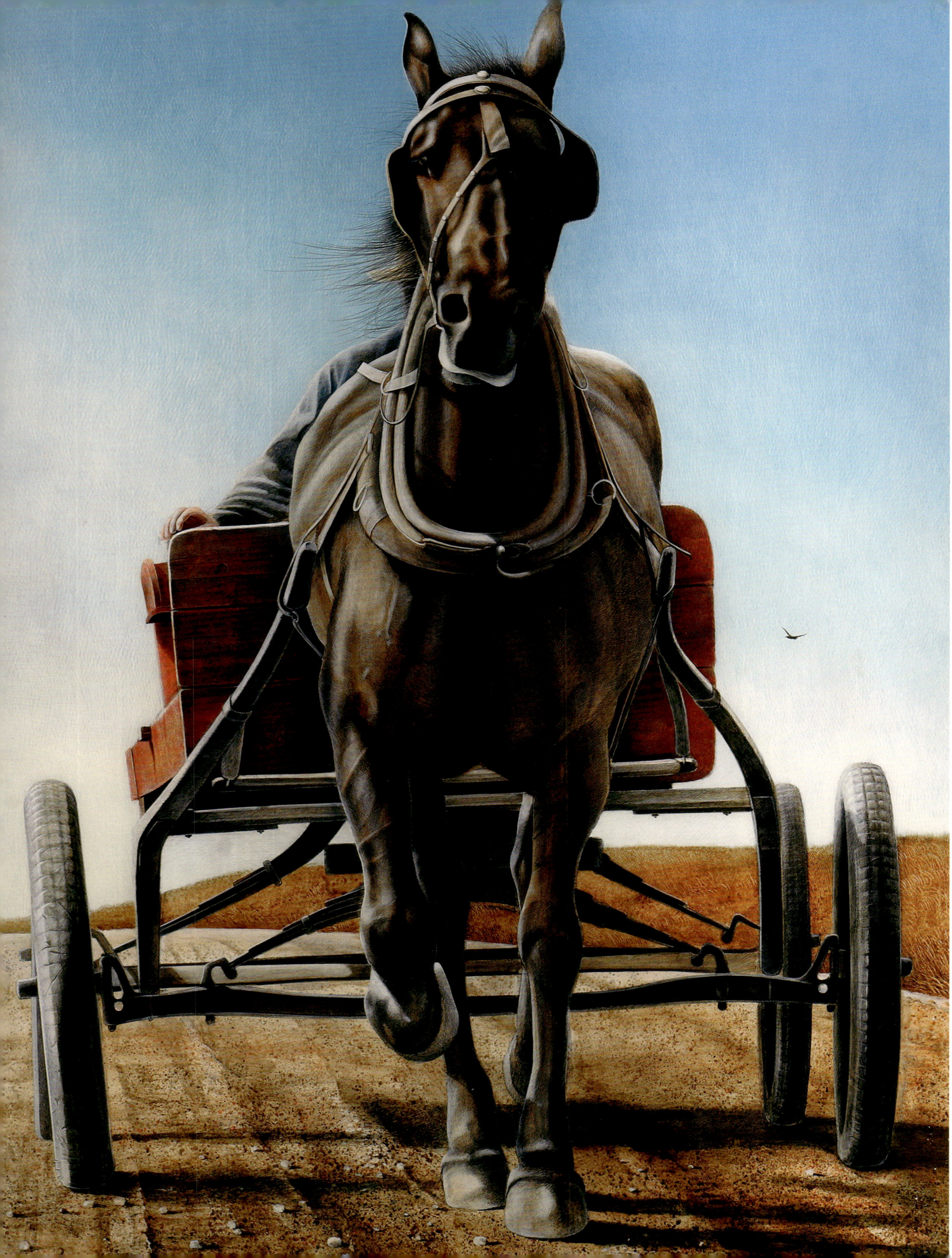

Raymond Williams proposed that "Culture is ordinary," but importantly, experience is tested in "the making of new observations, comparison, and meanings."[11]

As Amaya recognized, Danby's work appeared at a moment when realisms, including so-called photorealism, were in the air and debated, concurrent with critical debates about photography. American critic and artist Douglas Davis presented his lecture "Photography as Culture" in 1975, which, as with Williams's proposition, offers inclusiveness:

> I am contending that photography at its finest is a product of our culture, not a window on the culture. The photographic image should be read and judged exactly as we read and judge moments in life, if not art.[12]

Another characteristic of Danby's approach to painting is a stillness. The ordinary is ordinary yet made to feel palpable. Amaya wrote, "Danby proves [that] realism is more than just skilled labour capable of mirroring through precision-painting slices of real life that exist around us."[13] Accordingly, you don't have to be told what is happening in Danby's paintings. They simply are — a car abandoned in a wheat field, a girl sun bathing, a view into the windshield of a bus, a motorbike rider poised to enter the road. There is a stillness in Danby's *At the Crease* and *Pancho*, where nothing is happening and everything is seen. Other works do offer dynamic movement — *The Red Wagon, Trail,* and *Stampede* — although none are so far from stillness in their respective arrested moments. There is no meta-text, no drama, no cautionary tale. The ordinary is a truth that is only escapable if ignored.

Mario Amaya was the curator for the 1970 exhibition *Realism(e)s* and included Danby's *Pulling Out*. In his preface, he wrote:

> [Realism's] aim is not merely to describe, for that would be illustration. It attempts to state a point of view about recognizable reality as we know it, to interpret, to select, to inform, and to show not a substitute for words, but a parallel experience, and as such offers intellectual enjoyment as well as an emotional and tactile experience.[14]

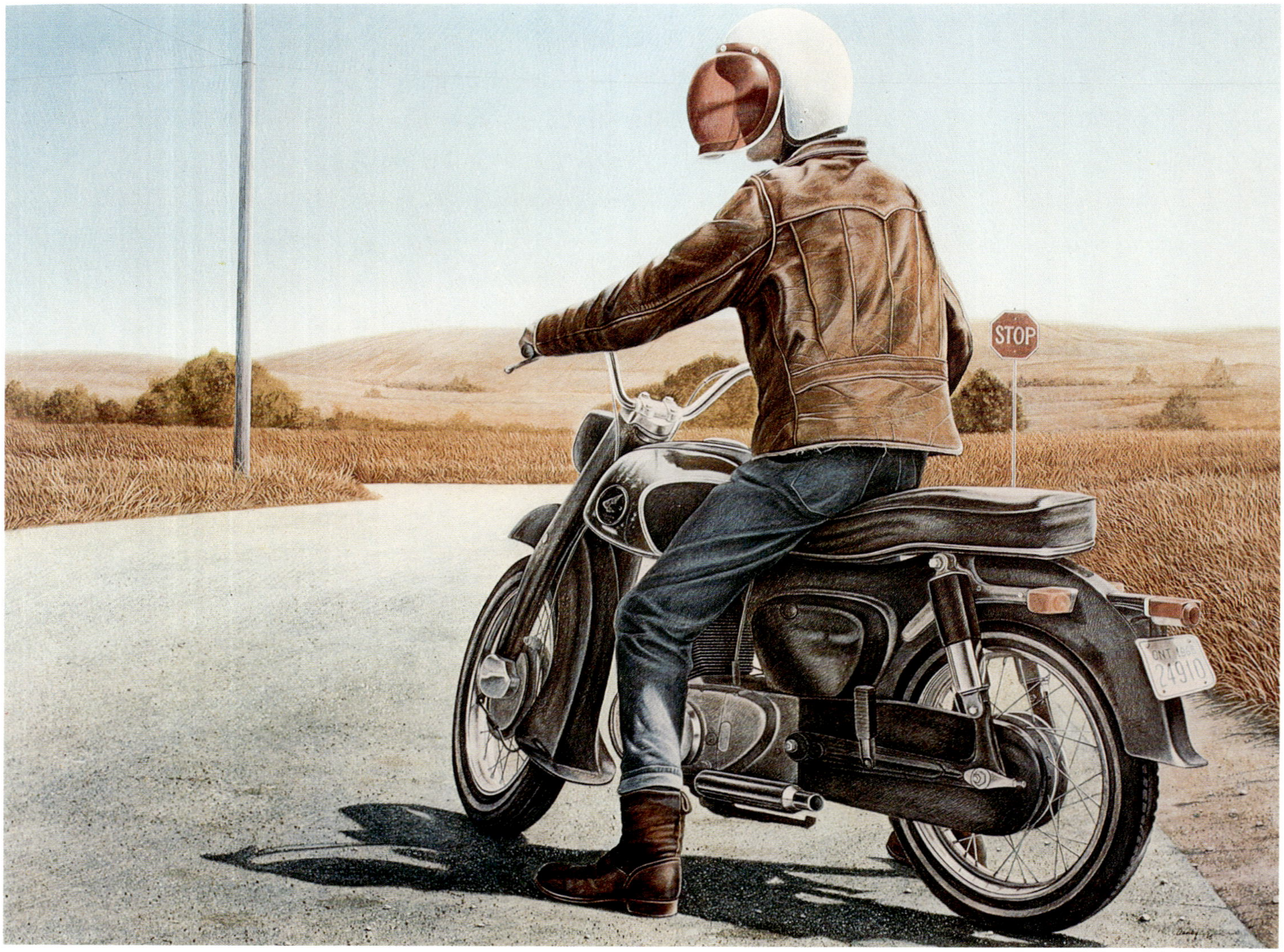

Linda Nochlin organized a formative exhibition titled *Realism Now*, mounted at Vassar College in 1968. She quoted French film-maker Jean-Luc Godard in her essay: "Style is just the outside of content and content the inside of style, like the outside and inside of the human body — both go together, they can't be separated."[15] Danby echoes this in his own commentary: "While the subject is ... the catalyst ... and [the] main focus, I want the work itself to become a synthesis of many elements ... light, colour, space, dimensions,

 Pulling Out, 1968

design, tone, texture, mood, tension... relative to my concept." He also elaborated on the challenges and pitfalls of "simply depicting" a subject.[16]

Australian academic Patrick Hutchings discussed the resurgence of realism in contemporary art in 1971, through an examination of the *Realism(e)s* exhibition, an eavesdropping through Amaya's selection:

> Here is our paradox — it is Danby who painted the *Easy Rider* picture,[17] *Pulling Out*, in the *Realism(e)s* exhibition. The nostalgia cracks; we are brought up face to face with a moment of our own time, in a hard and uncompromising image.[18]

Hutchings then commented on the Canadian scene:

> Contemporary Canadian realisms are all... a function of regionalism, and connoisseurs of the Canadian scene can place the landscapes very precisely.[19] But the regionalism, whilst it is resolutely provincial, is not restrictive. The painters are not mere topographers of their own landscapes, physical and sentimental: they have developed a vision which has a validity outside its own place.... A universal style of *quiddity*-painting [i.e. a "what it is" painting] comes out of small towns in Ontario, New Brunswick, and Newfoundland, but what comes out of the small towns is a big style. Ontological realism has a point to make; the provincials have a large vision.[20]

In his conclusion he stated, "contemporary art may — quite contingently — be nonrealistic: but realistic art, the imitation of the world, can always be contemporary. After all, the world is."[21]

This is a preface to the artist's own words to follow, Danby's reflections on life, art, culture, and society, but in his credo, published in 1984, he underscored what we speak of as the necessity of developing visual literacy: "We do not see with our eyes, but through them. The mind does the actual seeing, and it can only evaluate a visual experience according to its degree of visual awareness."[22]

NOTES

1 Mario Amaya, "Ken Danby," publication for a solo exhibition at William Zierler Inc. [gallery], (New York: 1972), n.p. It must be emphasized that (as he noted) Amaya was bringing the term "realism" into the twentieth century and contemporary time.

2 Linda Nochlin, *Realism* (London: Penguin Books, 1971), 13.

3 While today the adherence to a "pantheon" is in disrepute, it had a vigorous grip in the nineteenth century. A case in point is Paul Delaroche's *Hémicycle*, a twenty-seven metre-long mural completed for the École des Beaux-Arts in Paris in 1841, and which depicts the seventy-five "greatest artists of all time." The mural has its precedent and compositional framework in Raphael's mural *The School of Athens* (1509-11), depicting "all" the great Greek philosophers for the Apostolic Palace at the Vatican. Delaroche's choice of painters was his own, and reflects of prevailing taste and fashion in France. There were other such "tributes" done outside of France, each with a different cast of characters. See Francis Haskell, *Rediscoveries in Art* (Ithaca: Cornell University Press, 1976), 8-38.

4 Mario Amaya, *Realism(e)s* (co-organized by le Musée des beaux-arts de Montréal and the Art Gallery of Ontario, 1970), np.

5 Mario Amaya, *Pop as Art, A Survey of the New Super-Realism* (London: Studio Vista, 1965), 21.

6 http://edward-weston.com/edward-weston/. Retrieved 2 February 2016. Danby outlines his use of photography in the unpublished manuscript *Ken Danby: Closing the Millennium*, Danby Estate Archives (19 Feb 2002): 61-63.

7 Danby wrote that *At The Crease* was "a radical image and departure" for him. From Ken Danby untitled unpublished manuscript (Danby Estate Archives) "4/14/08": 114. Further citations as KD: UM. Danby also made note that when his dealer Walter Moos first saw it, it was with a "certain reservation." He then said, "Who would buy this?" Ibid., 113-14.

8 Danby wrote, "Pancho happily agreed to allow me to pour a bucket of water over his head every few minutes so that I could see the effects it produced." KD: UM "4/14/08": 118-19.

9 It should also be noted that *At The Crease* and *Pancho* came after Danby had already achieved public attention.

10 Danby listed the artists who had a significant impact on his approach to painting, a virtual checklist of the history of painting—his pantheon—from Leonardo da Vinci (Danby's "special favourite") to Edward Hopper, as well as twentieth century American abstract artists Franz Kline and Jackson Pollock. *Danby: Closing the Millennium*, 65. Danby also cites the influence of Norman Rockwell and N.C. Wyeth, the father of Andrew Wyeth, artists who do not rank highly in the canon of art history, in part perhaps because of their popular appeal. Danby's visit to the Andrew Wyeth exhibition at the Albright-Knox Art Gallery in 1962 has been noted many times as being an influential moment, and Danby recounts a visit to Wyeth's studio. KD: UM "3/17/08": 59. But to over-emphasize the Wyeth association is to diminish the broader view that Danby held. Danby also noted that his guide to painting "was and still is" *The Practice of Tempera Painting*, by Daniel V. Thompson, who cites the fifteenth century manuscript *The Craftsman's Handbook* by Cennino d'Andrea Cennini. KD: UM "3/17/08": 76.

11 Raymond Williams, "Culture is Ordinary," *The Everyday Life Reader*, ed. Ben Highmore (London: Routledge, 2002), 91-100, accessed December 27, 2015, http://artsites.ucsc.edu/faculty/Gustafson/FILM%20162.W10/readings/Williams.Ordinary.pdf

12 Douglas Davis, "Photography as Culture" in *Artculture: Essays on the Post-Modern* (New York: Harper & Row Publishers, 1977), 76. Danby used the camera and photographs as an aide-mémoire and compositional cue, but emphasized, "I rarely take a photograph that is interesting enough to replicate." *Ken Danby: Closing the Millennium*, 61-63. There are numerous photographic examples in the Danby Estate archives.

13 Amaya, "Ken Danby."

14 Amaya, *Realism(e)s*. The exhibition had a broad and wide perspective, and included the media-noted live cow orchestrated by Glenn Lewis and Michael Morris, and Joyce Wieland's text-quilts. Danby recounts Amaya's visit to his studio prior to the 1972 William Zierler exhibition: "After Mario's visit I seemed to gain incentive…which was rewarding enough." KD: UM "4/14/08": 107.

15 Linda Nochlin, *Realism Now*, reprinted in *Super Realism, A Critical Anthology*, ed. by Gregory Battcock (New York: E.P. Dutton & Co., Inc, 1975): 125.

16 *Danby: Closing the Millennium,* 65-66. I would propose that there is a cognitive process that "makes us pay attention" to the textural. The power of Albert Bierstadt's *Yosemite Valley* painting, 1868 (Collection, Oakland Museum of California), rests in the spectacle of light as it registers the vastness of land (or what the eighteenth century philosopher Immanuel Kant would term "God's work"). Effect, style, and subject come together in a way that presents a convincing experience through the work without ever needing to be there.

17 A reference to the 1969 landmark American counterculture "biker" film *Easy Rider*, co-written by and starring Peter Fonda and Dennis Hopper.

18 Patrick Hutchings, "Some contemporary realisms," *Concerning Contemporary Art: the Power Lectures 1968-1973*, ed. Bernard Smith (Oxford: Claredon Press, 1975), 117. Hutchings was a senior lecturer in philosophy at the University of Western Australia. Previously he had written on the work of Alex Colville for the National Gallery of Canada, Bulletin 8 (IV:2), 1966.

19 Although realism neither played out with the same vigour in Canada as it did in the United States and Europe, nor had the same historical roots in art, Danby's work did receive support and accolades. Toronto critic and art dealer Paul Duval championed Danby and others in several publications, including *High Realism in Canada* in 1974. In the Atlantic region there was the "Sackville school" — Alex Colville, who taught at Mount Allison University in Sackville, New Brunswick, from 1946 to 1963, was the progenitor for artists such as Christopher Pratt, Mary Pratt, Tom Forrestall, and D.P. Brown. Ontario regional artists include Jeremy Smith, Jack Chambers, and Hugh Mackenzie. A critical realism is evident in the work William Kurelek (Ontario) and Esther Warkov (Winnipeg), but forcefully presented as cautionary tales and the fantastic. Hutchings discussed Alex Colville and Jack Chambers at length in his Power Institute lecture.

20 Hutchings, 117.

21 Hutchings, 128. Linda Nochlin offers a resonant comment in her study of historical realism: "For the realist, horror — like beauty or reality itself — cannot be universalized: it is bound to a concrete situation at a given moment of time." Nochlin, 33.

22 Ken Danby, "The Artist's Credo," in Paul Duval, *Ken Danby: The New Decade* (Toronto: A Gallery Moos Book/Stoddart Publishing, 1984), 157.

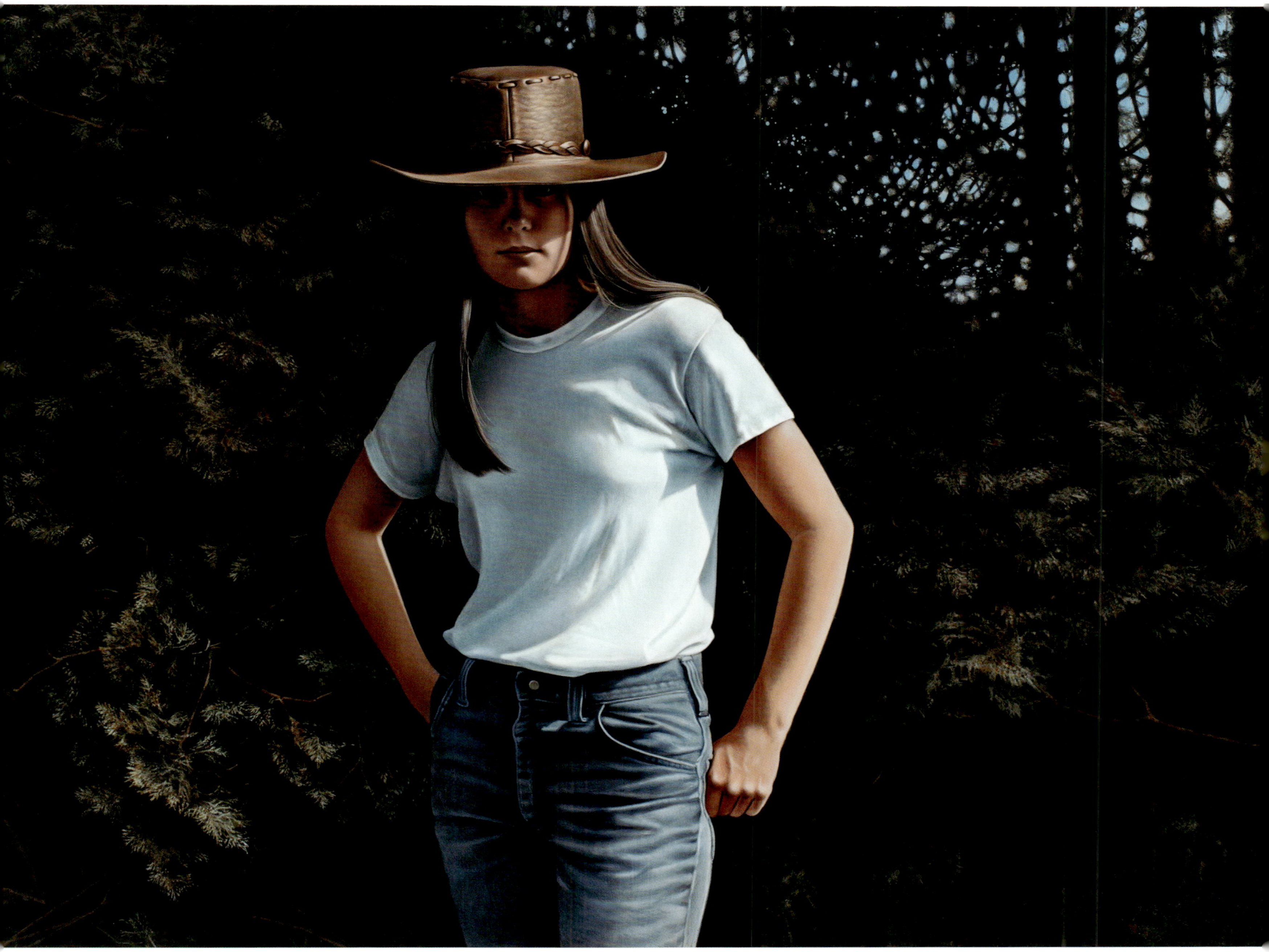

Leather Hat, 1975

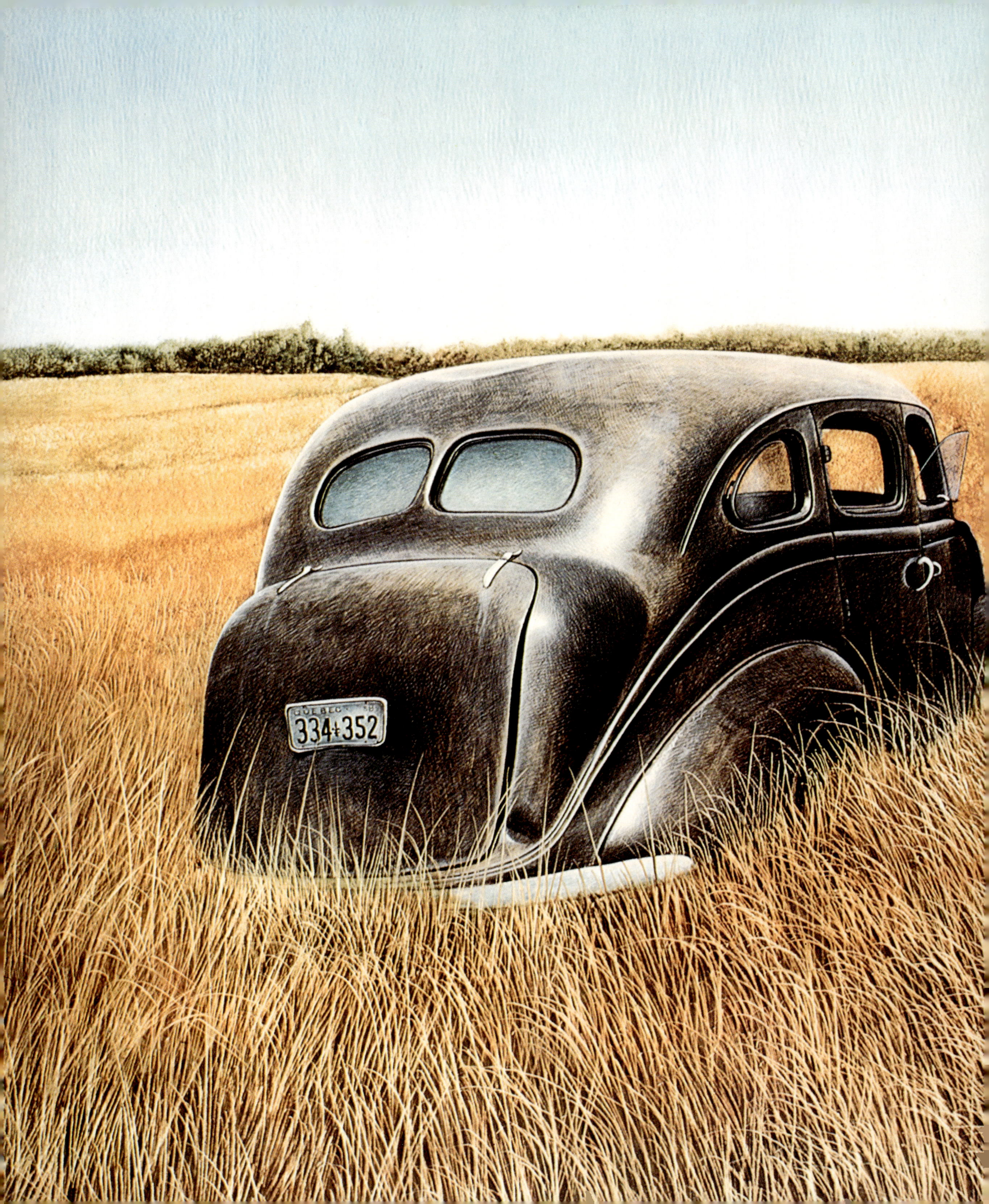
QUEBEC
334 352

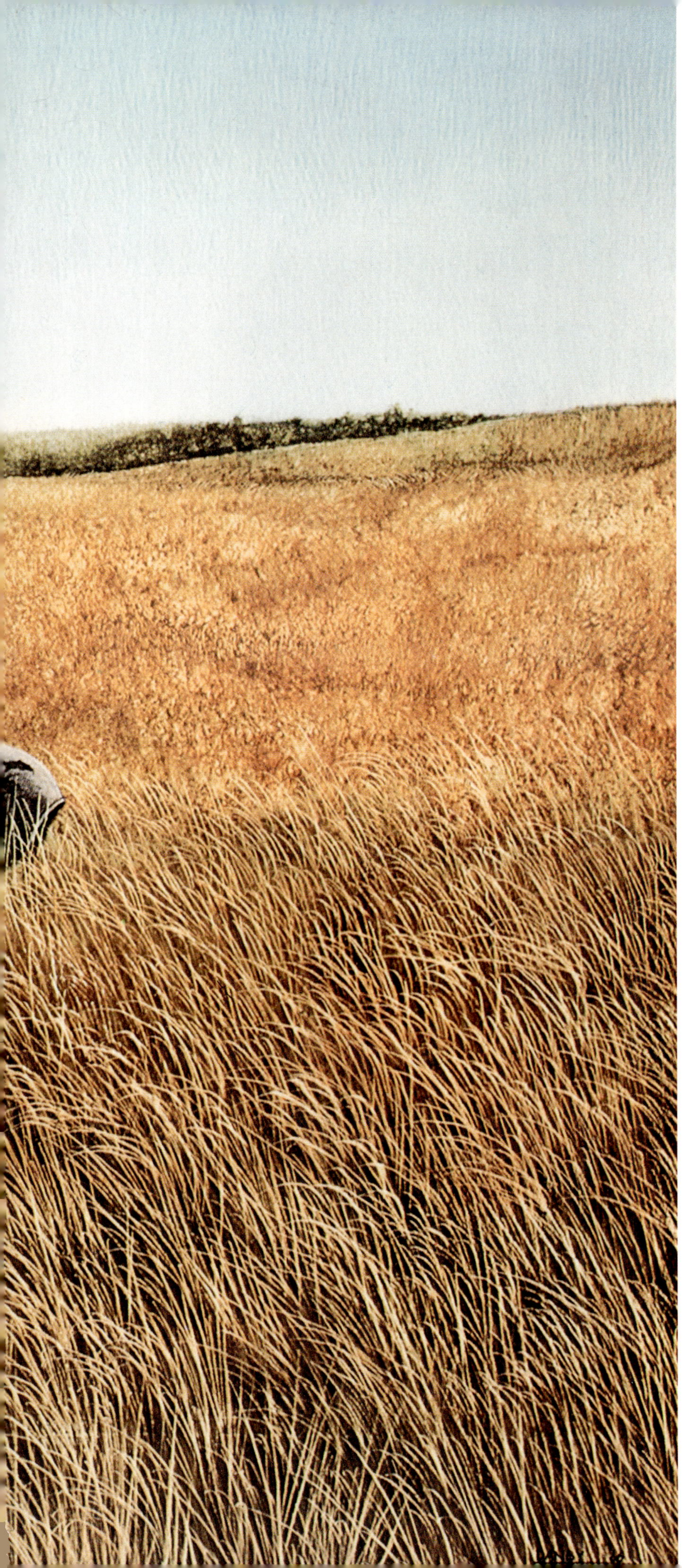

From the Summer of '38, 1966

overleaf: **Charter**, 1978

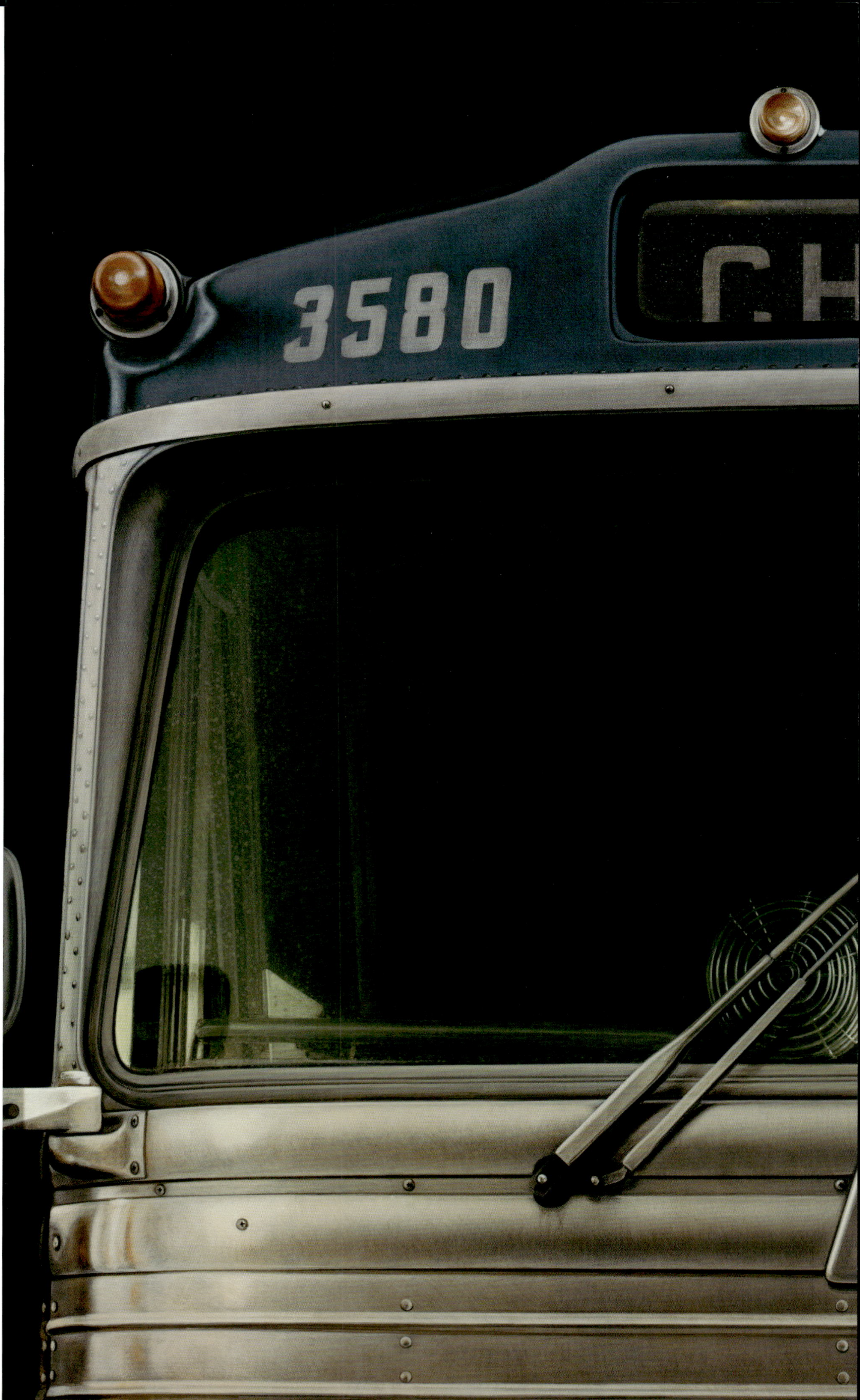

3580

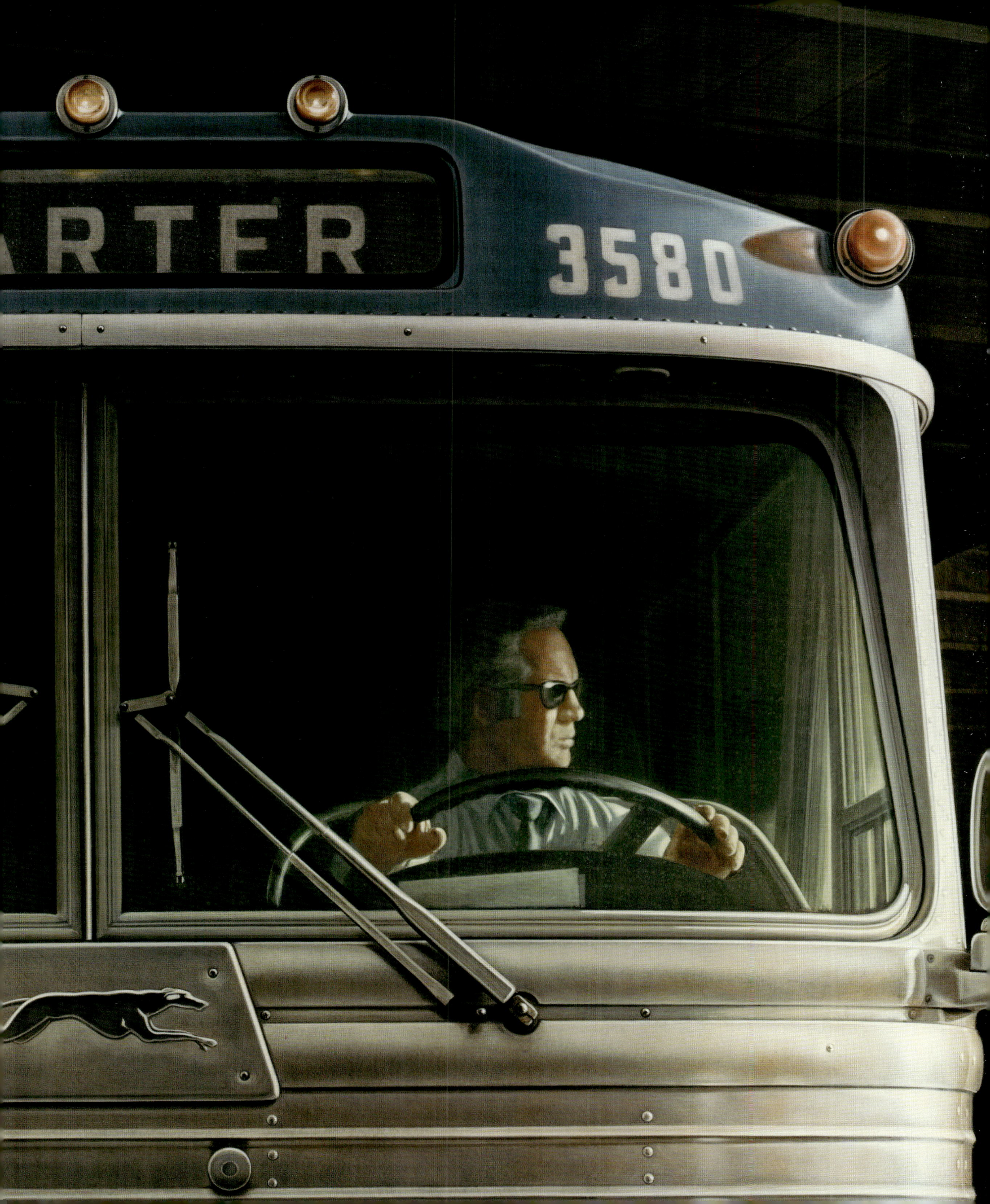
RTER
3580

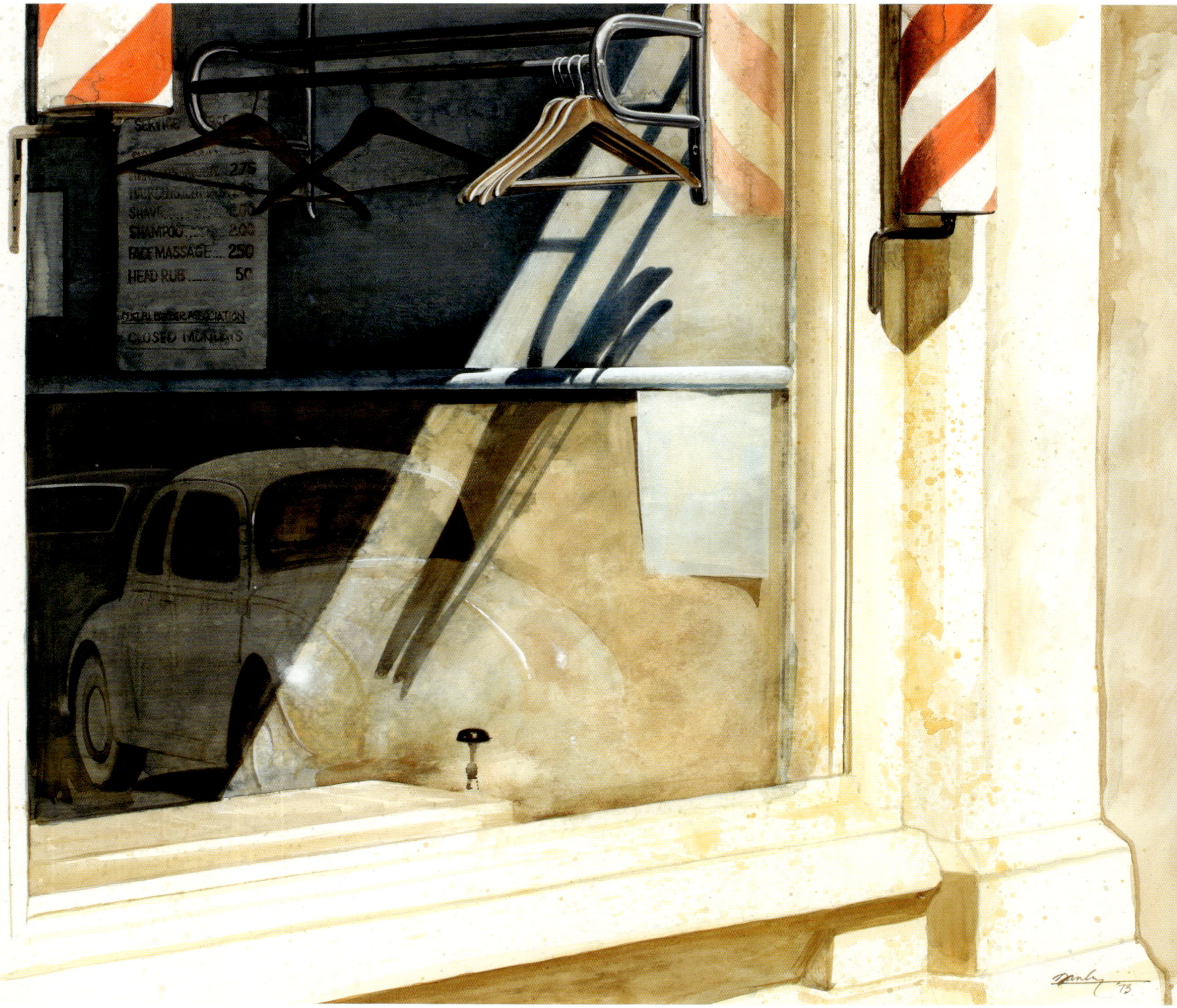

 Untitled (Barbershop), 1973

Ken Danby on the Artist's Life

1950s

Boyhood in Sault Ste. Marie

At the tender age of ten years, I learned from a guidance teacher that there were schools where one could learn to be an artist. I immediately determined that one day I would attend such a school, and upon returning home from my grade-six class that day I advised my parents of this decision. I'm sure their reaction was probably along the lines of "Oh that's nice, Ken." While I had exhibited a strong inclination and ability, and had become labeled as "the school artist," still it must have seemed like a very precocious and naive declaration to my parents — and not one to be taken all that seriously.

While growing up in Sault Ste. Marie didn't provide me with arts experience, it offered a marvelous small town sense of community, friendships, and profound influences that became building blocks for my future.

The major industry in the Sault has always been Algoma Steel. But a second was the Abitibi Pulp and Paper mill. Both my grandfathers worked there: Milton "Dan" Danby as a millwright, and Hereford "Harry" Buckley as a maintenance painter. Grampa Buckley would regularly supply my brother Marvin and me with lots of off-cut paper from the mill. We'd have pink, yellow, and white, green, blue — bundles of light coloured paper — to draw on. It was a godsend of inexpensive newsprint, which we used continually as young boys without worrying about making a mess or waste.

I was fortunate in having a number of teachers that encouraged my interests in art during my schooling. Glen McEachern, who was an inspiring teacher in my grade seven year, apparently saw something in my early efforts that caused him to respond with praise. In later years, he remained enthused and eventually became my first purchaser. When I was eighteen, he paid me five dollars each for two small oil paintings. I was thrilled! It was not just a pat on the back or words of praise, but a very positive response to my work. Within a few years, he died in an automobile accident on the Autobahn in Germany. In his memory, I presented an original serigraph of my son to Cody Public School. Many years later, I received a letter and package from his family. It contained the two paintings, which they felt Glen would have wanted me to have.

Charles “Charlie” Carrington taught art at the Sault Collegiate, and he introduced me to the old masters and the history of art. He would also set me up with plaster casts to draw in a studio room separated from the rest of the class, so that I could expand my learning beyond the programmed projects that my classmates pursued. And whenever there was an art workshop scheduled in the Sault, he would make sure that I was invited to participate.

Yet, notwithstanding the levels of encouragement from teachers and friends, I knew that I was unable to acquire the insights that I needed. To a great extent, I was trying to teach myself, with little opportunity to gain the required training or knowledge in the Sault.

When I left grade school with the growing aspiration to become an artist, I knew of the Ontario College of Art (OCA) and determined that I would go there following high school.

All went well with my plan until the end of my grade eleven year, when my parents suddenly realized that I was still steadfast about becoming an artist, and they put their foot down. They had assumed that my very youthful ambition would eventually pass — but now were realizing that it hadn’t, and they were most concerned for my future. “No,” they said, “It’s far too risky. You’ll end up starving.” Weeks of despondency and disappointment prevailed. After much soul-searching and anxiety, I agreed to take a special vocational exam at an institute in Sault Ste. Marie, Michigan, to assess my abilities and interests and to learn what better options were recommended for me. I don’t remember the actual results, but it was finally decided that I should study to be an architect (as close to “art” as was allowable).

. . .

During winter, many evenings and Sundays were spent at Wilcox Park, which had an outdoor rink with boards and light poles, a few blocks from our home. I recall long sessions of skating, hockey, snow shoveling, flooding of the ice, and often limping into the wooden shack to warm my frozen feet near the pot-bellied stove. We'd shake the balls of snow from our mitts, letting them hit the stone with a steaming sizzle, loosen our skates to ease the pain.

The comings and goings of skaters were always pronounced by the bang and squeal of the wooden doors. The walls were covered with initials burned into the planks with the hot poker from the pot-bellied stove. We all drank nearly frozen water from the same ladle and bucket, and often the last bit was splashed onto the stove for sizzling effect.

We played pick-up hockey, alternately picking players as they arrived, and if someone of better ability left or arrived, we'd juggle the teams to keep us competitive. No equipment was worn, other than by the goalies. But then, we often didn't have goalies as such, so we'd alternate standing in the nets. Rules prohibited hoisting the puck, and the slapshot didn't exist. Yet often the puck would be bounced over the boards to be buried in the high snow banks, with the corresponding delay to find it. Competition often caused bruised shins, elbows, and heads. Occasionally a more serious fight was called for, but in the end, a spirit of fair play prevailed, and bragging rights carried over for the winners around the hot stove.

As I grew older and was allowed to stay out later at night, I'd help with the final cleaning and flooding of the ice for the next day's use. Following this, the lights were turned off, the fire in the stove extinguished, and the shack locked up by the caretaker.

Then I'd head off with my skates hanging from my stick slung over my shoulder, and trudge the four blocks to home. I have vivid memories of the crisp silence in the air after such an evening, broken only by the squeaking of my boots in the cold snow. Often the black sky sparkled with a million stars shimmering like jewels in the night. If the northern lights were dancing overhead, I'd stop and marvel at this amazing phenomenon and then quicken my page to share the news at home. There was magic in the air.

. . .

At thirteen, I joined the Sault's Air Cadet Squadron. I remained a member of the squadron for five years — until I was eighteen and left the Sault for art college. The whole experience remained a marvelous and enjoyable one for me. Not only was I a high achiever in the cadets, but early on when the squadron decided to create a pipe band, I learned to become the bass drummer, the guy who keeps the beat, who wears a leopard-skin apron and twirls the drumsticks in unison with the tenor drummers. Of course, we wore kilts, Canadian Air Force tartan, with spats and highly polished boots.

Our squadron was highly ranked as one of the best in Canada, in fact, *the* best, at least twice in my years. Spit, polish, and discipline became the norm. I learned to put a shine on my boots and brass buttons that would glisten from a hundred yards. Learning to take and, later, give orders in precision marching and interaction in workshops with other cadets was great character building. The camaraderie of colleagues, the pride of presentation, the self-control, and the discipline were all factors that would benefit my future.

Sports played a significant role in my youth. I enjoyed playing hockey, baseball, football, and competing in track and field, mostly. I'd never suggest that I was an athlete but I certainly enjoyed an avid participation in sports. As a high school student, I competed successfully in many track and field events, especially the running events. I began a regime of running two or three miles a night and loved it. I reveled in the feeling of fitness and stamina that I developed.

Being an aspiring artist while still participating in sports appeared to be at odds with people's expectations. How could a big, strapping young fellow be keen on art and athletics at the same time? Artists and athletes were supposed to be on opposite ends of the spectrum. But, I discovered that Tex Coulter, a football star with the New York Giants and later the Montreal Alouettes, was also a famous artist (whom I once met briefly when he was visiting the Sault). He drew marvelous portraits while still performing as a professional athlete. So much for stereotyping. Another variant of this theme is one that I have received often over the years, when on various occasions I've met people who have declared, "But you don't look like an artist," as if there is a particular "look" that an artist should have. I'd take it all with a grain of salt, and a chuckle. I don't think one has to "look like an artist" to be one. In fact, I've met too many wannabes who posture themselves as being artists and adopt as artsy a look as possible in order to play the role. I went through that stage as an art student — you know, paint splattered jeans, black turtleneck sweater, the prerequisite beard, etc., but after a time, one grows out of it — usually.

Art School in Toronto

In September 1958, freedom arrived. I finally took the train to Toronto to begin my studies at the Ontario College of Art.

My first few weeks at the college were exciting. I was totally enthralled by my opportunities to learn from instructors that had developed fine reputations as important artists, such as Jock Macdonald, Rolly Murphy, John Alfsen, Carl Schaefer, Fred Hagan, and Eric Freifield, to name a few.

During that first year, called the Foundation Year, students would get a grounding in multiple disciplines, from life drawing to calligraphy to art history to sculpture and industrial design — a whole gamut; and I learned quite a lot. I was constantly drawing at every opportunity on my own, filling sketch pads and books with sketches of Kensington Market, the ROM, back alleys, people, trees — even my left hand if I was lacking a subject — for a number of pen and ink studies. I felt that I was gaining almost as much from my free-time drawing excursions as I was from school.

The first half of my second year went quite well. I was as obsessive as ever toward my now specialized studies in drawing and painting. But I slowly became more and more disenchanted with both the courses and the prevailing philosophies of art. At one point, one of the instructors actually told me that if I had any aspirations to become a serious painter, I would have to be an abstract impressionist. This was the doctrine of the day, but it didn't sit well with me. Yet I tried. I appreciated learning abstract fundamentals from someone like Jock Macdonald, whom I admired, and who often invited some of us students to his home for good talks. I began to understand the reasoning behind such image making and it then became more acceptable to me, but could I devote my career solely in this direction? I doubted it.

My social life was thriving, but my satisfaction with OCA was diminishing. Yet, I was enjoying my year, with many additional rewarding experiences. Graham Coughtry, one of Canada's finest abstract painters, became a part-time instructor at the college that year and ultimately a friendly acquaintance. I attended a poetry reading at the Greenwich Gallery on Bay and Gerrard Streets, where a young Montreal poet by the name of Leonard Cohen was performing for the first time in Toronto, and managed to have a rewarding conversation with him afterwards.

I received a portrait commission from a Toronto lawyer whom I'd met the year previously, and I sold two or three other paintings. I was commissioned to create a special relief wall sculpture for a lounge in the Sault. Not bad for a second-year student.

This was also the year that I discovered both jazz and folk music, which became significant elements of my life as a young artist. Pete Seeger and the Weavers were making headlines at Carnegie Hall and in US folk clubs. They came to Massey Hall in Toronto for a concert, which was sold out weeks before, but I managed to get tickets. Somehow, I found myself attending an after-concert party with them and ended up in conversation with Fred Hellerman, (one of the Weavers). I recall asking him, in a rather naive fashion, "What kind of music do you personally listen to, Mr. Hellerman?" I've always remembered his answer. He said, "Good music," and I learned a lesson. There are really just two kinds, good and bad, and it's up to the individual listener to make the judgment. I realized that the same principle applies to the world of art.

I didn't return to school the following year. I "dropped out," as they say. However, I didn't quit without thoroughly appraising my reasoning beforehand. I asked advice from many experienced sources, including instructors Fred Hagan, Jock Macdonald, Eric Freifeld, and Graham Coughtry. I also went to visit Duncan Macpherson, the renowned cartoonist for the *Toronto Star*, to ask his opinion. They all offered the same advice, which was: staying in school wouldn't improve my chances of succeeding in the world of art. The certificate of graduation would be relatively meaningless, and I should follow the path that seemed right for me. I left the school for the summer after my second successful year and returned home to the Sault to dwell on my decision.

I applied for work as an artist at the Sault's television station, CJIC, and was hired as a set designer/painter and general assistant in the studio. I learned to operate the camera, help with the boom mike, and set up the studio for various shows and interviews. But I also learned how to create interesting and compatible backgrounds for the shows. Often when the studio was not in use, I'd set up shop with my cans of paint and my portable record player and work away with my favourite jazz playing beside me.

As the summer advanced toward fall, I told my parents that I would not be returning to OCA. They were upset by this, as it appeared to them to be a juvenile decision, and they felt strongly that I should carry on for the full four years and get my graduation certificate. In their eyes, it would be an accredited qualification that I had achieved something, especially since I had aspired for so many years to get to OCA, something they had eventually helped me to do. For me to then simply quit was just something they couldn't comprehend. "If you're going to start something, finish it," they said. In my eyes, it would be another two years with little to show for it, except a piece of paper. Clouds of disappointment and concern for their son's future hung heavily in the air.

I knew that I was a problem for them and that I had to find another avenue of direction. Also, I was now twenty years old, and it was time for me to move on.

1960s

Life as a Young Artist

One day, in summer, 1960, I met with my singer friend Mary and her boyfriend from Toronto over drinks. He informed me about a new television station in Toronto, which would be the first in Canada to employ colour in television broadcasting. CFTO was owned by John David Eaton, John Bassett, Foster Hewitt, and Joel Aldred, with no expense spared in making it one of the best facilities in North America! Mary's boyfriend said, "You'd better get to Toronto fast if you're interested, because they just began hiring employees."

So I resigned from CJIC, (which was really just a summer job, although I could have stayed on), packed my bag, and took the train to Toronto. The next day, I went to the CFTO offices, temporarily located in John Bassett's *Toronto Telegram* building at Melinda and Bay Streets, and made an application as a scenic artist. I became the first one hired, in large part thanks to my varied experience over the summer at CJIC.

I had a two-floor apartment over Benny's Cigar Store on Yonge Street. A couple of art-college friends moved in, which helped with meeting the rent. Around the corner, on Gerrard Street, the Coffee House was *the* meeting place for artists, writers, and musicians, and its Gerrard Street Village location was in its prime, with Av Isaacs's Greenwich Gallery then nearby on Bay Street, and Jack Pollock's Art Gallery a block behind. I was a frequenter of the village and enjoyed the company of many. We'd have long philosophical discussions over coffee, play chess, listen to poetry readings or folk singers, and I could often be found filling my sketchbooks, if on my own.

I was also exploring various directions for my painting. Knowing of the almost total pre-eminence of abstract expressionism of the day, combined with what I'd been told and taught during my two years at OCA, I continued painting abstracts. But I also needed to find employment in order to survive.

Then one day I saw an advertisement in the *Toronto Telegram*, inviting applicants for the job of graphic artist. I applied and was immediately hired. I began work at the "*Tely*" in May of 1961. I was twenty-one years old and was now employed as a designer by one of Canada's major newspapers. My parents were very pleased. My work consisted of designing and completing finished art for the promotion department of the *Telegram*; special brochures, full page ads, illustrations for various *Tely* journalists, and whatever came my way. I enjoyed it.

My life was improving. I was gainfully employed as an artist and I continued to paint often. Meanwhile, Yorkville was developing quickly as the new village and folk clubs and

Ken in his apartment studio
in Toronto's Yorkville district, ca. 1960
(photographer unknown)

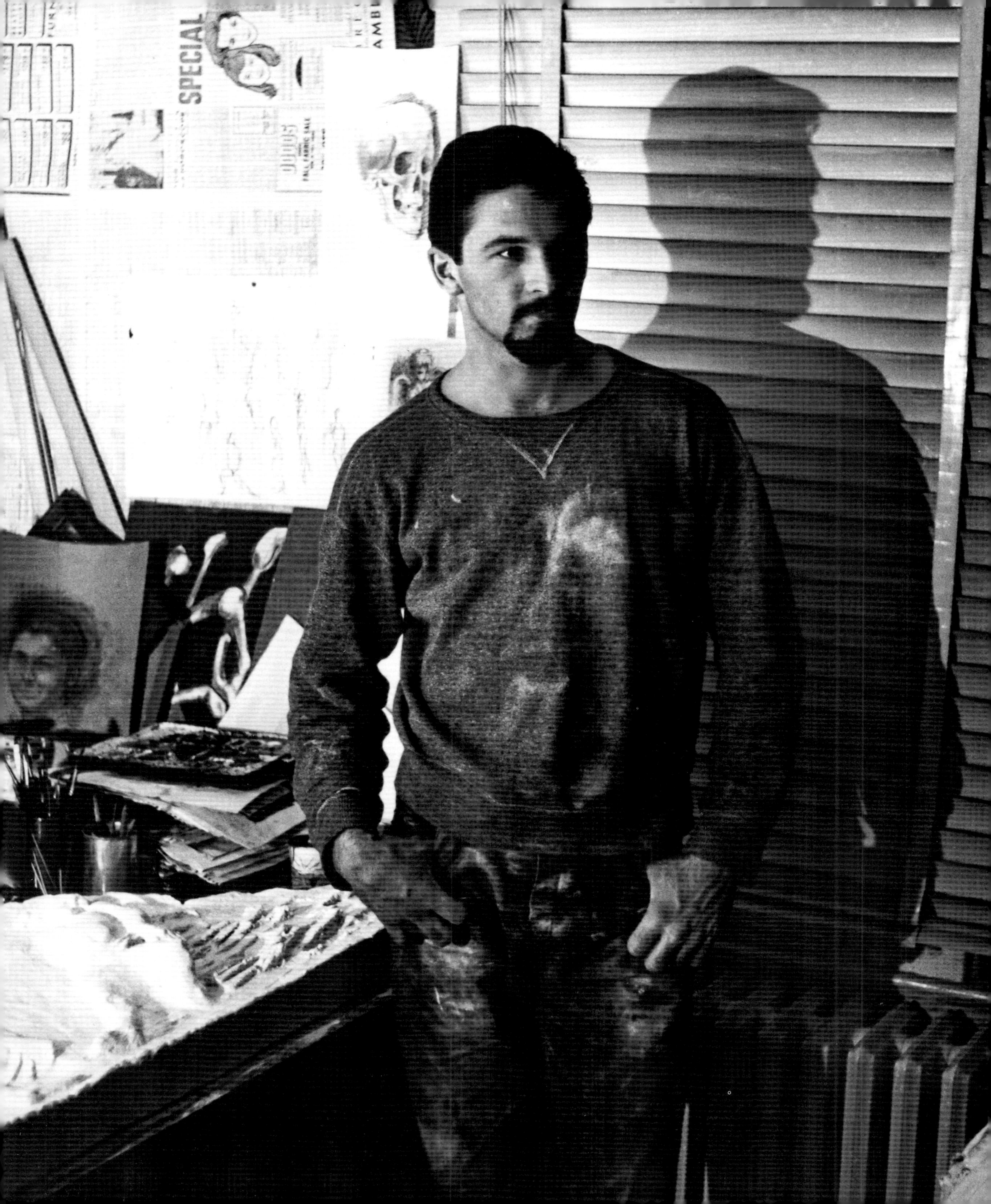
SPECIAL

coffeehouses were opening in abundance. The Village Corner was where I first met Ian Tyson, Sylvia Fricker, and later, performers such as the Two-Tones, a duo comprised of two fellows named Terry Whelan and Gordon Lightfoot. Ian and Sylvia were not yet a team, but individual performers. But within months, they were rehearsing together and being managed by another friend-to-be, Ed Cowan, who just happened to also work for the *Telegram* promotions department.

Over the next two years or so, I became a fixture on the Yorkville scene as well as often frequenting the entertainment spots just south of me on Yonge Street below Gerrard, and I loved being in the midst of such creative energy.

For a few months I alternated between the Yonge Street strip and the Yorkville folk clubs. Yonge Street beckoned with the Le Coq d'Or Tavern, the Brass Rail, and the Colonial Tavern, that featured performers such as Ronnie Hawkins and the Beau-Marks; at various times, Yorkville's audiences were entertained by the Travellers, Ian & Sylvia, Bonnie Dobson, Buffy Sainte-Marie, and even Rich Little, the impressionist. And of course there were still my favourite jazz haunts to enjoy, including the First Floor Club. My nightlife had a great deal to choose from and often included socializing with the performers afterwards at one or another artist friend's pad.

One day a club acquaintance named Carl Noylander asked me if I would like to share part ownership of a new folk club. After hearing his proposal, I agreed and together we created the Gate of Cleve, at 161 Dupont Street. I created the physical setting and Carl provided the capital. And we both worked hard to generate business.

In November 1961, I had an exhibition of my abstract paintings at the Pollock Gallery on Elizabeth Street in the Gerrard Street Village. Jack Pollock was enthused with my efforts and generated quite a successful show. He sold five paintings out of the ten or twelve comprising the show. While I was pleased with the results, I really didn't feel fulfilled by the work, and I wondered how long the abstracts would keep my interest.

My work at the *Telegram* was creative and interesting. Although I wasn't generously paid, it enabled me to support myself and indulge my variety of activities, while continuing to try to find my way as a painter. Meanwhile, the Gate of Cleve was barely holding its own. If I ever had an idea that it might be financially successful, it wasn't happening; but then we didn't expect to make money, just remain viable as a folk club. I decided to move on and let my partner, Carl, take over.

Jack Wall invited me to occupy the second-floor space above his club, the Fifth Peg. We built a separate washroom with a toilet and shower facility within, and I managed to make the place livable, with a small bedroom area at the rear, which had a door leading onto the flat roof outside. The rest of the space was all studio.

Jack had also taken on the role of producing the second Mariposa Folk Festival and suddenly, I was to be the art director for that summer's event, which again meant promo and program design work, including a revised version of the poster. The original design in 1961 was done by Ian Tyson and it worked very well, so I decided not to alter its essential image.

In the summer of 1962, the second annual Four Seasons Outdoor Art Exhibition took place at the Four Seasons Hotel on Jarvis Street, across from CBC Studios. The Four Seasons was owned by Murray Koffler and he'd initiated the exhibition the year before. Eventually, it would become the Toronto Outdoor Art Exhibition in Nathan Phillips Square and the largest event of its kind in North America. I decided to participate and acquired an entry. I set up a display of a few drawings and three or four abstract paintings for the weekend's show. I was soon surprised to learn that one of the paintings was chosen to receive the purchase award for the Four Seasons. The adjudicator was the then-director of the National Gallery in Ottawa, Alan Jarvis. I was delighted! Later, the organizers came to me to ask if I would allow my winning painting to be exchanged for a smaller work, at the same price. I said, "Sure." So they then selected a painting of an abstracted nude figure and I kept the actual winner (a completely non-objective gouache painting on paper), which I've enjoyed ever since.

For months, I had been painting in a much more representative style, experimenting with a realistic approach, which was for me challenging and satisfying. My subjects were basically still life, but my drawings continued to depict observations of life around me, including performers, guests at the club, and friends. I knew that this direction was against the grain of what the art world was embracing, but it was a much more comfortable fit for me.

I resigned from the *Telegram* at the end of October in '62. I was free and easy, and having a lot of fun. As long as I could pay my way, I saw no reason to settle down. Besides, I was apprehensive toward the very notion. I wanted to be free, to paint, not work nine-to-five in a production job. And although I enjoyed my *Telegram* experience, the work had become rather boring for me. It was time to move on.

In November, I received a phone call from a folk singer friend who was performing in New York's Greenwich Village and who needed some help returning to Toronto. I liked the idea of visiting New York and I said I would go. I also had another reason for making the trip. Buffalo's Albright-Knox Art Gallery had a month-long exhibition of the work of Andrew Wyeth, the American painter. After the visit to New York City, we began the journey to Buffalo, stopping overnight somewhere along the way in order to arrive the next day for a lengthy visit to the Albright-Knox.

I had read about Andrew Wyeth and I had seen a few reproductions of his work. I knew also that he was the son of N.C. Wyeth, the famous American illustrator who had fueled my imagination as a young boy with his illustrations for the classics, such as *Treasure Island*, *Last of the Mohicans*, *The Black Arrow*, *Kidnapped*, and many others. I expected to see...well, I wasn't sure what I expected. But what I saw bowled me over. Big paintings and small, dozens of egg tempera, watercolours, and drawings, all done with an amazing realist fidelity and yet a fabulous sense of abstract design and composition as well. He had combined the genres! In my mind, he was reinforcing the merits of working realistically and abstractly at the same time. One didn't have to paint gibberish to include abstraction in the work. As he was quoted as saying, "Abstraction is the best thing that has happened to realism."

I think I more or less stumbled around the gallery for a few hours, absorbing the work from a distance and scrutinizing it up close. Here was the reinforcement that I needed! Here was a validation of my itch, already implemented, to work in a realistic mode. I now knew that I needn't feel insecure about where I wanted to direct my work, or feel out of touch because of what was in vogue in the galleries. Here was a major museum presenting a major show by a realist painter. It was okay, after all! What a breath of fresh air for me as a young artist.

I returned to my Toronto apartment, with a renewed enthusiasm for my future directions in painting. I recall resting in my studio, assessing the work that I'd been attempting, and realizing how inadequate it was. It was a good insight to bring home, and I would remain aware of it in the future.

My life above the Fifth Peg was becoming more difficult. The future of the club was uncertain, and I was owed money by many clients for a variety of design work and wasn't getting paid. I was becoming more and more frustrated with my work as a freelance designer, and the kind of clients I was dealing with at that time. Besides, to my mind, it was only a means to an end, which was to support myself in order to paint.

I decided to attempt to interest a gallery in my paintings, and began to assess which of those might be the best candidates for me. Months earlier, I had shown some early work to Av Isaacs of the new Isaacs Gallery. He wasn't very positive at the time, so I scratched that as a possibility. But his framer, who had a gallery across the street, had framed a drawing for me, and I remembered him offering to display my work. His name was William Kurelek, later to be a most prominent Canadian artist. (He soon closed his gallery to work exclusively for Isaacs, as his framer.)

I narrowed my list of possible galleries to three: Jack Pollock's gallery, where I'd shown my abstracts in '61, Dorothy Cameron's gallery, up the street from Isaacs, and Gallery Moos Ltd. on Yorkville, recently relocated from Avenue Road. Jack Pollock came to my studio flat above the Fifth Peg to see the work that I'd been doing. He was positive but hesitant. He said, "Keep it up, let's see what develops." Dorothy Cameron stated on the phone that she would only look at slides of my work, which I couldn't afford to have taken. Finally, I called Gallery Moos, and spoke with the owner, Walter Moos. Walter said, "Come and see me with your work." I asked when this might be convenient, and he said, "Why not today? Come this afternoon." I agreed.

Walter asked a lot of questions regarding my awareness and the extent of my commitment. We talked about the work and identified areas where improvement might develop. It was a full afternoon of compatibility and encouragement. Finally, he told me that if I continued to work hard in the direction I'd shown him, he would be willing to represent my work. He then purchased a drawing outright and wrote me a cheque for thirty-five dollars. Positive indeed! I was most pleased, and greatly relieved. As a young, twenty-three-year-old artist, I was determined to justify Walter's vote of confidence.

Not long after this, I moved from the Fifth Peg to a studio apartment building in Rosedale. (Located right behind it was the Studio Building of Lawren Harris and the Group of Seven, an auspicious location, to say the least.) I had finally realized that my painting would be compromised by the buzz of activity at my Fifth Peg flat, and I felt that I needed this change. It was a first small step toward removing myself from the Yorkville scene.

In 1963 I completed a painting of my cat Kimbo walking along the top of a brick wall beside the chimney. I called it *Fur and Bricks*. It was my first egg tempera painting, a medium that I was enjoying, but that I was having to teach myself to use. I delivered *Fur and Bricks* to Gallery Moos and Walter decided to enter it in the Montreal Museum of Fine Arts Annual Spring Show. Walter also asked if I could have enough new work available to participate in a March exhibition. I could, and delivered it to the gallery for framing. This would be my first exhibit at the gallery, a three-man showing of drawings and watercolours by Martin Berkovitz, Waltraud Markgraf, and myself, three very divergent artists. The show was well responded to, and even drew very positive reviews in the press. Soon after the show opened, I received a letter from Evan Turner, the director of the Montreal Museum, informing and congratulating me on the fact that *Fur and Bricks* was selected by the jury for the Jessie Dow Prize as the best painting in other media, for the Spring Show. Included with the letter was a cheque for $250. I was elated!

Immediately thereafter, the museum selected me as one of two or three artists to receive prominent news coverage in conjunction with their event. As a consequence of my Jessie Dow Prize and the resulting publicity, Gallery Moos extended its exhibition for an extra week. As it happened, the museum's publicity was extensive and reached

The Art Dealer (Walter Moos), 1983

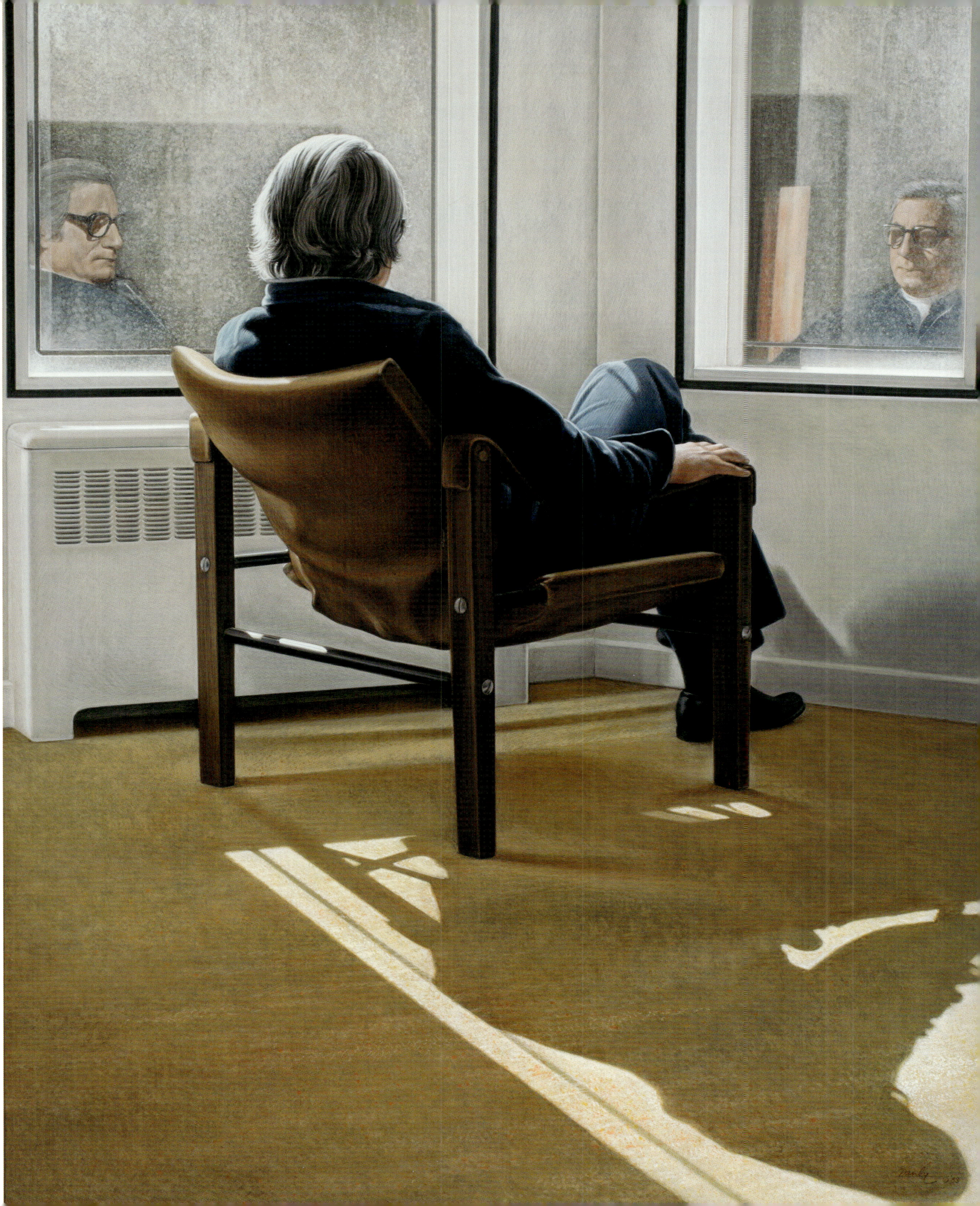

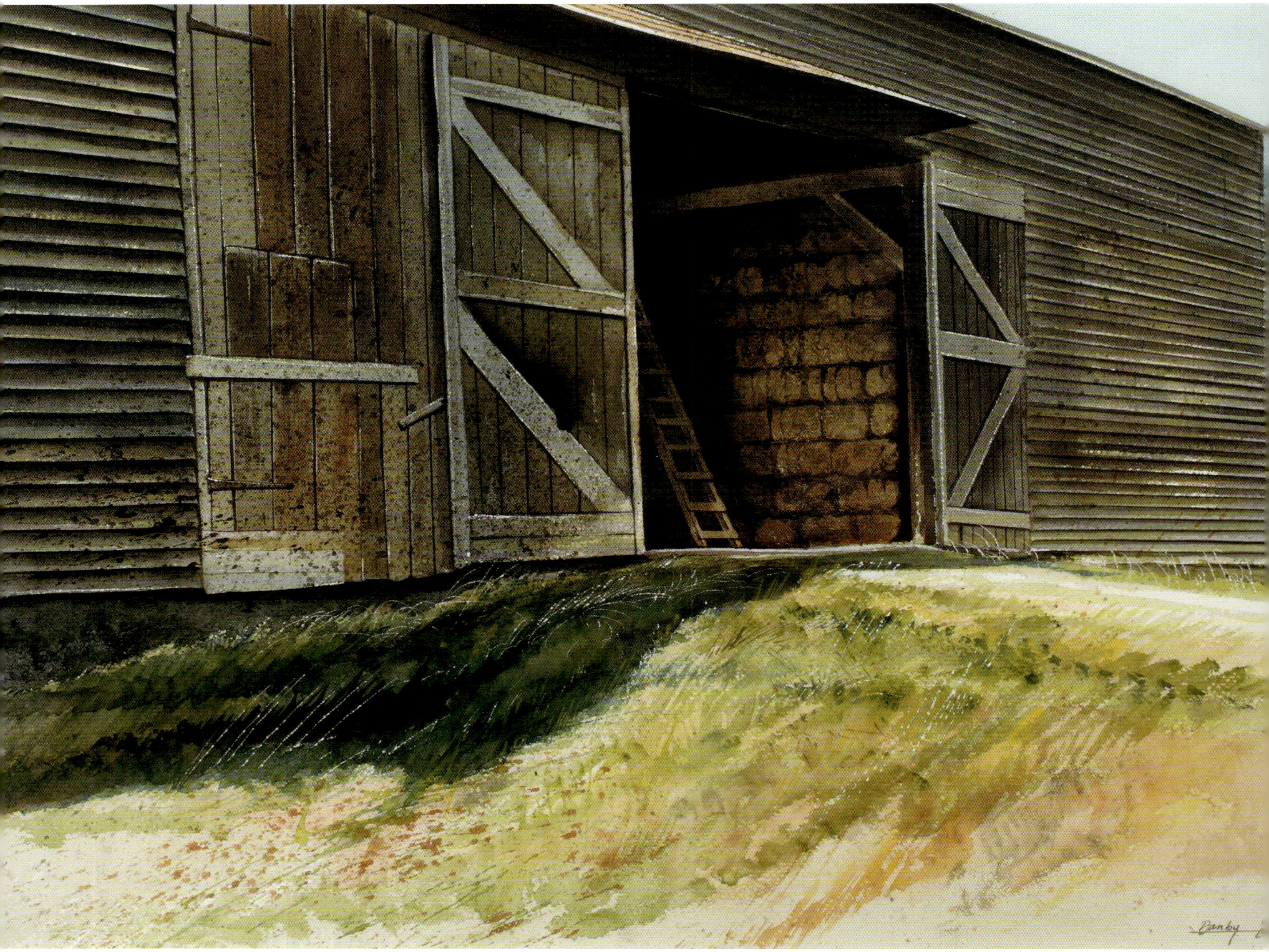

 Barn Door, 1967

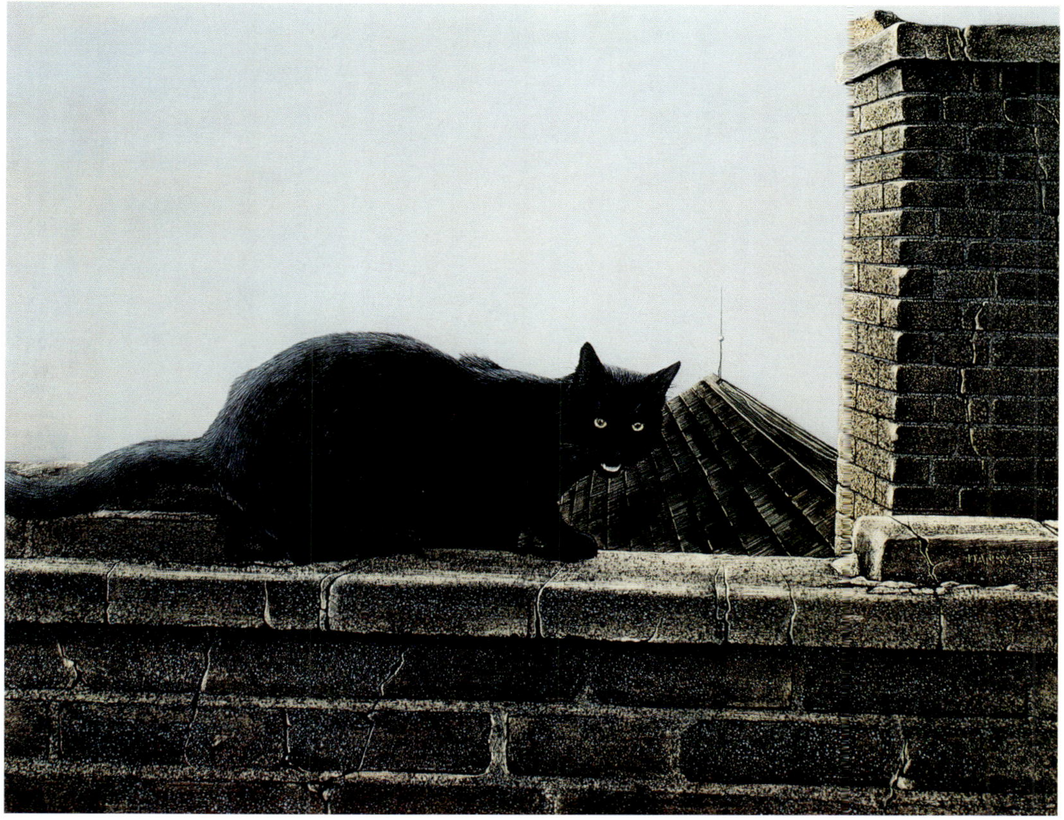

a national level. Suddenly, as an artist, my name became known. Walter decided that we should plan to have a one-man exhibition in the fall. I could feel the pressure of the event as soon as we decided to do it. Walter agreed to finance the opportunity for me to devote myself full time to the task, and I began to wonder what I would do and where.

In 1964 I rented a small log cabin at the village of Richards Landing on St. Joseph Island, near Sault Ste. Marie, right beside the water and a few short miles from my parents' cottage, and settled in. It was here that I met Judy Harcourt, who later became my wife and mother to my three sons. During this period, I was having challenges with my painting. Since my first egg tempera (*Fur and Bricks*) of the year before, I had continued to learn and experiment with the medium on my own.

Fur and Bricks, 1963

Egg tempera is a centuries-old painting medium, in use long before oil painting was developed. Where linseed oil is the vehicle that binds the pigment in oil paint, a solution of egg yolk performs the identical task in egg tempera. It is a water-based medium, dries very quickly, and is applied to a specially made panel that has been coated with a plaster called gesso, which is sanded to a smooth surface. As a porous ground, the gesso absorbs the paint, as well as holding it on the surface. Egg tempera is especially well suited for translucent work, as one can actually control the degree of light reflected or held within the painting. It is also the most permanent medium known, in terms of its light fastness. Colours maintain their richness over centuries without change. However, it requires much preparation before use, as it is not available ready-made (in its proper form), unlike other mediums.

My guide was and still is *The Practice of Tempera Painting*, by Daniel V. Thompson, in which he cites a manuscript from the fifteenth century by the Italian painter Cennino d'Andrea Cennini, called *The Craftsman's Handbook*. Teaching oneself such a complex medium is not an easy task; in fact Cennini himself discouraged this, insisting that we "must study under a master," which is all very well, if you can find one.

My ultimate problem didn't so much involve the mixing or application of the paint, which I became quite comfortable with, but the application of a final varnish to the finished painting. In spite of following the Thompson translation carefully, the varnish would highlight irregularities, which troubled me. As a means of avoiding this, I eventually took a short cut and simply sprayed each new painting with a satin-finish acrylic spray fixative, which seemed to solve the issue quite well. Yet I continued to feel there must be another solution that I was missing. Who could I ask?

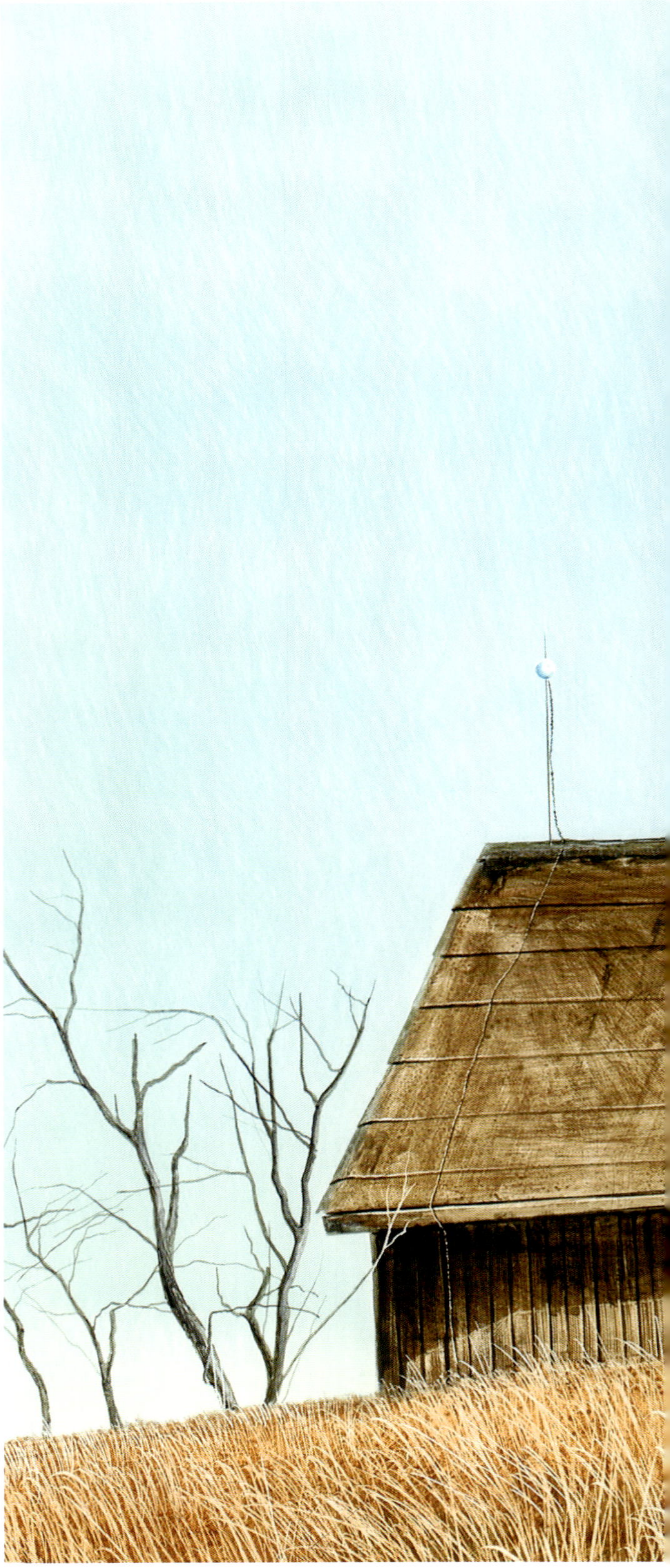

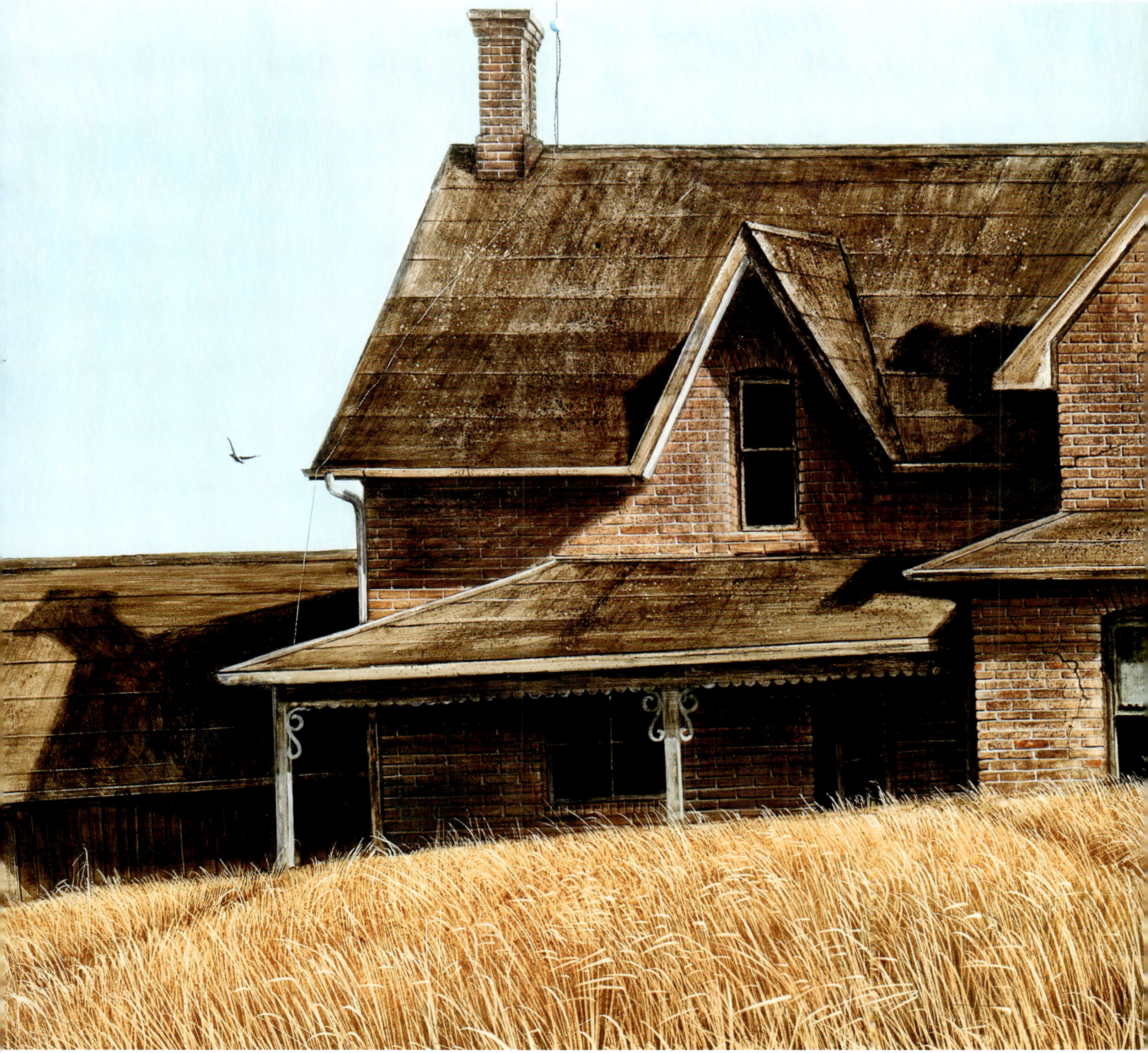

Early Morning, 1965

Well, I thought, why not try Andrew Wyeth? He was the only painter that I was aware of who had years of experience with egg tempera, and as I regarded him as something of a mentor, through his strong influence on me. He was the logical source. I decided to travel to Pennsylvania and attempt to meet with him. Upon describing these thoughts to my artist friend Jim Kerr, from the *Telegram*, he said he'd like to come along. Our chum Peter Dawes decided to join us and we were soon on the road on my pilgrimage to meet the master. It was a bit foolish, I know, but win or lose, we would have an adventure.

We arrived in the countryside north of New Wilmington and found a motel. The next day, we drove to Chadds Ford in the early afternoon, and after eventually locating the Wyeth property, we boldly decided to drive in. I got out of the car and walked toward the first building in front of me. The door opened and Andrew's wife, Betsy, stepped out to confront me with, "Can I help you?"

I nervously explained that I had just driven from Canada specifically with hopes of being able to ask her husband some technical questions about egg tempera. She listened to my plea and then advised me that Andrew wasn't available, but she added (taking pity on me I'm sure), "If you call tonight, between six and six thirty, he'll speak with you." With that, she wrote down the phone number and gave it to me. I thanked her profusely and promised to call.

We decided to enjoy a fine meal at the Chadds Ford Inn that evening, just down the road, and were there well before six p.m. I soon made my call and Andrew answered, having expected it. Once he realized that I was quite conversant about egg tempera, he warmed up immediately and we had a most interesting conversation, which lasted the better part of a half-hour or so. He informed me that the varnish problem was one that he had also experienced and that his solution for some time had been identical to mine, the use of the acrylic spray. But he eventually learned of a better answer, which was a mixture of water and egg yolk, which after applying could be carefully polished with a silk cloth, to a firm and even finish, and this was now his practice. Of course, this was very interesting to me and prompted further questions and answers that he was happy to offer. I thanked him very much for his kind help. He asked me to keep in touch and wished me well. I felt that my pilgrimage had succeeded most admirably.

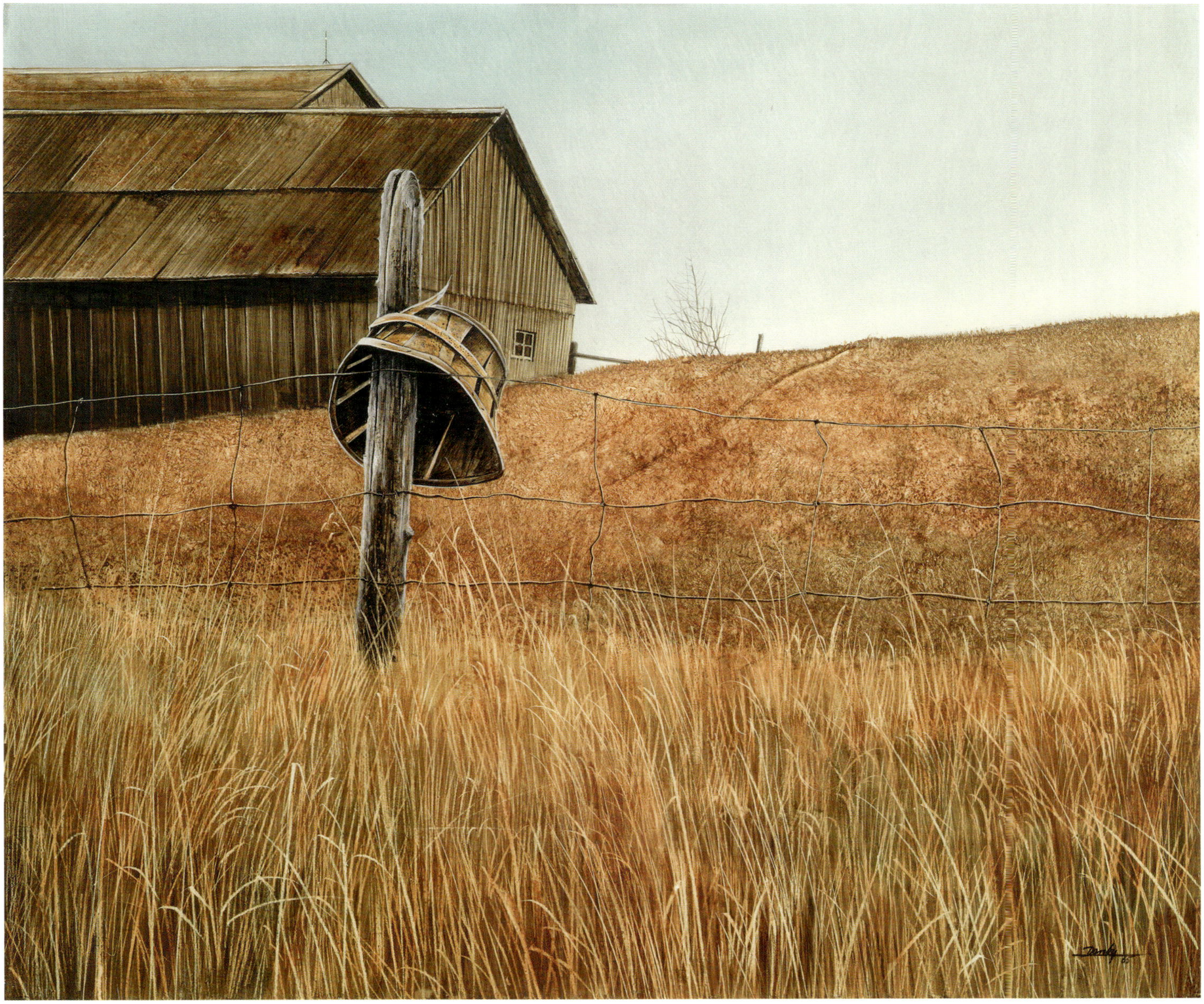

Guidepost, 1965

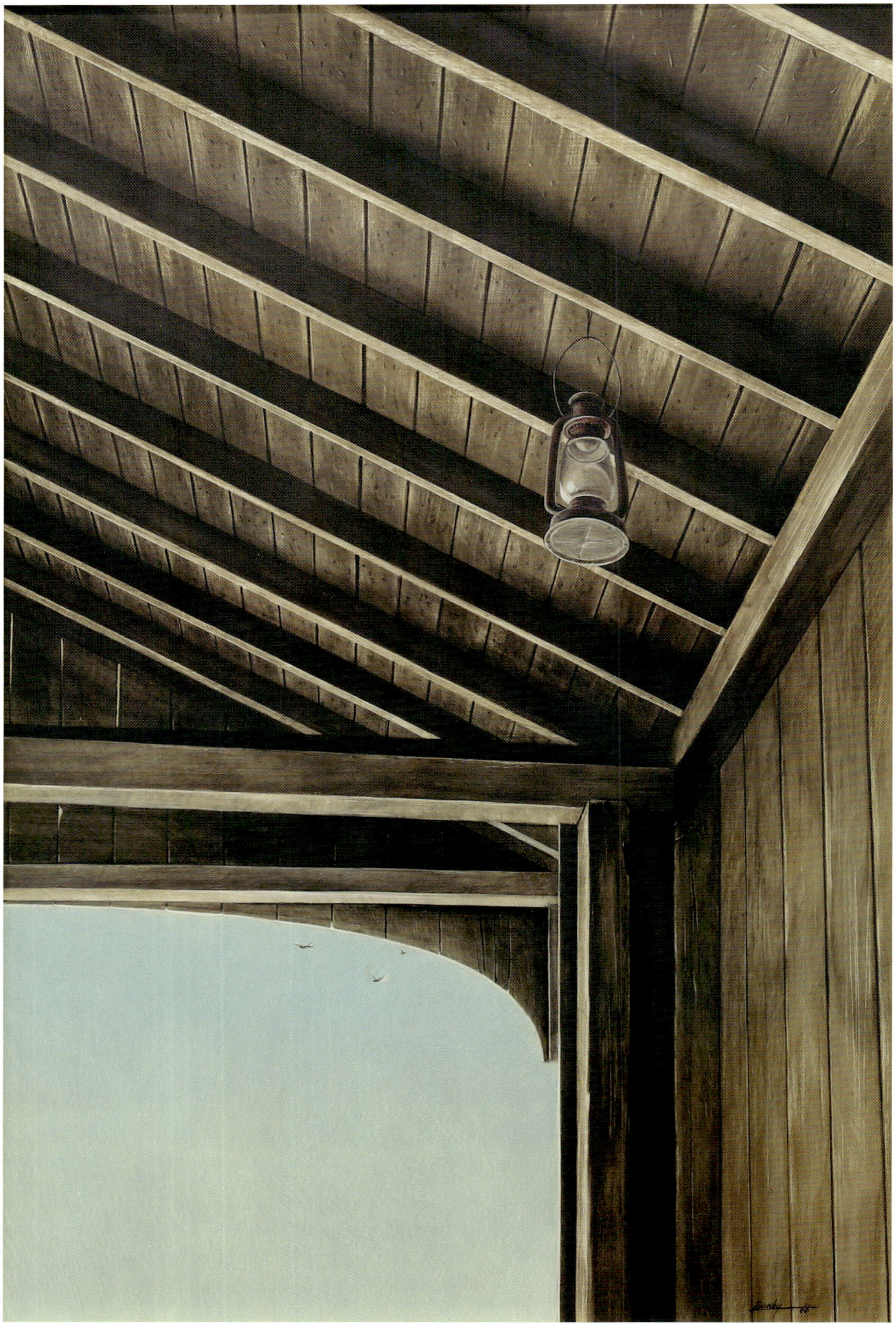

 Kerosene Lamp, 1966

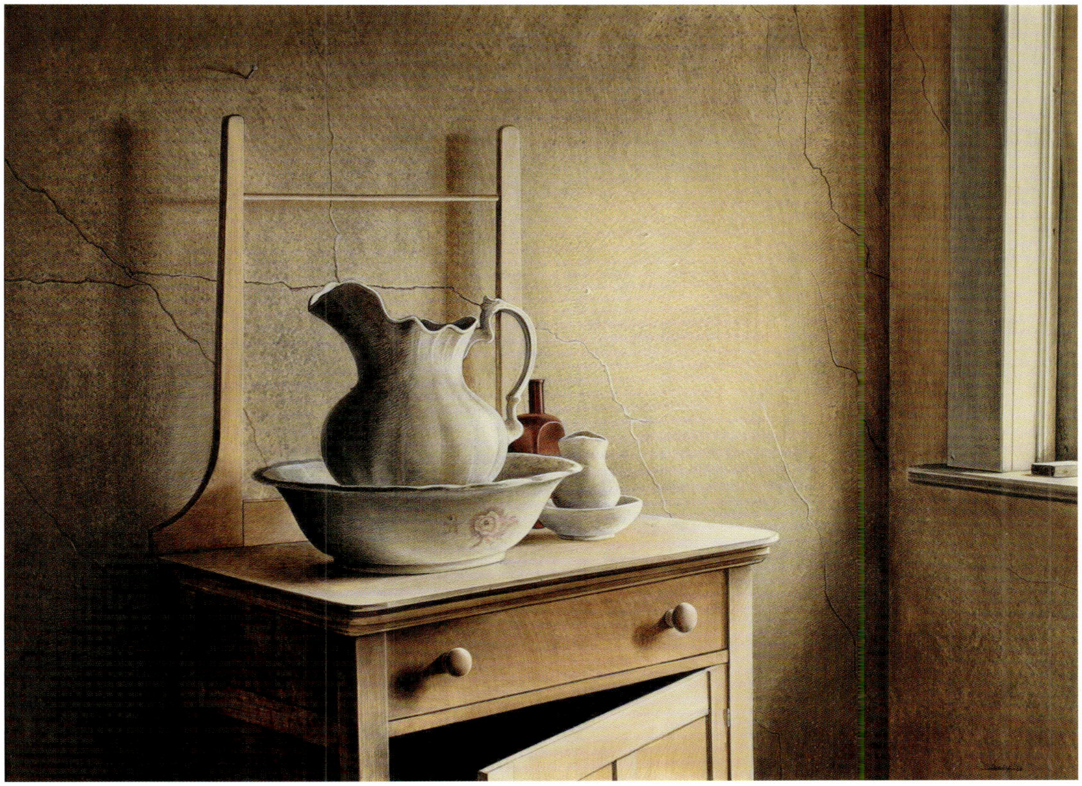

The Rose Bowl, 1966

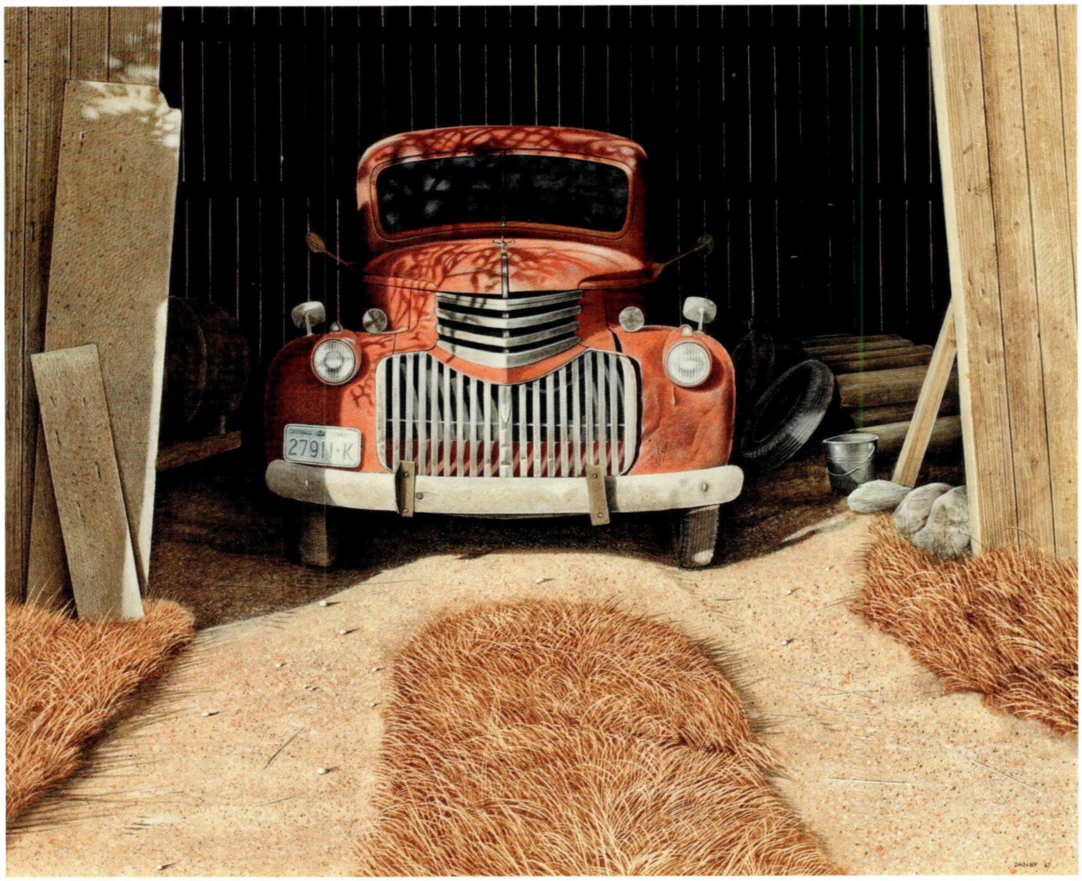

The Pickup, 1967

Settling Down

Judy and I married and lived in Toronto for awhile, but after our son Sean was born, I began to have hopes that we might be able to find a home in the country, so my habit of exploring rural areas of the province for interesting subject matter took on a new meaning. I had a great affinity for stone buildings and undulating, rather than flat, land. I also wanted to be near water. All of these characteristics usually prevailed with old mill sites. So I acquired a collection of ordnance maps from the government offices, and used them to navigate to mill sites when on my sketching trips in the countryside, eventually covering most of southern and eastern Ontario. I always returned with a better understanding of where I might find an appropriate property.

At the top of my list of preferences was Armstrong Mills, just outside of Guelph. The retired miller and his wife lived on the property in a stone house on the hill above. I saw him on the property during a second trip, and enquired as to its availability. He refused to even consider it.

We had been attracted to a large stone coach house in Guelph a year before, but after a closer look we decided against it. The real-estate agent then began calling me in Toronto in hopes of persuading me to buy it. I told him that I was much more interested

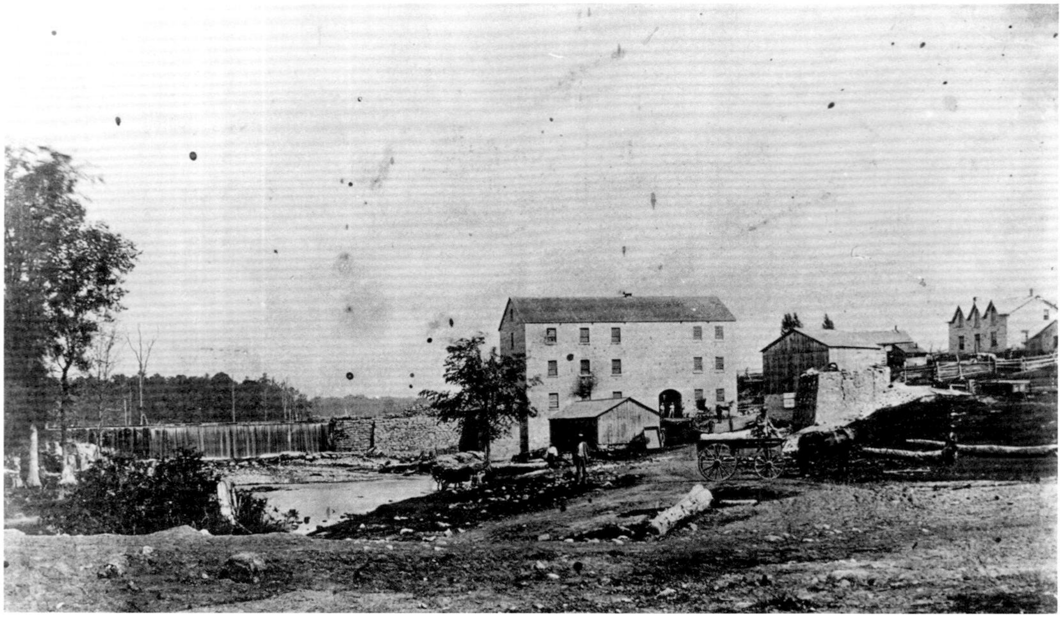

The earliest known photograph of Armstrong Mills, ca. 1860
(photographer unknown)

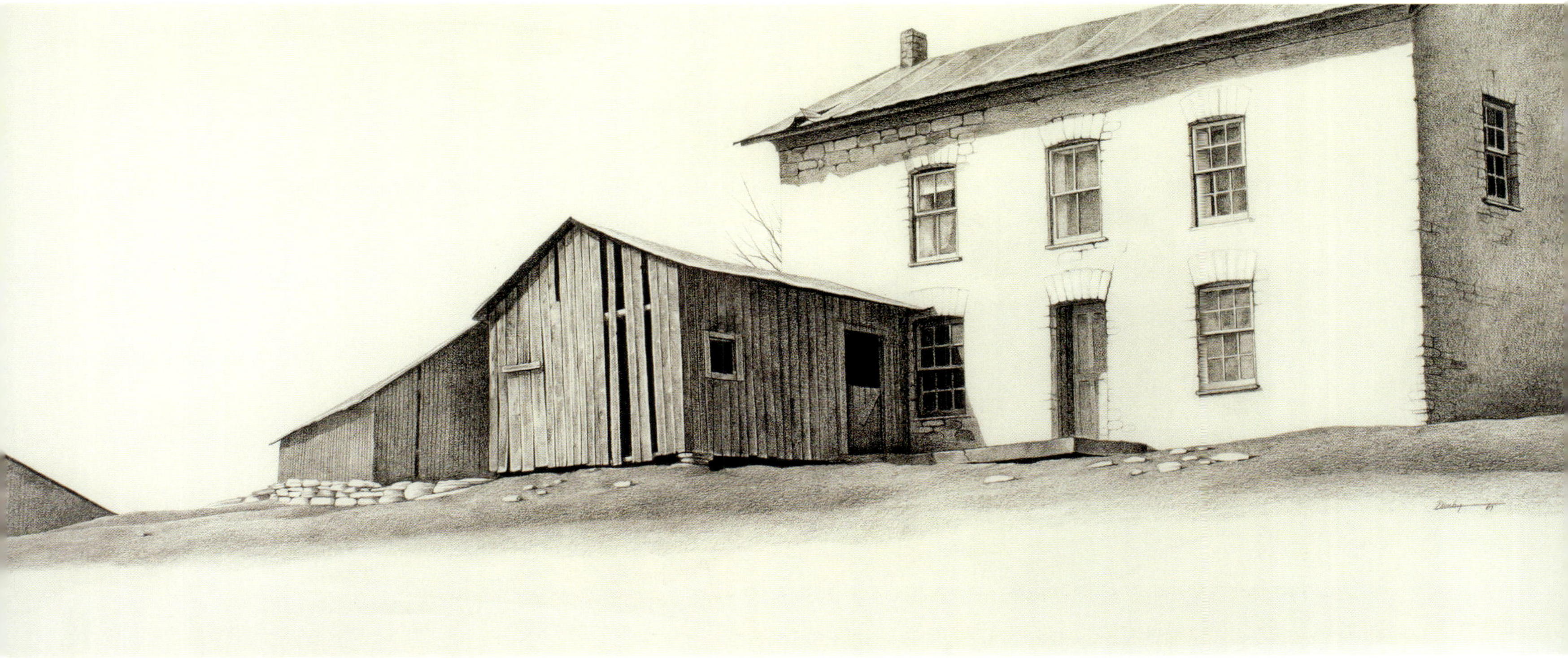

in the old mill property and described its location. He promised to see what he could do. Almost a year later, he called to announce that the owners had made an offer to sell. Would I go for it? He described it as a bargain, naturally. In reality, the owners had decided to make the offer to get rid of the pestering agent, and had named a price that they thought would effect this. I agreed to the proposal, conditional upon an assessment of the property. The assessor's opinion was that the property was not worth the asking price, by far. While I found that to be of interest, it wasn't a sufficient deterrent for me. I saw its potential, and was convinced that I wanted to acquire it.

We moved to our newly acquired property near Guelph in December 1967, in time to settle into the miller's stone house before Christmas. It was a happy time, with friends and family visiting, and Sean having his second birthday. There was a first-floor room that had two windows and offered privacy. This became my studio for the next two and a half years.

Untitled (Stone House and Sheds), 1967

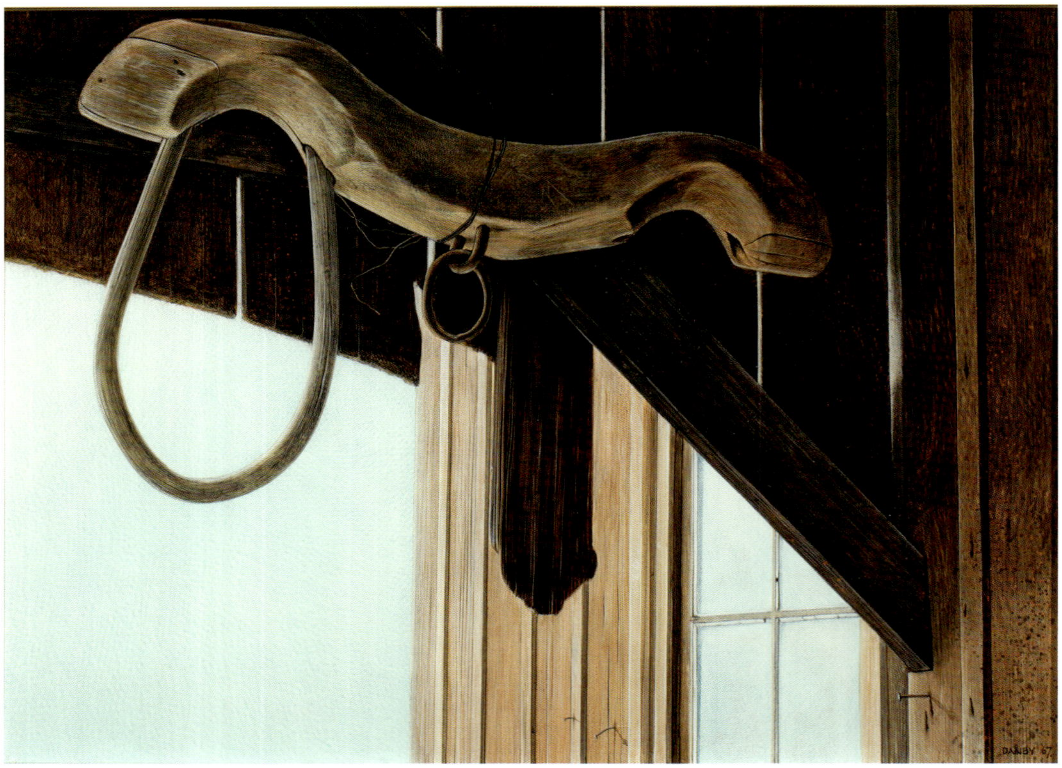

Bleached Yoke, 1967

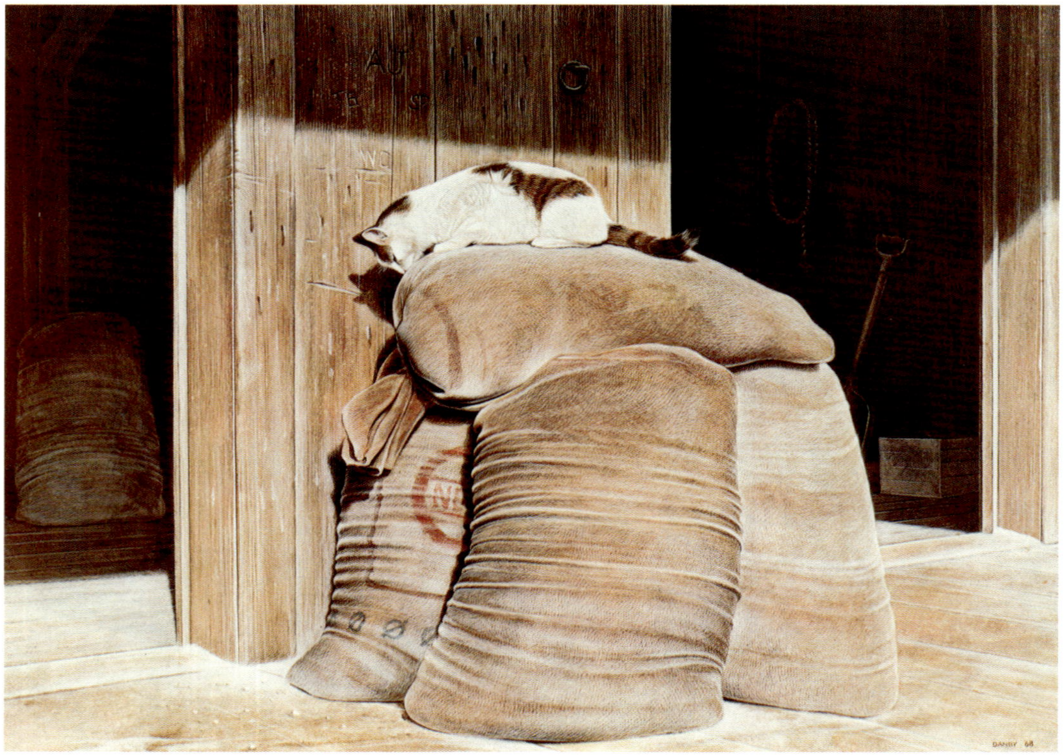

The Mill Cat, 1968

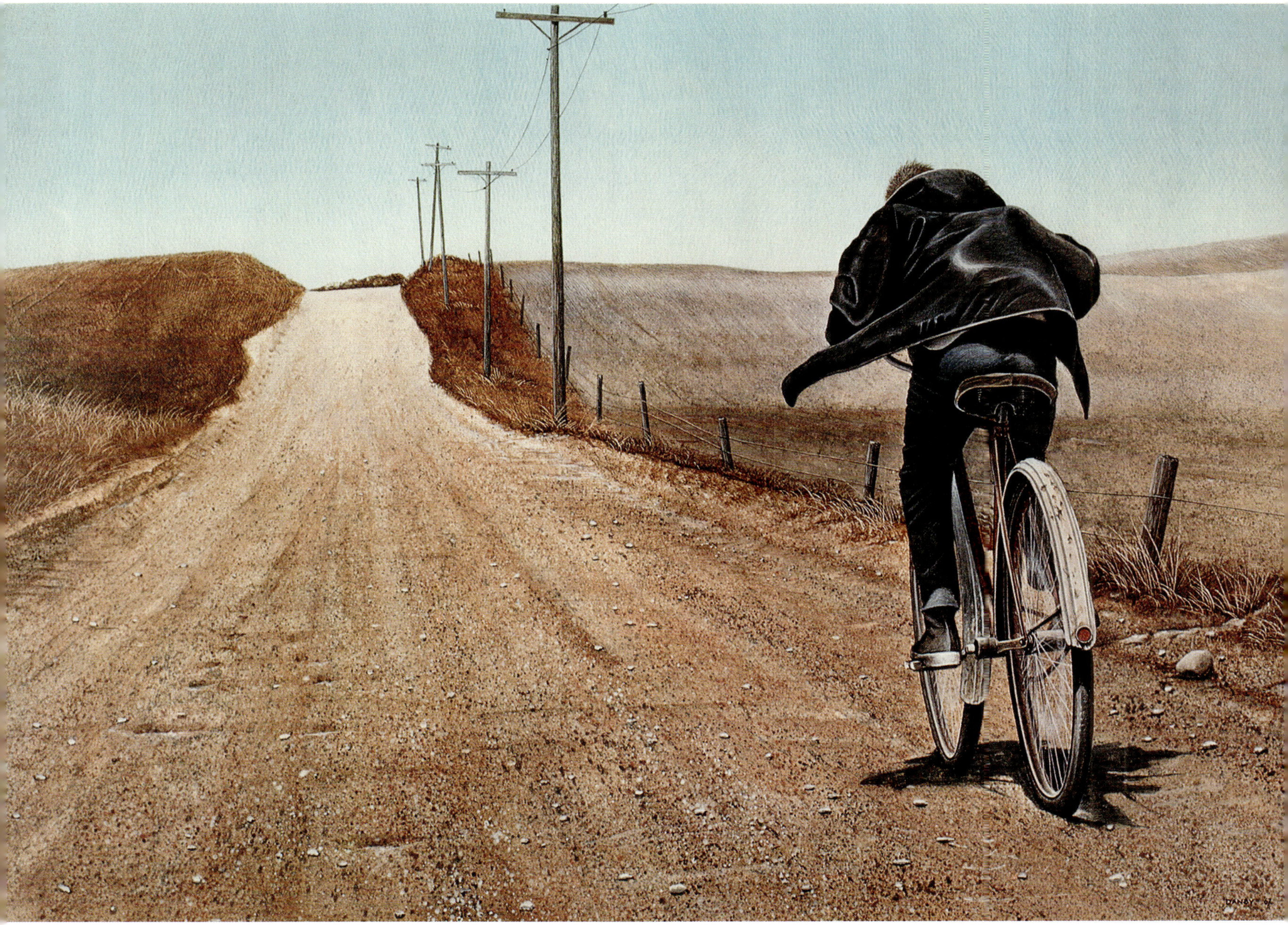

Towards the Hill, 1967

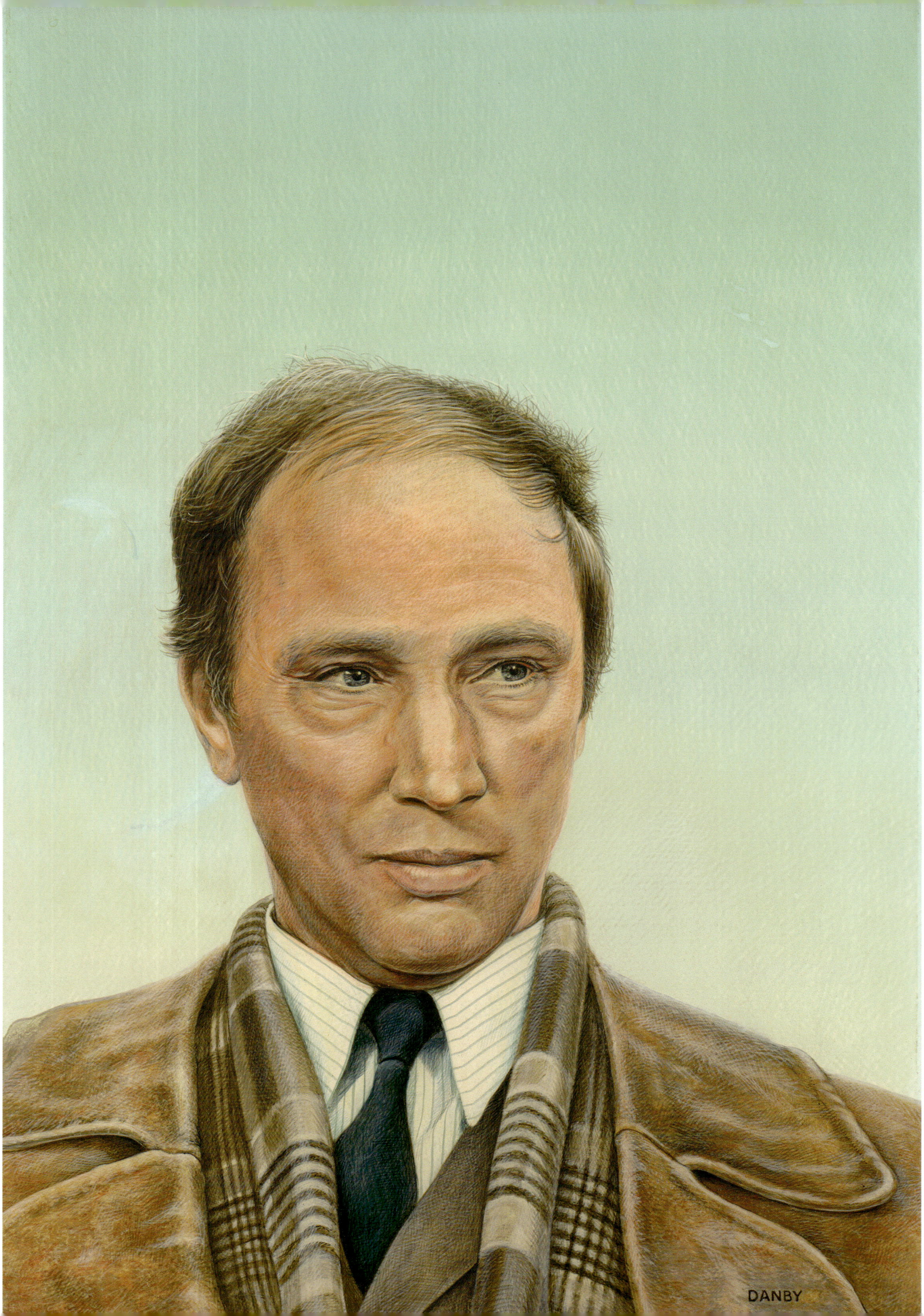
DANBY

. . .

One evening in spring of 1968, I had a phone call from Walter. He'd just received an overture from *Time* magazine asking if I could create a portrait of Pierre Elliott Trudeau for the cover of the magazine. They were placing their bets on his winning the leadership and they wanted the portrait ready to go to press as soon as possible. Walter felt that this would be an important commission and exposure for me and was pleased when I said I would do it. The question was, how? Could Trudeau pose for me? There were many other answers to be resolved, as well.

A week or more went by as *Time* scrambled to set up a posing session with Trudeau, who by then was criss-crossing the country on his campaign tour. Meanwhile, they sent me a folder of black and white photographs and articles. All of the photos were of an animated, speech-giving variety with very little to offer me, but one or two had enough potential that I began preliminary pencil drawings for a concept that appealed to me. I wanted to depict him with a dignified but determined look, in his then-trademark leather overcoat.

The delay from *Time* kept me waiting as my deadline approached. They advised that Trudeau would pose for me in a special photo session in Newfoundland, and that the resulting photographs would be couriered to me immediately thereafter. Meanwhile, I decided that I couldn't wait any longer and began my painting based on my drawing concepts. I knew that if I missed the deadline, my efforts would be all for naught and they would simply use photography for the cover. I had four days left.

Three and a half days later, the portrait was finished, and so was I. I was exhausted, having persevered for the entire eighty-four hours without sleep. Walter arrived within an hour or so with the package of photographs, which *Time* had sent to him, instead of directly to me, from Newfoundland. It was just as well, since when I saw them I felt that my concept was much better. The portrait was carefully wrapped and Walter delivered it back to Toronto. I collapsed in a long-overdue sleep for a whole day and night!

Not long afterwards, I received a congratulatory letter from the editor, declaring the cover portrait to be "the best she had seen in her twenty-four years at *Time*." *Time* magazine's bet then paid off. Trudeau won the leadership vote and the portrait appeared on the cover of the April 12, 1968, issue.

. . .

During the summer of 1968, I had confirmed my need for an improved studio facility. The compressed confines of my one small room in the stone house were too restricting for my work, as well as too compromising for our family needs. Along with the stone house and the mill, on the property there was a barn with a stone rolled foundation, located at an angle between the house and the mill and only about seventy-five feet away from each. This would become my new studio building, and work began in November with plans that I had drawn up. It was to be completed in January, so the work accumulated for the '68 show would be the last to be created in the stone house studio.

Each successive period of work culminated in a new exhibition, but more than that, it was a learning process that provided me with continuing improvement in both my technical handling of my media, and my conceptual response to my visual experiences. A year or two earlier, a major collector of my work, Peter Bronfman of Montreal, advised me to paint fewer works which, he explained, would create "higher values." I replied, "But Peter, then I wouldn't learn as much." He agreed that my point was a valid one, but continued to stress that my work should have much higher prices. "That will come, over time," I replied.

The '69 show at Moos did reflect higher prices, as the post-opening newspaper reviews readily reported. As with my previous exhibitions, there was a lineup outside the gallery on a cold December day. But this time the lineups began in the early afternoon for an opening that wouldn't take place until that evening! I looked out the window of the gallery, just after lunchtime, and saw a young man jogging about to keep warm, while his blanket and newspaper rested on the steps. I soon learned that he was a law student and that he was determined to buy a work from the show when it opened. (He did!) I bought him a cup of coffee and thanked him for his persistence. Within the hour, others had arrived to join the line and it continued to grow throughout the afternoon. The next day a story in the *Toronto Star* was headlined, "Lineups Like the CNE for Danby Show." The exhibition was sold out within hours of the doors opening at eight p.m.

1970s

Working at the Mill

My work was advancing well toward having my annual exhibition at Gallery Moos, opening on December 8, 1970. It would feature my newly created serigraphs for the first time, and therefore fewer paintings. Yet I'd been working long hours on my egg temperas as well. While there would not be much of a quantity (there were only three), two of them were my largest. *The Armstrong Miller*, a portrait of George Parkinson, who posed for me below the mill that I purchased from him three years earlier, and *Reflections*, a study of our neighbour's son, Neil Foote, who posed for me standing waist deep in the river directly beside the mill. The third tempera painting was of a more modest size, and titled *Boom Hook*. There were also a good number of watercolours, drawings, and studies.

I was finally understanding how to paint with egg tempera, after seven long years of trial and self-learning. Suddenly, revelations offered themselves to me that I hadn't anticipated, and I realized that they could only have materialized through the long process of learning by design. In spite of my continual references to Cennini's treatise on tempera painting throughout the years, my insights only arrived after seven years of working with the medium, which I realized was just as he had proclaimed to his readers that it might be.

The large windows of my studio building faced the stone mill, where work was progressing on the new roof and structural revisions as the New Year began. A large crane was on hand for many days and was lifting massive beams and other materials into place, with workers busy working on scaffolds. Every day multiple decisions were required that pre-empted my ability to address my work in the normal manner. However, I was able to intersperse these, with my brother Marvin's assistance, and began focusing on new work as often as possible. I saw the realization of the mill's rejuvenation through my window, and it was a profound motivation for my productivity. More often than not, I would work the night shift to make up for lost time during the day, and it became my habit.

Walter Moos had arranged for me to have my first exhibition in New York, to take place in February '72 at the William Zierler Gallery, on Madison Avenue, across from the

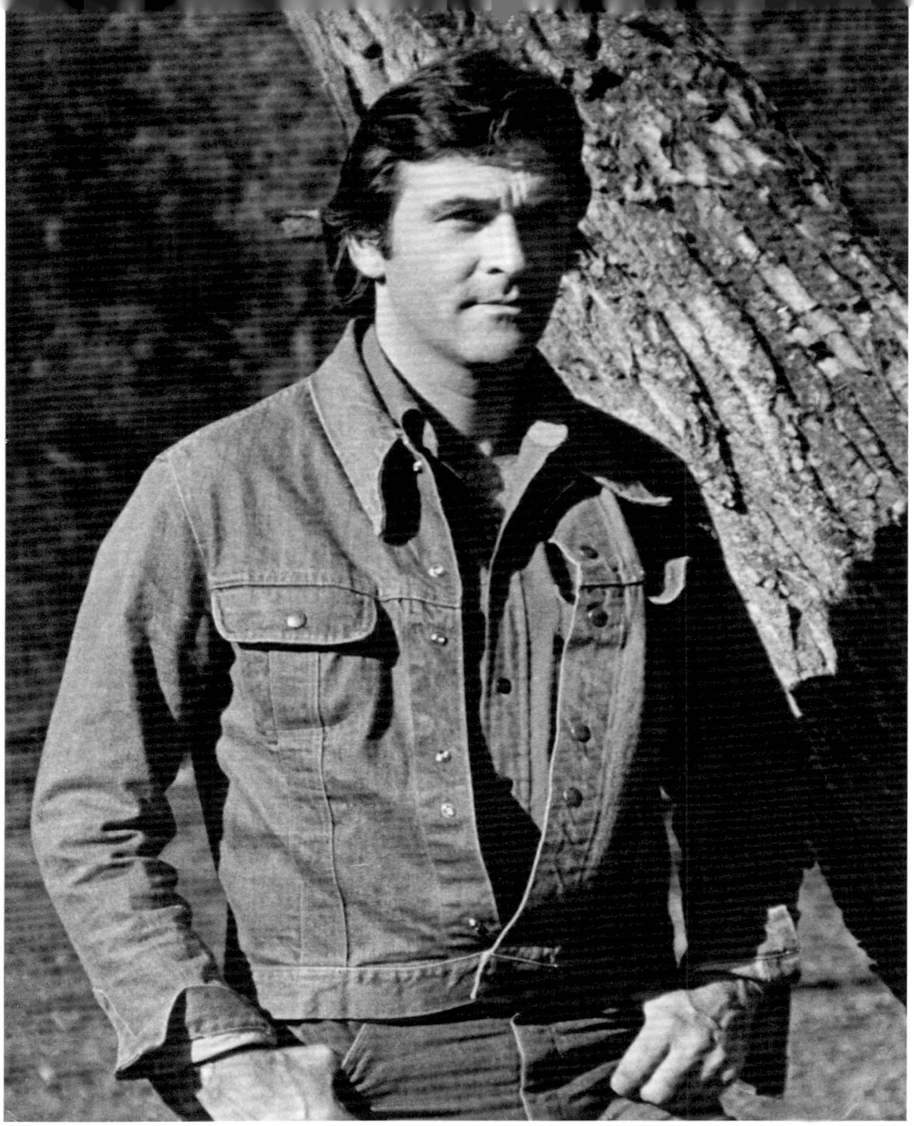

Whitney Museum. This meant that I would need to have a very productive year indeed, if I was to fulfill the commitment for new works for a Gallery Moos December exhibit, as well as an early February show to follow. Yet I remained confident that I could meet the challenge. In fact, as well as an increased painting objective, I managed to deliver four serigraph editions to Moos that year, including *Bobsled*, *Mill Wheel*, *On the Gate*, and *Early Autumn*.

My painting schedule improved when the first phase of the mill work was completed, in late March 1971, and I even managed to celebrate the mill's new look when it became the subject for a tempera titled *Blowing Up*. With my motivation spurred on and my opportunities to respond to my visual world increased, it was a very busy year. I completed thirteen temperas as well as a number of watercolours and studies. Along with *Blowing Up*, the temperas included *Delicious*, *His MGB*, and *Snooker* — to my mind, all major efforts.

Portrait of Ken Danby, 1975
(photographer unknown)

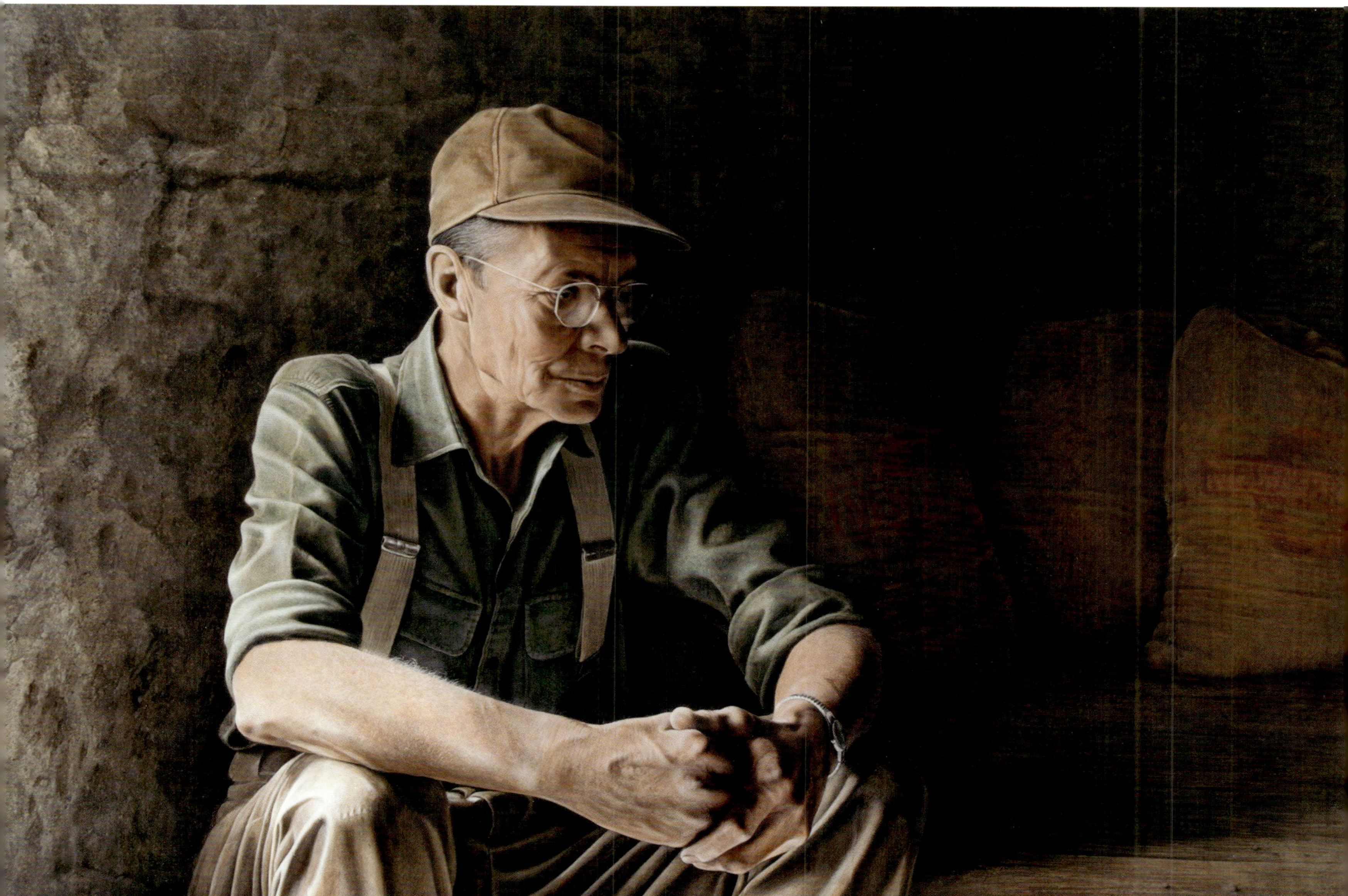

The Armstrong Miller, 1971

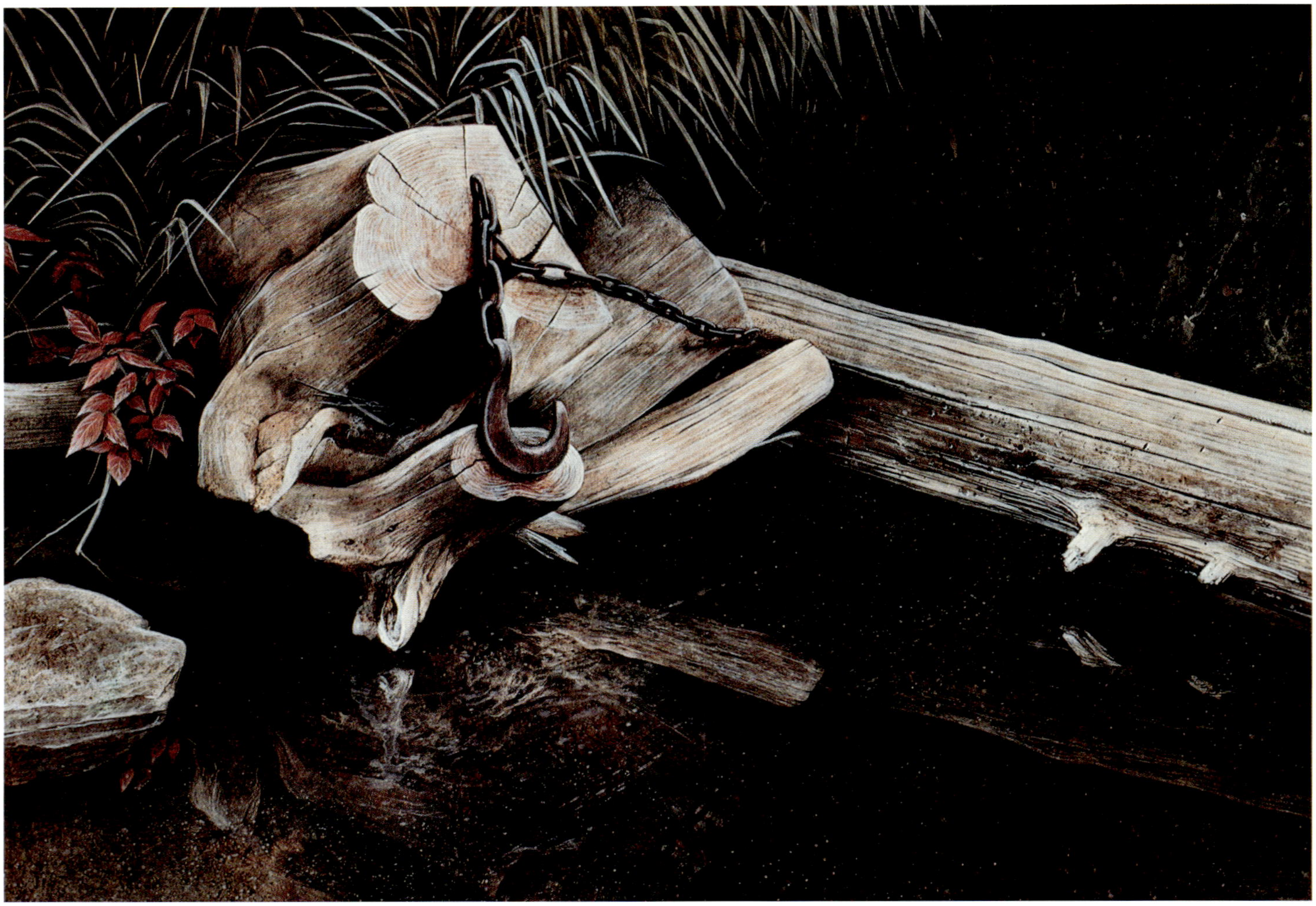

 Boom Hook, 1970

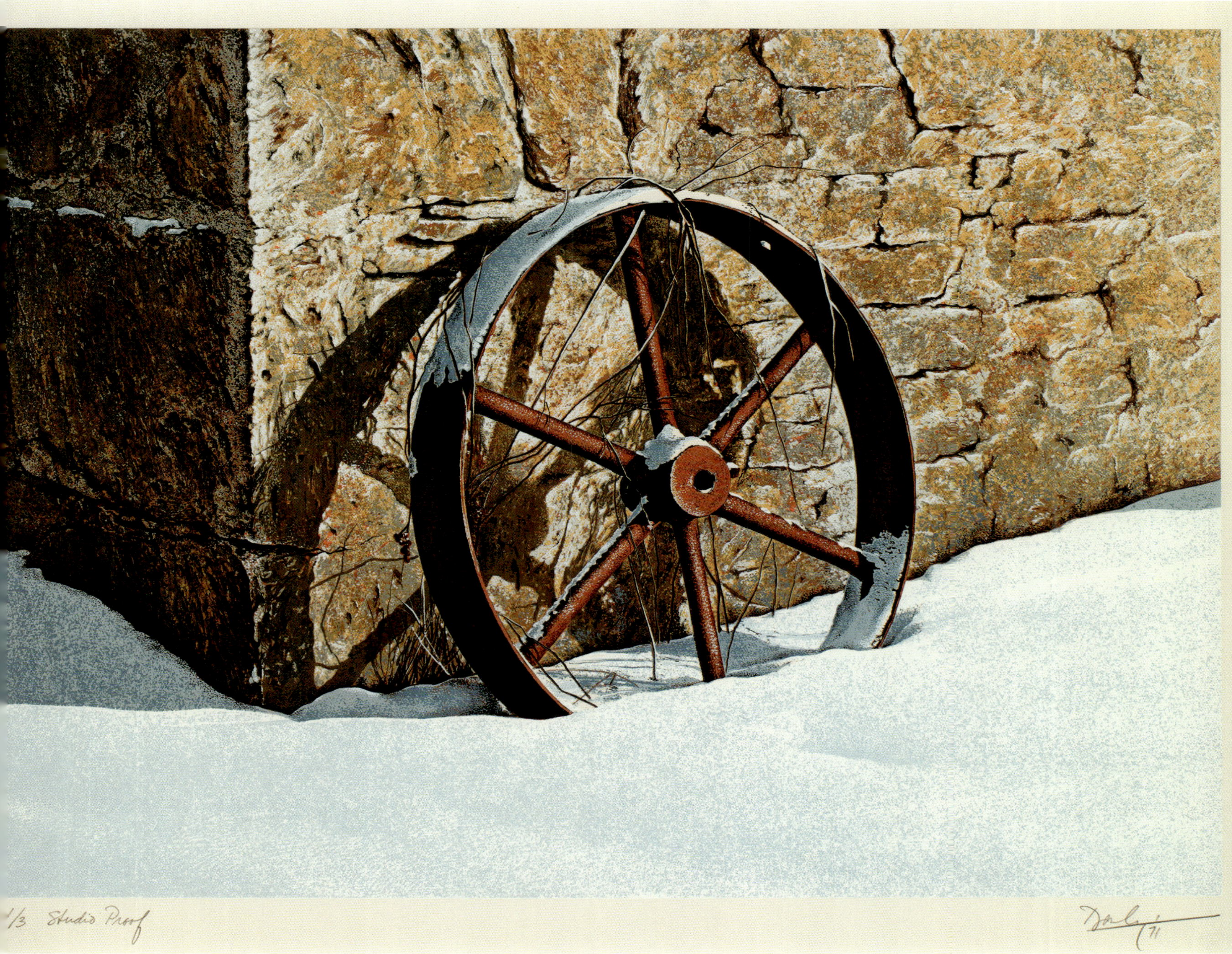

Mill Wheel, 1971

overleaf: **Blowing Up**, 1971

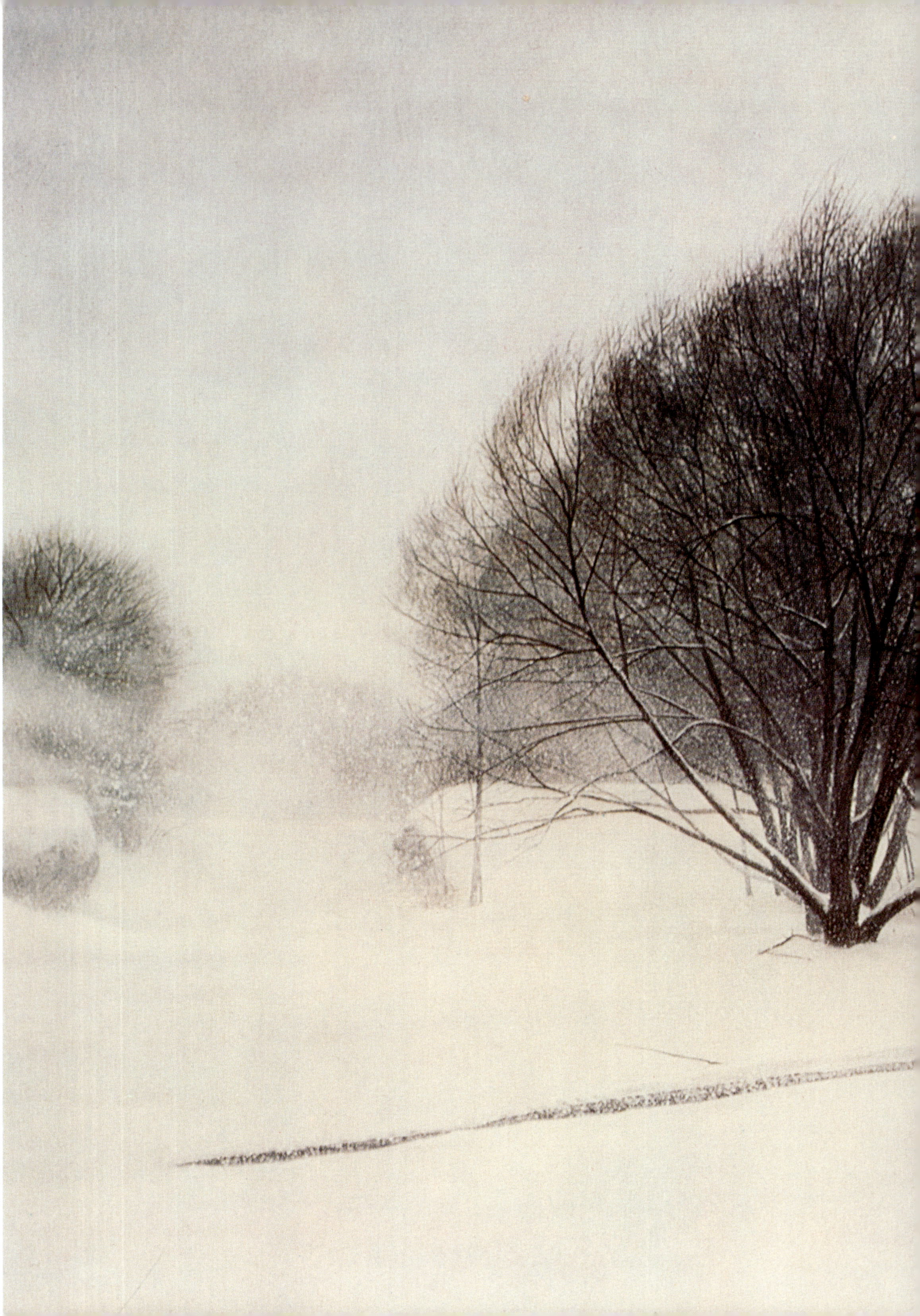

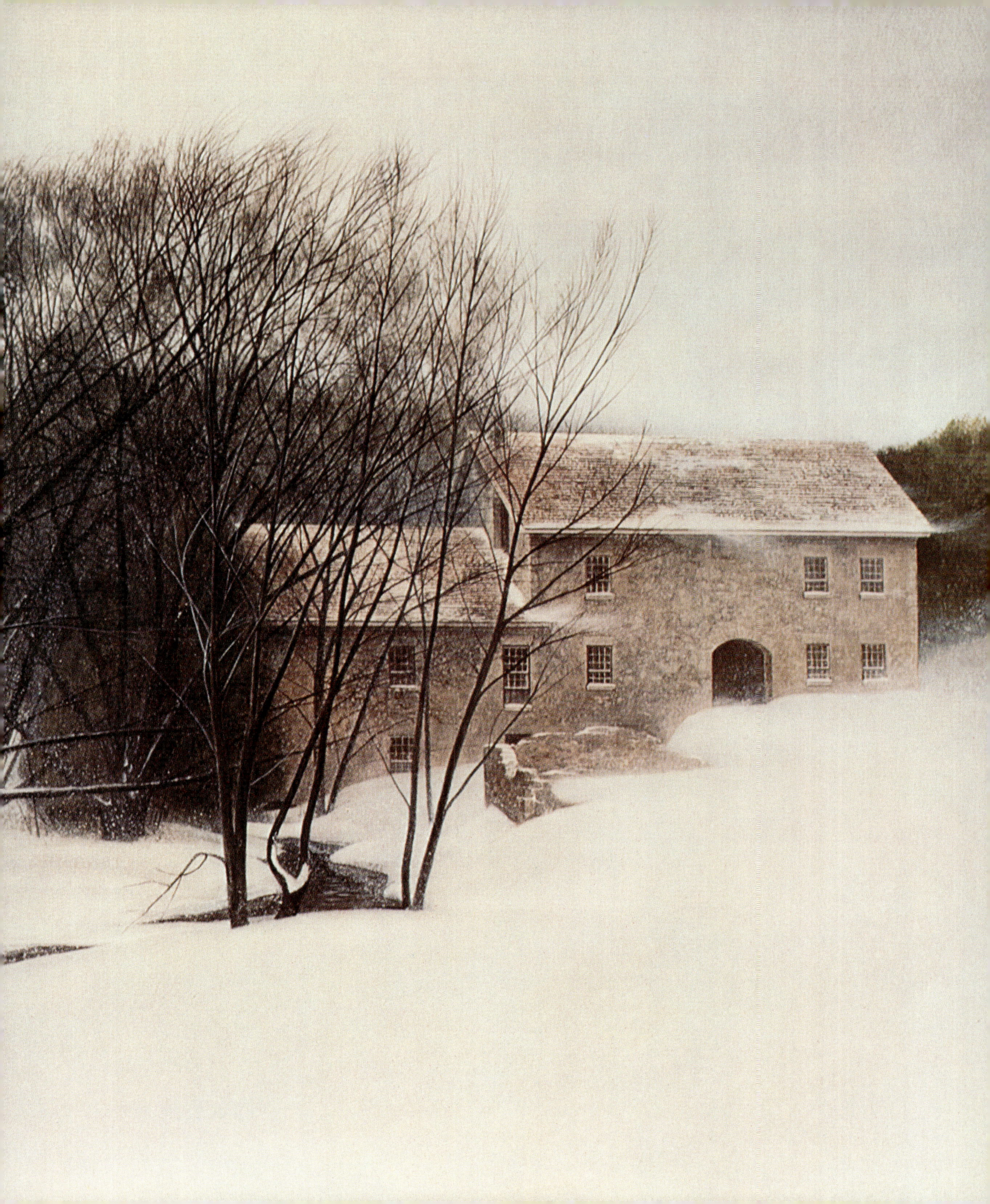

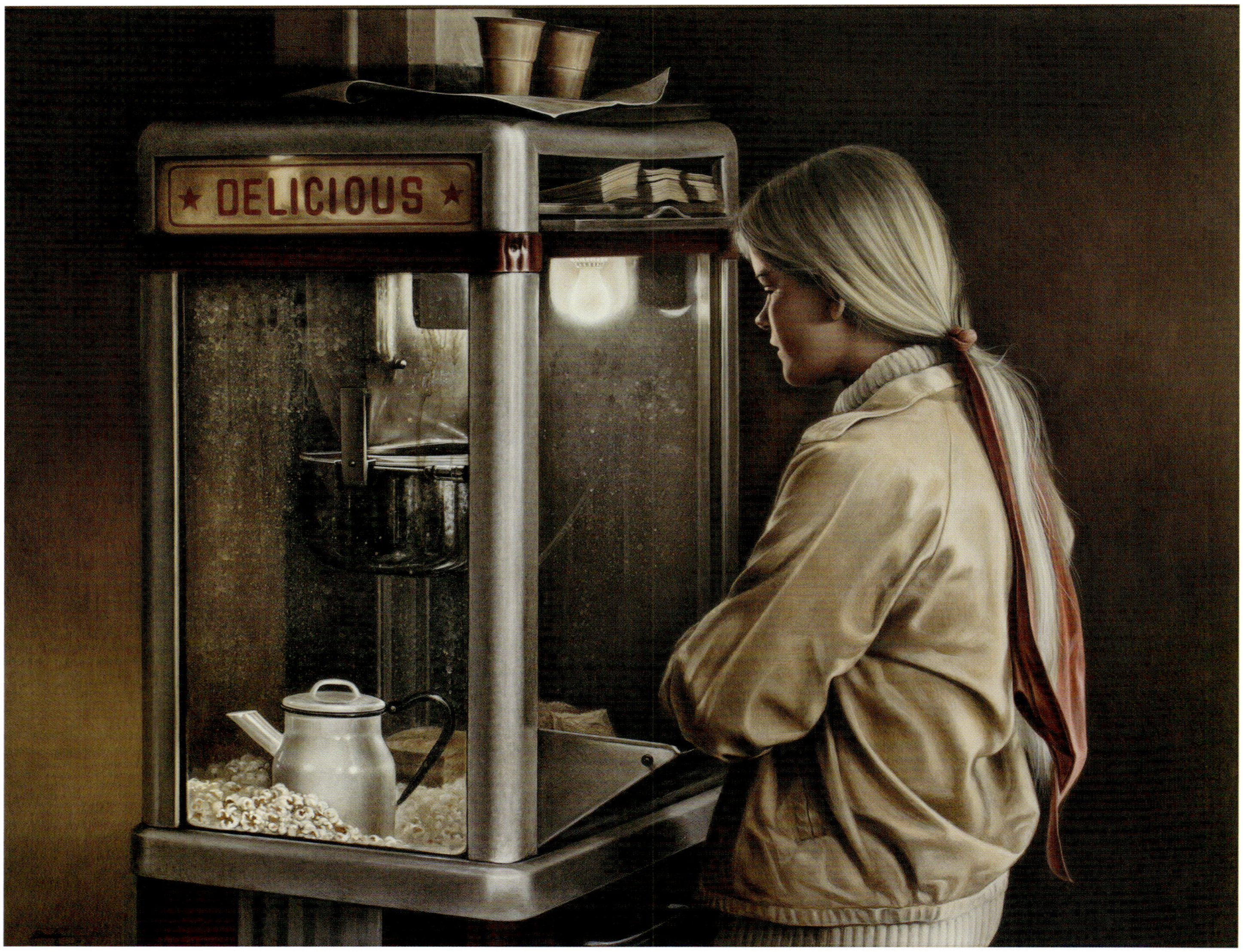

 Delicious, 1971

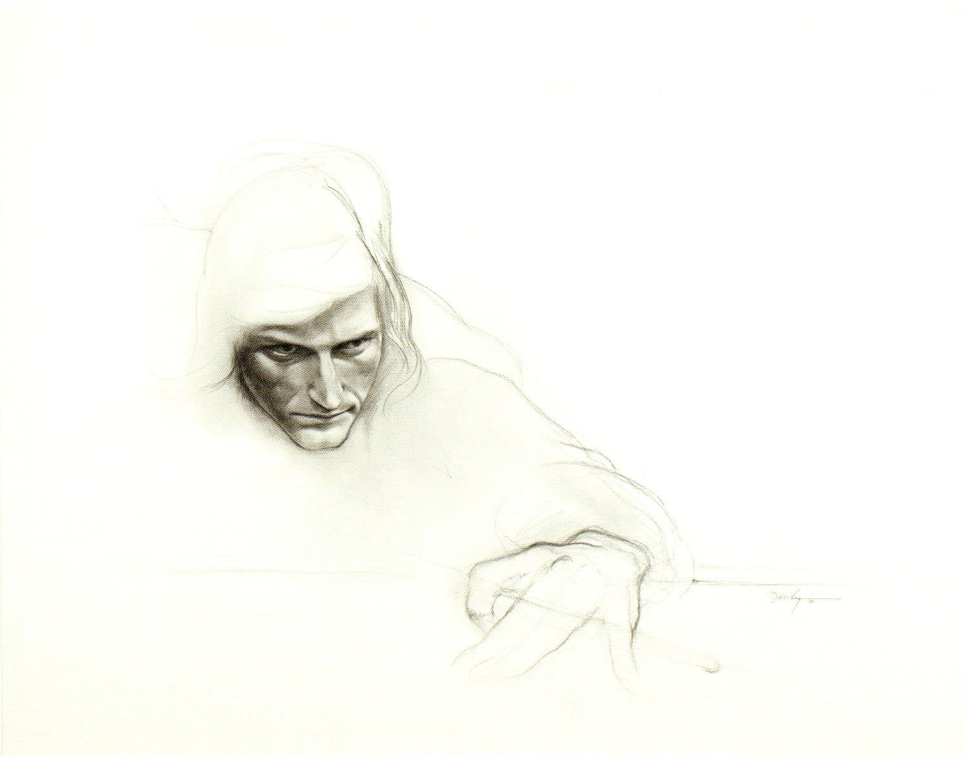

Study for Snooker, 1971

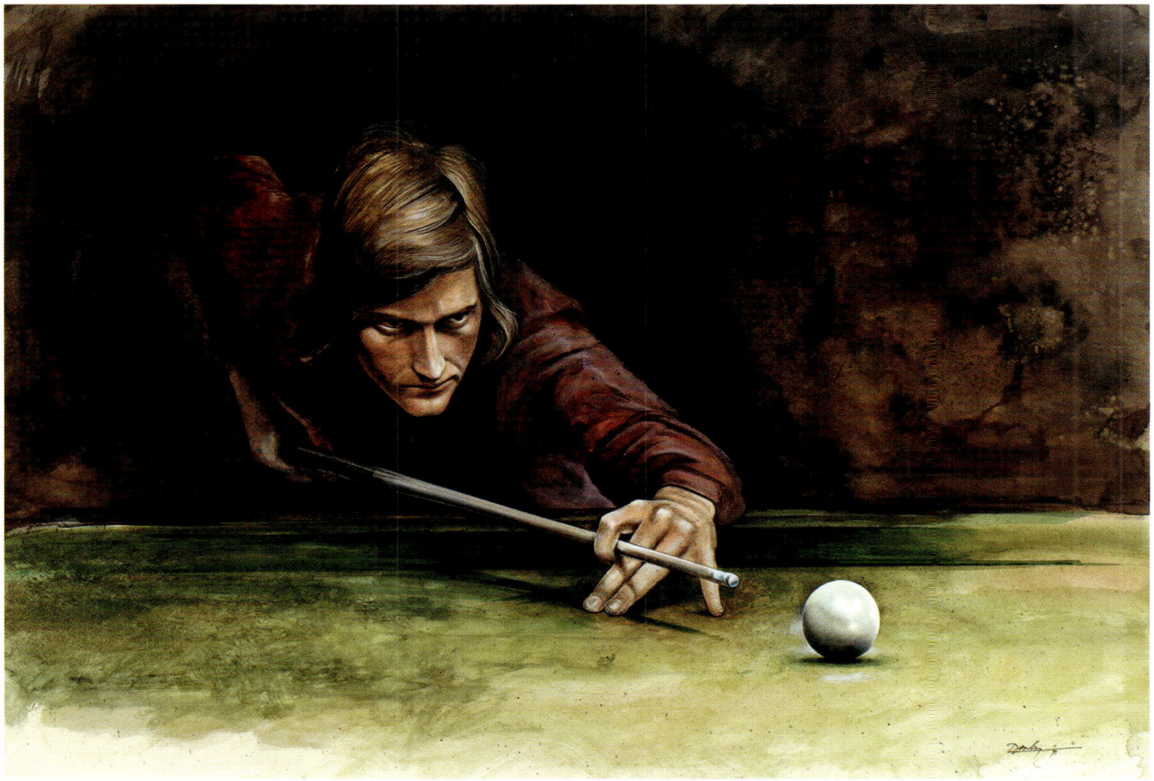

The year also saw a selection of my work exhibited in Paris, at the Biennale des Jeunes, through September to November (including the large tempera, *Reflections*, painted the year previously), and my serigraphs exhibited in Zurich, Switzerland. I was pleased to learn of the European interest in my work.

As the year advanced, I realized that no matter how determined I might be, the calendar would simply not provide enough time to complete all new work for two exhibitions just two months apart, and I refused to allow the work to be compromised in the attempt. I discussed the problem with Walter and with Bill Zierler. We agreed there could only be one satisfactory answer. Works that were sold at the Moos exhibition in November-December would have to be made available, on loan, to bolster the presentation in New York. In this way, Bill Zierler's gallery wouldn't have as much to sell but he would, more importantly, have a much stronger presentation, which we all agreed was the more important issue, since this would be my first New York showing.

A week after the Moos opening, Walter brought a visitor to my studio, Mario Amaya, chief curator of the Art Gallery of Ontario. Mario had agreed to write an introduction to my catalogue for the New York show in February. He wanted to meet me and discuss the new work in order to gain insights for his forthcoming efforts. We enjoyed a few good hours of conversation, interspersed with first-hand looks at a few new temperas and watercolours. Later, he responded with a very insightful essay for the catalogue.

Of course, once again, the Moos opening sold out, and later, a number of the temperas went to New York on loan, for February. The New York show received admirable attention and reviews, as well as sales! One of the works was acquired by the renowned Hollywood actor, Henry Fonda. Another ended up in Paris in the collection of the noted fashion designer Daniel Hechter.

In early March 1972, I began work on a new serigraph, the first of three to be created that year. It became *The Skates*, a twenty-two-colour effort that resulted from my having painted a watercolour study of my skates, left at the back door, following a game of shinny on the river ice. The following morning I had discovered them, dusted with a bit of evening snow and bathed in the morning sunlight. Later, I felt that I could improve on the study and decided to create the image as a serigraph rather than as a tempera.

Realizing that *The Skates* epitomized my interest in hockey, I began to reflect again on a significant experience of two and a half years earlier. With a few friends and young neighbours, I had been playing shinny on the river ice. It was my first return to hockey after nearly ten years of absence from the game. Afterwards, I had vivid recollections of skating in on the goalie, who was wearing a mask. It wasn't that I was surprised by the mask. I was certainly aware of its place in hockey through Jacques Plante's equipment innovation in the '60s, but this was my first occasion to find myself actually facing a masked goalie at ice level.

The image, and the idea of it, locked into my mind for a long time, as often happens from my experiences. Yet, whenever I thought about the idea as a painting, I'd dismiss it as being too *Sports Illustrated* to be taken seriously as art. But, finally my image of *The Skates* persuaded me to think of it again, and I began to realize that as a personal experience, it was worthy of being pursued further.

I enlisted the help of my young neighbour and borrowed his goalie equipment to assess in my studio. Then I found a local goalie willing to pose for me. The result of considerable effort through the following summer months, it became a tempera painting of an anonymous goalie, titled *At the Crease*.

As it happened, the third individual to view *At the Crease*, after Judy and my brother Marvin, was my young son Ryan. Just twenty months old at the time, he came into the studio with his mother, and I picked him up in my arms and carried him over to see my finished painting. He took one look and suddenly burst out crying! Scared stiff! It was amazing! I couldn't calm him. It was pure fright and he wanted out of there! While we laughed about this afterwards, I was thrilled! If my painting could cause such a response from a one-and-a-half-year-old boy, I knew it was potent. *At the Crease* was completed in August and was included in my exhibition at Gallery Moos, which opened on December 9.

The exhibition once again generated an advance lineup at the door and sold out overnight! When I delivered *At the Crease* to Walter Moos, he looked at it for some time,

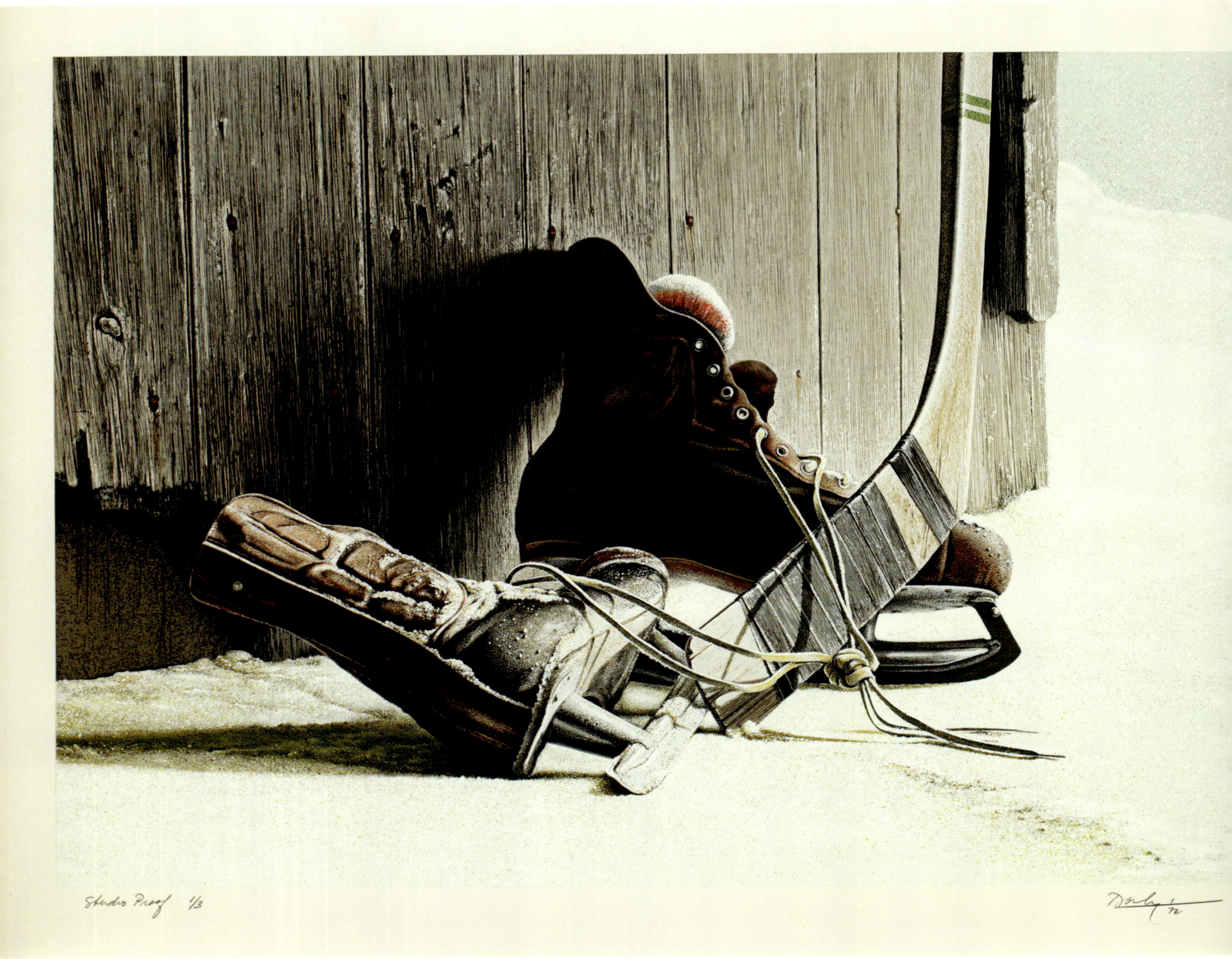

 The Skates, 1972

with a certain reservation. He then turned to me and said, "This is a strong painting, Ken. But, what am I to do with it? Who would buy this?" I replied, "I don't know, I just had to do it." Despite Walter's doubts about finding a buyer, it sold to a major collector the day before the show officially opened. Earlier, in September, the hockey world and all of Canada was focused on Team Canada and its dramatic come-from-behind win over the Russians in the "Super Series" of '72. When my painting was exhibited, many people, including in the media, assumed that it had been inspired by the Team Canada series. But in fact, the painting was completed well before the series began and really had nothing to do with it. In hindsight, one might say that my timing was good, which I think is true, but it was absolutely pure coincidence.

And so, the guessing game had begun: who's the goalie in *At the Crease*? I've been asked this question countless times over the years, and the reality is, the goalie is not intended to represent any particular player, but simply the personification of a goalie.

Years later, a woman expressed to me her admiration for the painting and described it as, "The one you did of Ken Dryden." I thanked her for her appreciation of the work but added, "It's not Ken Dryden." She paused, thought for a moment, and strongly said, "Yes, it is!" I responded by saying, "But, I'm the artist, and I assure you it is not Ken Dryden." She then grew more animated and determined, replying adamantly, "Yes, it is!" I suddenly recognized her point and apologized. "Well, of course you're right — it's whomever you want it to be."

Since 1972, *At the Crease* has been the work that I am most recognized for creating. It has become my identification in the minds of those familiar with it. They may not know of the artist, but they know of this painting.

In his 1978 publication *Colombo's Book of Canada*, the author John Robert Colombo, identified *At the Crease* as a visual icon, on a par with CBC's or CN's logos as a Canadian symbol. Upon seeing a reproduction, Andrew Wyeth described it as "a terrifying and exciting image." My biographer, Paul Duval, defined it as "possibly the finest sport picture in Canadian art." And so it went. I had obviously created something that made an impact, and it had been achieved only through the gradual lessening of my reluctance to respond to it as a subject.

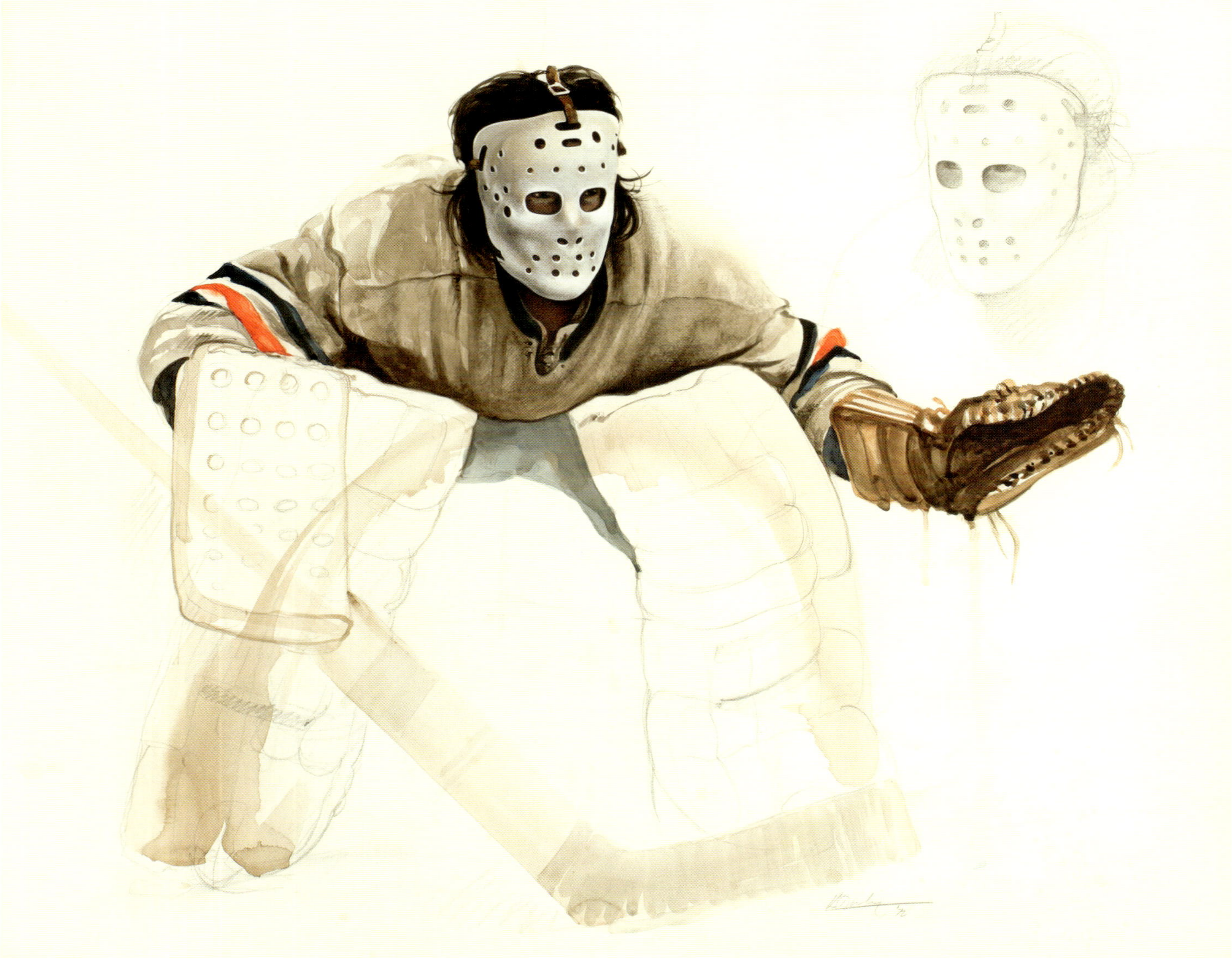

 Study for At the Crease, 1972

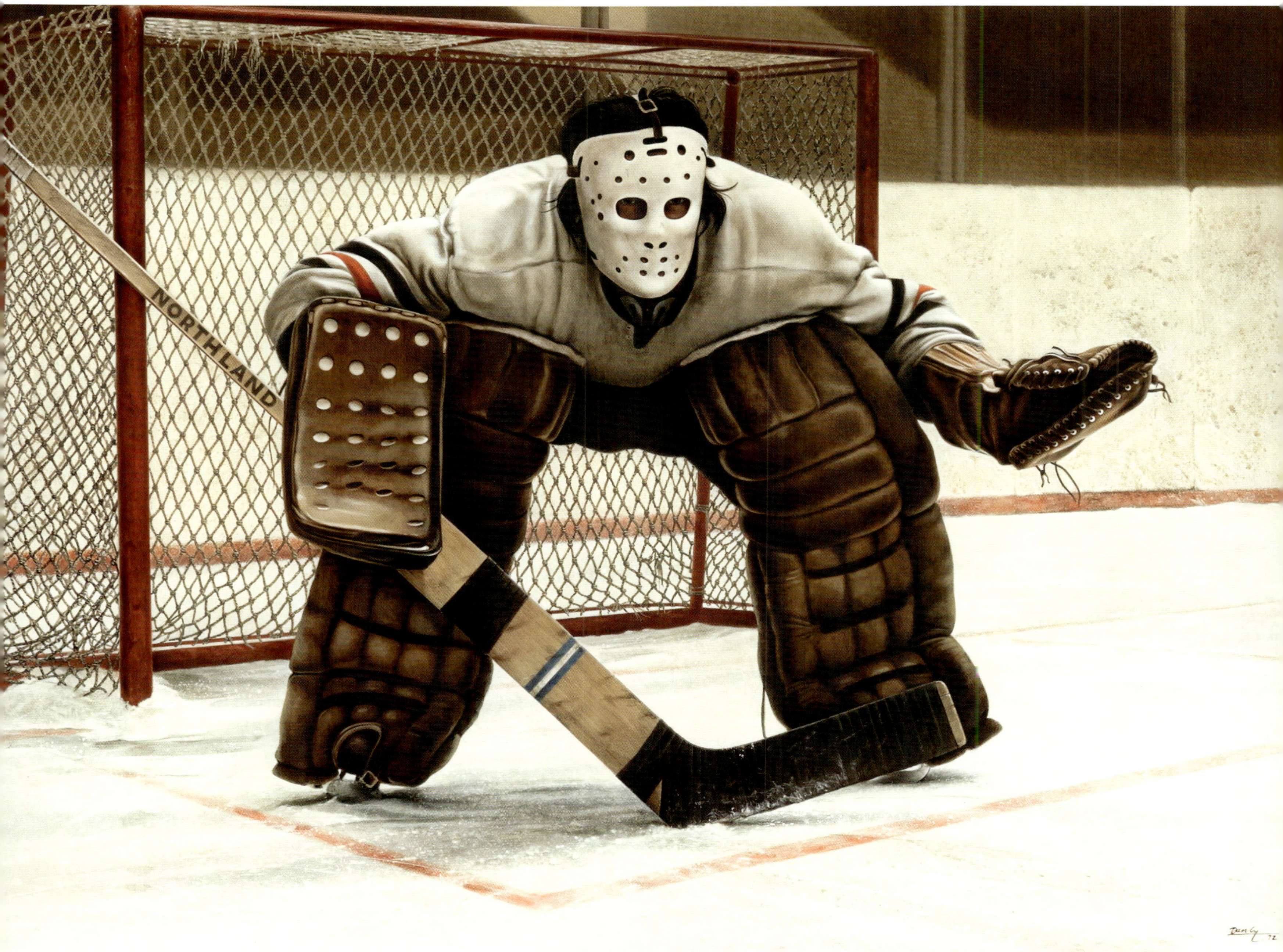

At the Crease, 1972

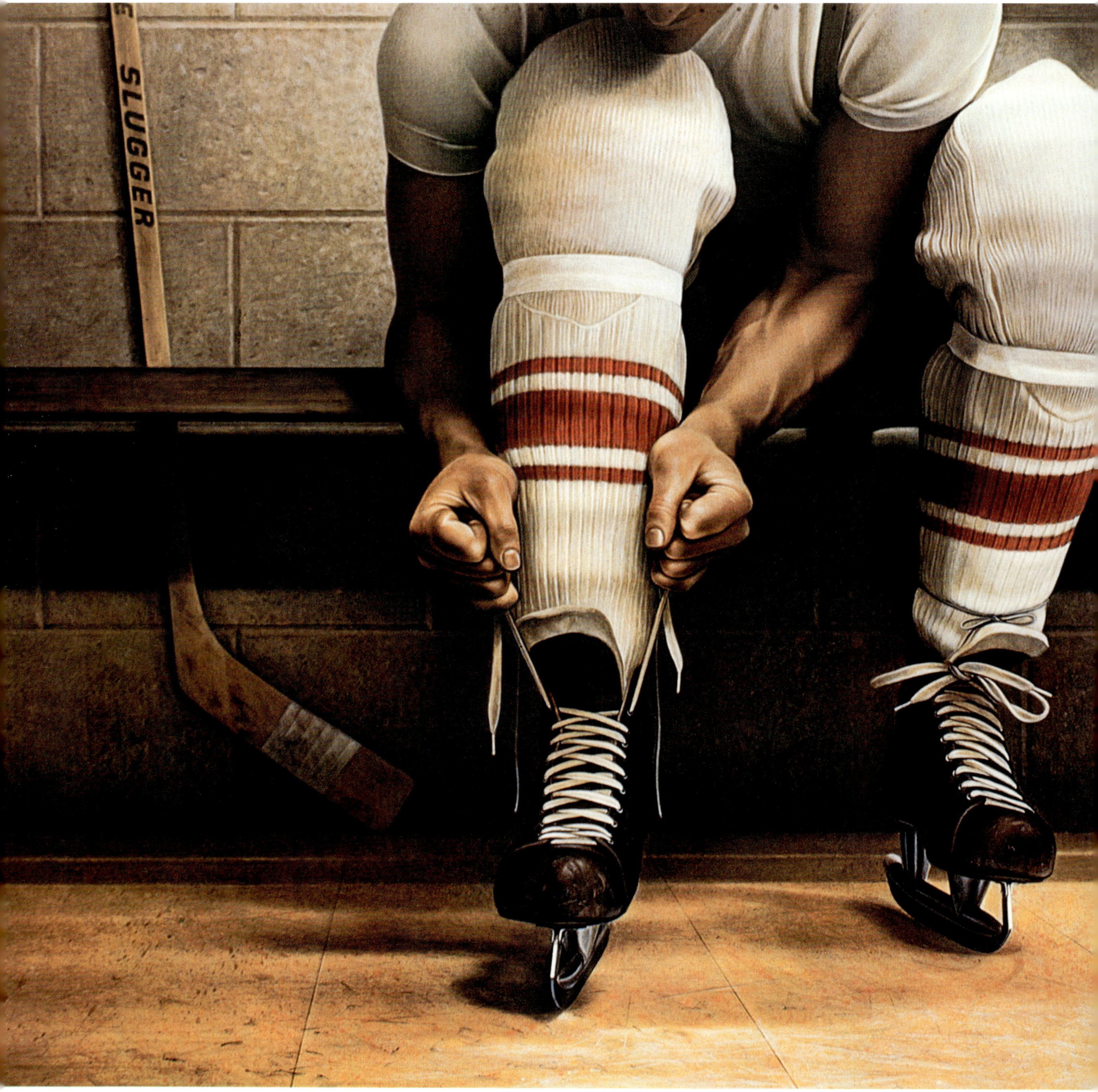
SLUGGER

Over the years since, a number of critics have accused me of deciding to paint *At the Crease* because, they presume, I knew it would be a popular image. What a shallow accusation. In fact, the opposite is the reality. It was a work that took two and a half years of reticence before I let it happen. And, as was evidenced by my dealer's response, there was no preconceived idea that anyone would even want to acquire it. At the time, it was a radical image and a departure for me, in broadening my subject matter beyond the themes of the rural life that I had been focused on. While painting it, I began to realize that sport could also be a legitimate subject in my art, as it's always been an important element in my life. It also caused me to understand that I was responding to a deeply felt urge prompted by my experiences, rather than just my visual encounters, which I believe had been happening previously in my work, but not to the same degree.

While painting *At the Crease*, I had contemplated the need for protective equipment and of suiting up for the game, and I recognized this as a pre-game ritual that I'd experienced countless times in the past. In January 1973, I was invited to join a team of old-timers in Guelph, called the Guelph Goodtimers. The familiar ritual of preparing for the game confronted me in the dressing room. I had one of my teammates pose for me and the result was *Lacing Up*, which became a tempera painting and, eventually, my second well-known image of hockey.

While *At the Crease* was certainly the bold centerpiece of my '72 exhibition, another tempera created that year was a stark contrast to it. *The Sunbather* was a nude-like portrayal of our neighbour's daughter and our babysitter, Lynn Gray. I had asked Lynn to pose for me, lying on a yellow chaise longue, which ultimately became a large serigraph called *Sunning*. During the session, we took a break and Lynn sat on the grass with her arms folded over her knees which immediately struck me as a much more contemplative pose and the one that I preferred to focus on.

Lacing Up, 1973

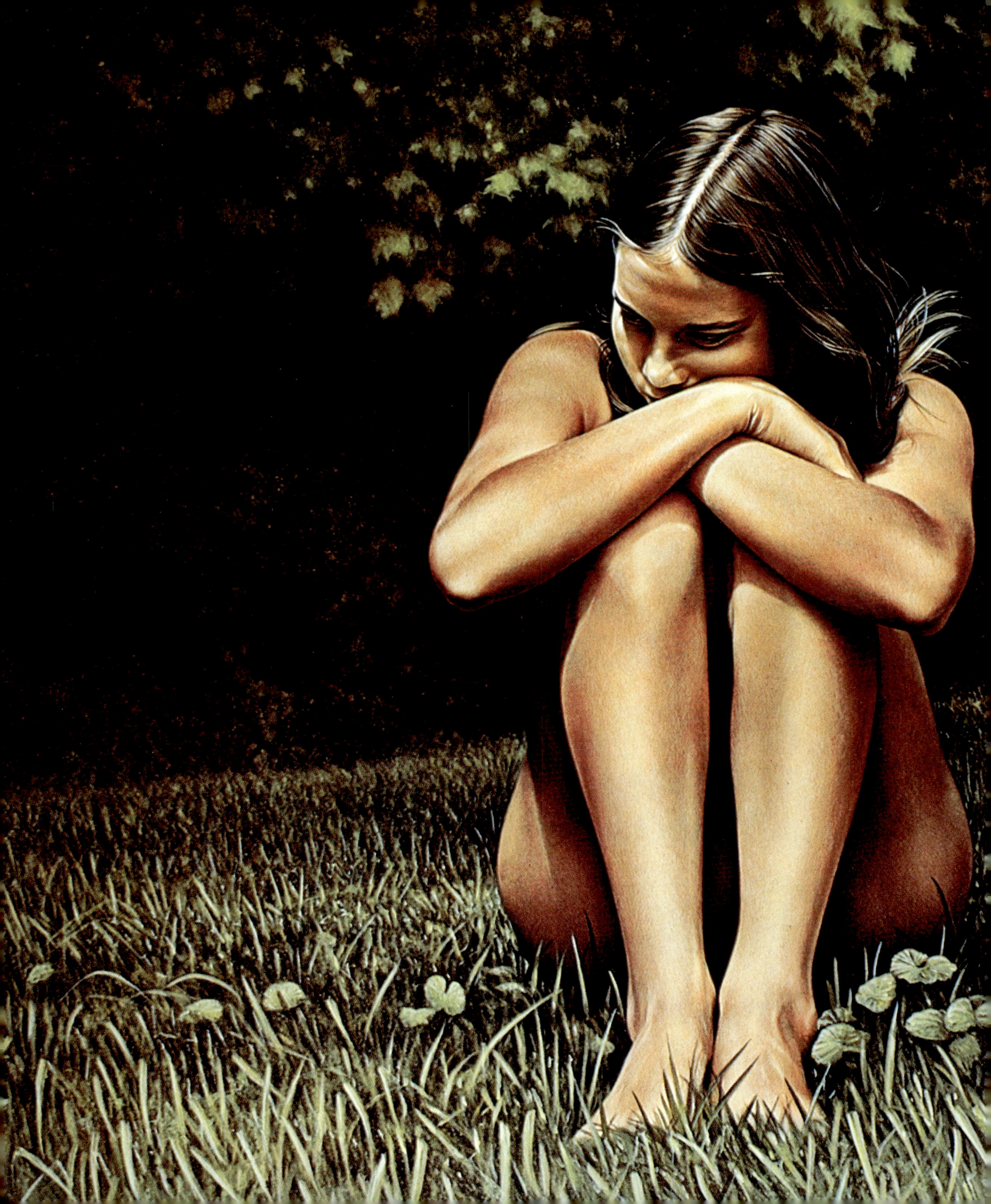

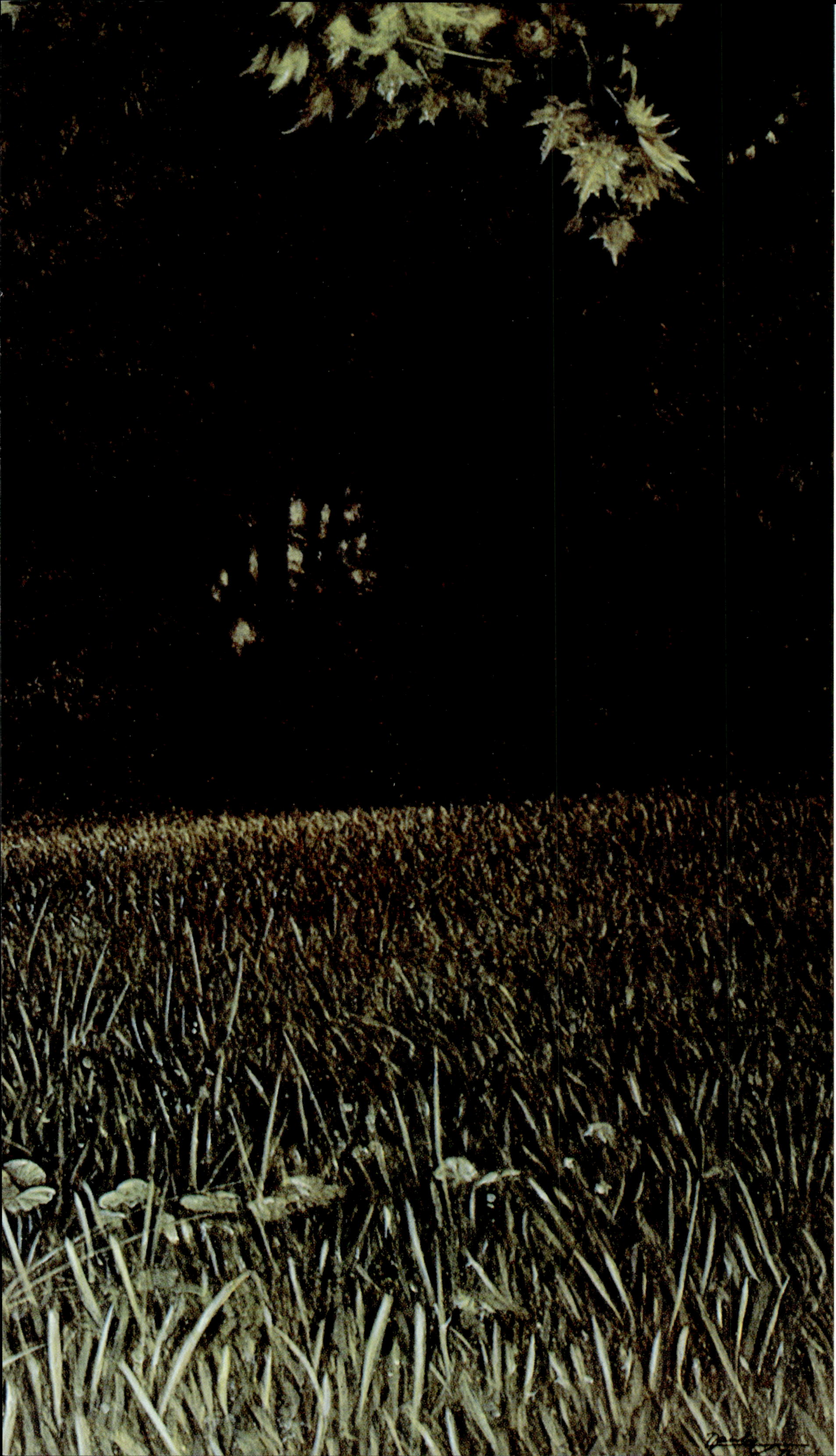

Sunbather, 1972

. . .

Another work that had percolated in my mind from at least three years earlier was a painting of my friend and neighbour Raymond Mur, who had moved to Canada from Spain and was known to all his friends as Pancho. We had met in 1968 and shared many good times together over family visits and socials.

In a spiritual sense, Pancho was larger than life. He was exuberant and full of energy, a magnetic personality that filled whatever room he entered.

One evening in 1970 Judy and I had visited Pancho and his wife Hilda for dinner. It was pouring rain, and after parking our car, we ran to the kitchen's enclosed porch and closed the door behind us. While we removed our wet coats and boots, the door opened again and there was Pancho. He was illuminated by the light of a single bulb over the door, wearing a yellow rain slicker, and was dripping wet. He had been out in the rain for quite a while, finishing some tractor work, and he had immediately come to greet us. We entered the kitchen, greeted Hilda, and shared an enjoyable evening together over drinks and dinner.

From that evening on, I couldn't shake the image of Pancho in his yellow slicker from my mind. Whenever he was the subject of a conversation, or when we spoke on the phone, this image would suddenly return to my memory bank. Eventually, more than three years passed before I realized that it simply had to be painted and I asked him to pose for me. He was thrilled by the idea. But he no longer lived at his farm, and he didn't have his yellow slicker.

I purchased a yellow poncho at Hercules Army Surplus in Toronto. We then arranged a number of posing sessions, which took place in the garage below my studio. The first session didn't work very well. Pancho arrived with a fresh haircut which wasn't what I was looking for. (This has occurred with a number of my models over the years and it's always disconcerting.) However, he happily went through the motions of posing simply to test the waters of what I was trying to find, and we agreed on another session a few weeks later, with no haircut.

When the time arrived, Pancho again looked like himself, and we set about trying to find a pose that pleased me. After a number of trials, I decided that a hands-on-hips,

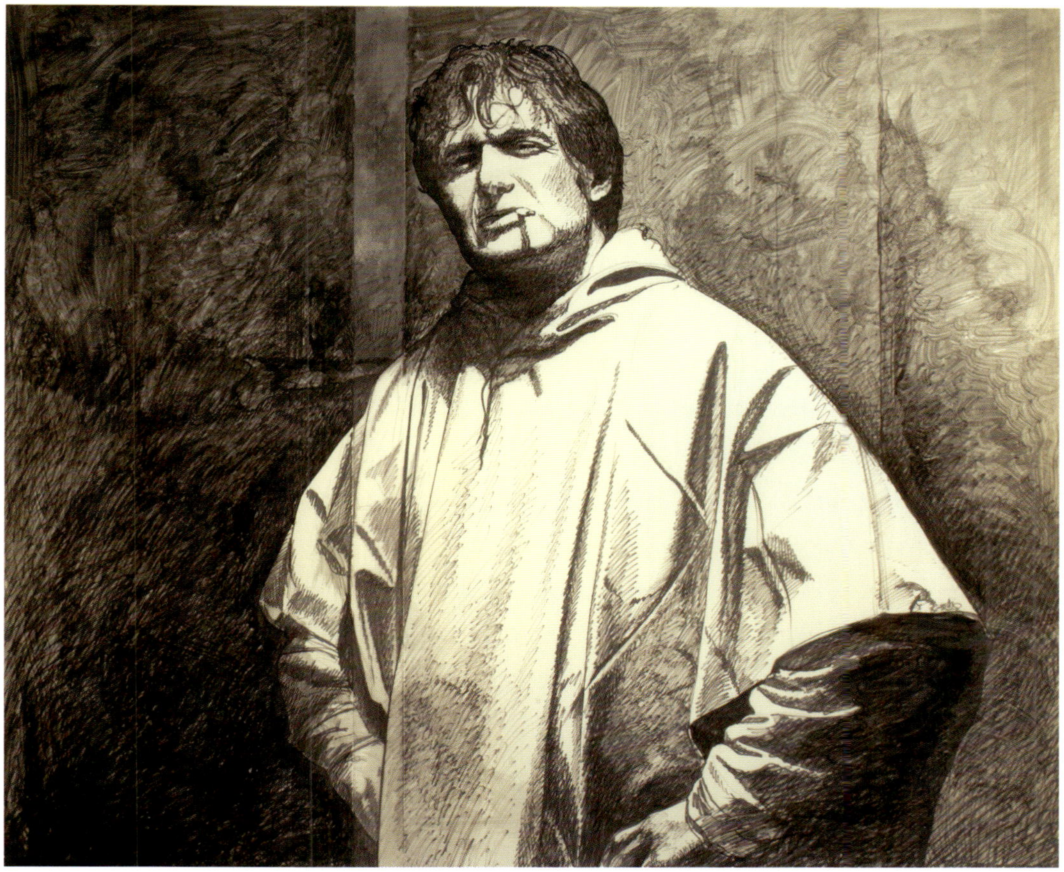

face-on view was what I wanted, but then I still sensed that it wasn't enough. I explained my concern and Pancho happily agreed to allow me to pour a bucket of water over his head every few minutes so that I could see the effects it produced. Later, I asked him to add the cigarette and decided to include it, as well. As we worked together to create the image I wanted, I told him that he had become a conquistador and he loved it.

The painting consumed many months of challenging work. I reached the stage of wanting to add the raindrops running down the yellow poncho. I hesitated, unsure of how I could capture this important detail. After an attempt at careful placement of a few drops, I stopped, realizing that it had to be much more spontaneous. With certain apprehension, I mixed a large bowl of diluted paint and then paused. I was contemplating the idea of splashing the paint onto the painting and actually letting it drop down

Drawing for Pancho, ca. 1973

naturally, while attempting to control it by tipping the panel when needed. If it didn't work, I'd risk ruining months of effort! I paced and worried for about half an hour, building up my courage. As it dried in rivulets of dripping paint, I rapidly controlled it as well as I could and it worked! Then I set about highlighting the actual water drops while breathing sighs of great relief.

When I showed the finished painting to Pancho, he was very pleased and proud. A week or two later, Walter Moos came for a visit and viewed the new painting. Not usually one to offer superlatives, he stood in front of it for some time, then turned to me and said, "There are very few artists in the world who could do this." And I was very pleased.

During the afternoon opening of the Zierler Gallery, in December 1973, I was engaged in a conversation with a number of visitors, when someone caught my eye as he walked through the door. It was Pancho himself! He had travelled all the way from Guelph to New York by bus to be at the gallery opening, at least a twelve-hour trip! I was astonished and delighted. We greeted each other warmly and I introduced him to many in the gallery. Before long he had become the centre of attention as he held court in front of his painting. Pancho took the long trip back to Guelph the next day after his unexpected arrival at the gallery. He had certainly been an inspired addition to the opening.

On May 3, 1975, I was shattered by a phone call from my friend Pancho's wife, Hilda. "Pancho's dead!" she exclaimed. I couldn't believe it. He was too young, too vibrant. It didn't make any sense! "What happened?" "He was working in the garden and just suddenly collapsed," she sobbed. "Within half an hour, he was gone!" He'd had a massive heart attack at the age of forty-three.

Judy and I drove to the house and tried to console Hilda and their two young daughters, Kathy and Teddy. Others arrived with similar intentions. It was a sorrowful day. The funeral took place three days later. I was a pallbearer. For the longest time afterwards, I often thought of how grateful I was for having painted *Pancho* and how proud he was to have been painted. As a result, it seems that his image will have a long life, indeed.

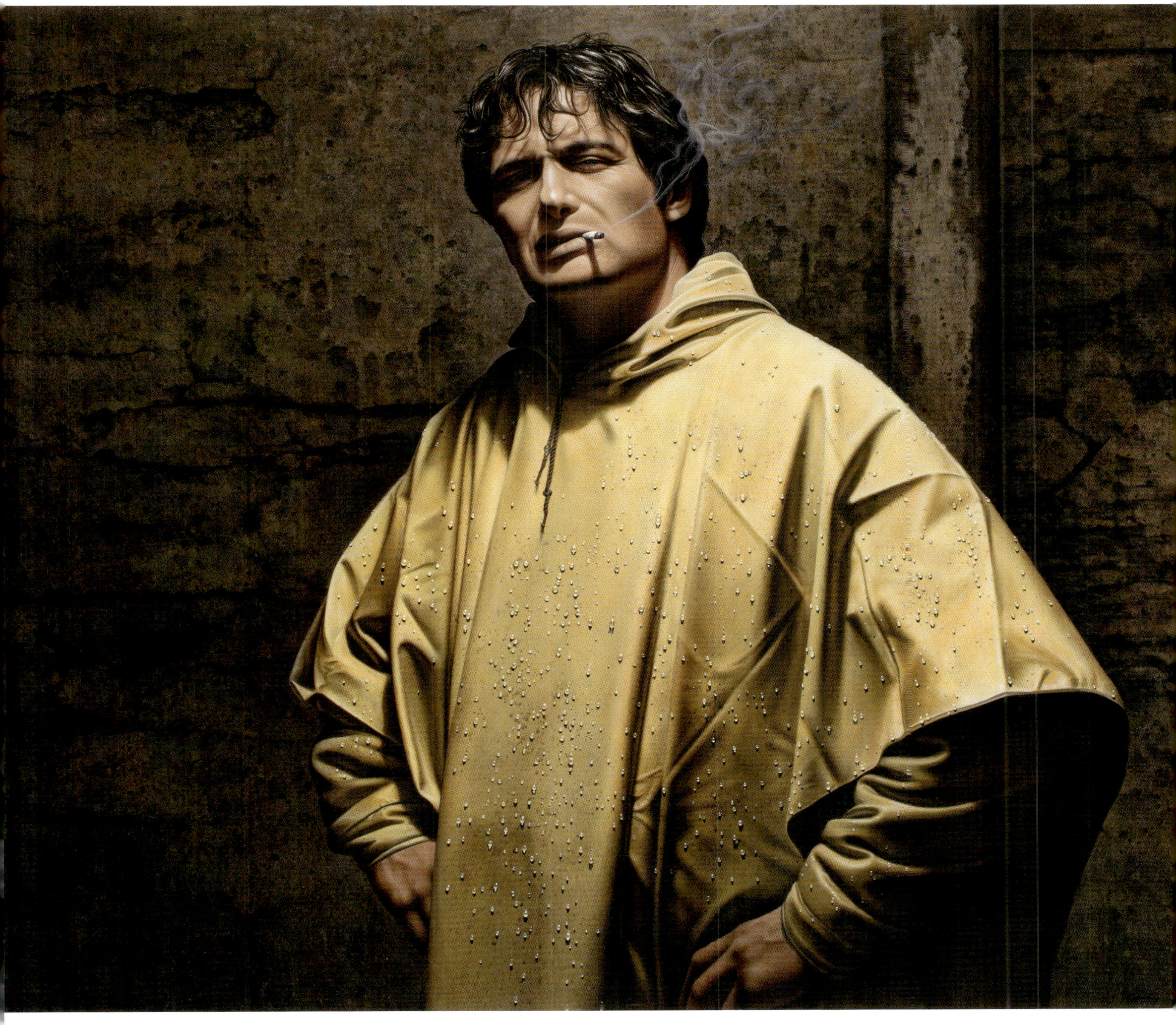

Pancho, 1973

. . .

In the first week of March 1974, I received a letter from the architect responsible for the design and construction of a new civic centre in my hometown of Sault Ste. Marie. It was both an inquiry and an invitation for me to create a large painting for inclusion in the new building under construction on the waterfront. The only criterion was for it to have some relevance to the Sault. I responded with interest, especially since I've always maintained a strong affinity for my hometown. I proposed the theme of the painting to be the Soo Locks, the canal that connects Lake Superior to the lower waters of St. Marys River and the North Channel into Lake Huron. It was not only a symbol of the Sault, but also the busiest shipping canal locks in the world.

My concept for the painting consisted of a head-on view of the locks, with the gates opening slowly as a large freighter waited to pass through from behind. The freighter that I hoped to depict was called the *Yank Canuck*, the only freighter to be registered in Sault Ste. Marie. I made a number of inquiries and learned that the ship was, in fact, currently at berth in the Sault, at the Algoma Steel docks, and that there was a delay in her departure, due to a Great Lakes pilots' strike. I waited for many days, hoping for word of a settlement, and then decided to go regardless, as it wasn't happening.

My dad met me at the airport. While driving to town, I explained what I was attempting to do and that I needed to see both the ship and the canal from water level. He was keen to help and said he could arrange for a friend to assist me with a small aluminum boat and outboard motor. The next day all was arranged and we met with Dad's friend downriver from the locks. Once aboard, we headed for the gates with the hope that I might soon be able to see them opening.

However, due to the pilots' strike there was no freighter traffic, so waiting for recreational boats or the tourist sightseeing vessel to pass through were the only alternatives. When it occurred, it was quite exciting and exactly as I'd anticipated, only more powerful. Once the upper gates were closed and the water released downstream, we were subjected to a rush of current and swirling eddies that made it extremely difficult to remain stationary, which was my need. Yet, once the lock had completed its voluminous release, the water calmed, and the gates began to open.

Following two or three episodes of this, and a lot of photos taken with my 35mm camera, I felt I had enough visual information to serve my needs. Then we entered the lock, to be raised to the higher level for entering the channel above where we found the *Yank Canuck* at the Algoma Steel dock. After shooting a roll or two of film, I had completed my first-hand research and we reversed our course to return to the boat owner's dock downriver. I thanked him for his kind assistance and then Dad and I drove to the locks to consult with the lockmaster regarding questions that I had. He was very helpful and invited me to call him if further information was needed. Meanwhile, he provided me with a couple of schematic diagrams and measurements of the locks.

Once in the studio, I was faced with the task of combining the images of the locks and the freighter in an authentic manner, and I realized that I would also need measurement of the ship to accomplish this. Once again, my dad assisted me. One of his colleagues in the Sault's Rotary club was "Skipper" Mansetti, who had owned the ship. Soon I received a set of drawings that provided for my needs.

Over a number of weeks, I diligently created studies and watercolours that assisted me in the pursuit of a final image for the painting. One of these became my attempt to assess how close I could advance the position of the freighter toward the gates, without sacrificing credibility. I called the lockmaster on two or more occasions to confirm this as I kept waiting to bring it farther forward, for increased dramatic effect. We finally settled on a closer distance when I agreed not to quote him on it!

On July 7, 1975, my completed tempera painting *Opening the Gates* was delivered to Sault Ste. Marie, and on the 26th, I attended the official opening of the new civic centre, where it was unveiled. Everyone was very pleased, and I was grateful to have been able to contribute to my hometown's celebration.

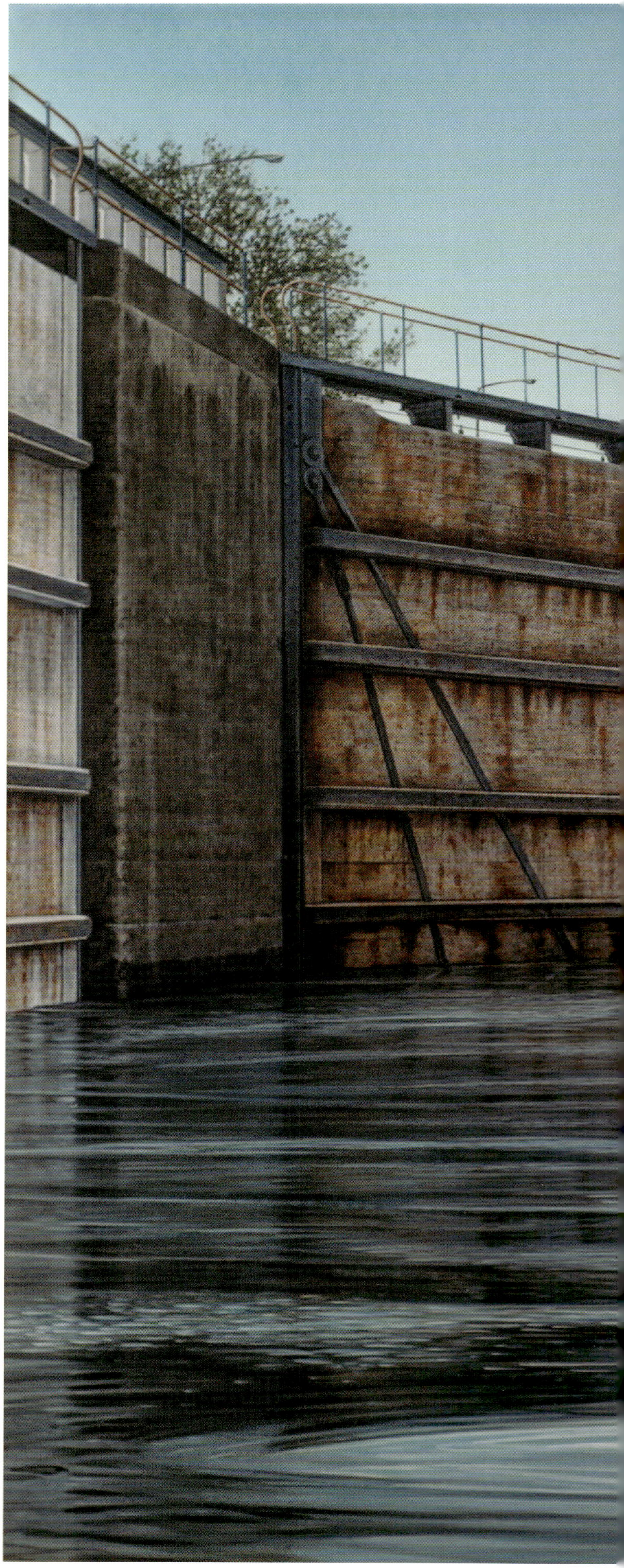

84 **Opening the Gates**, 1975

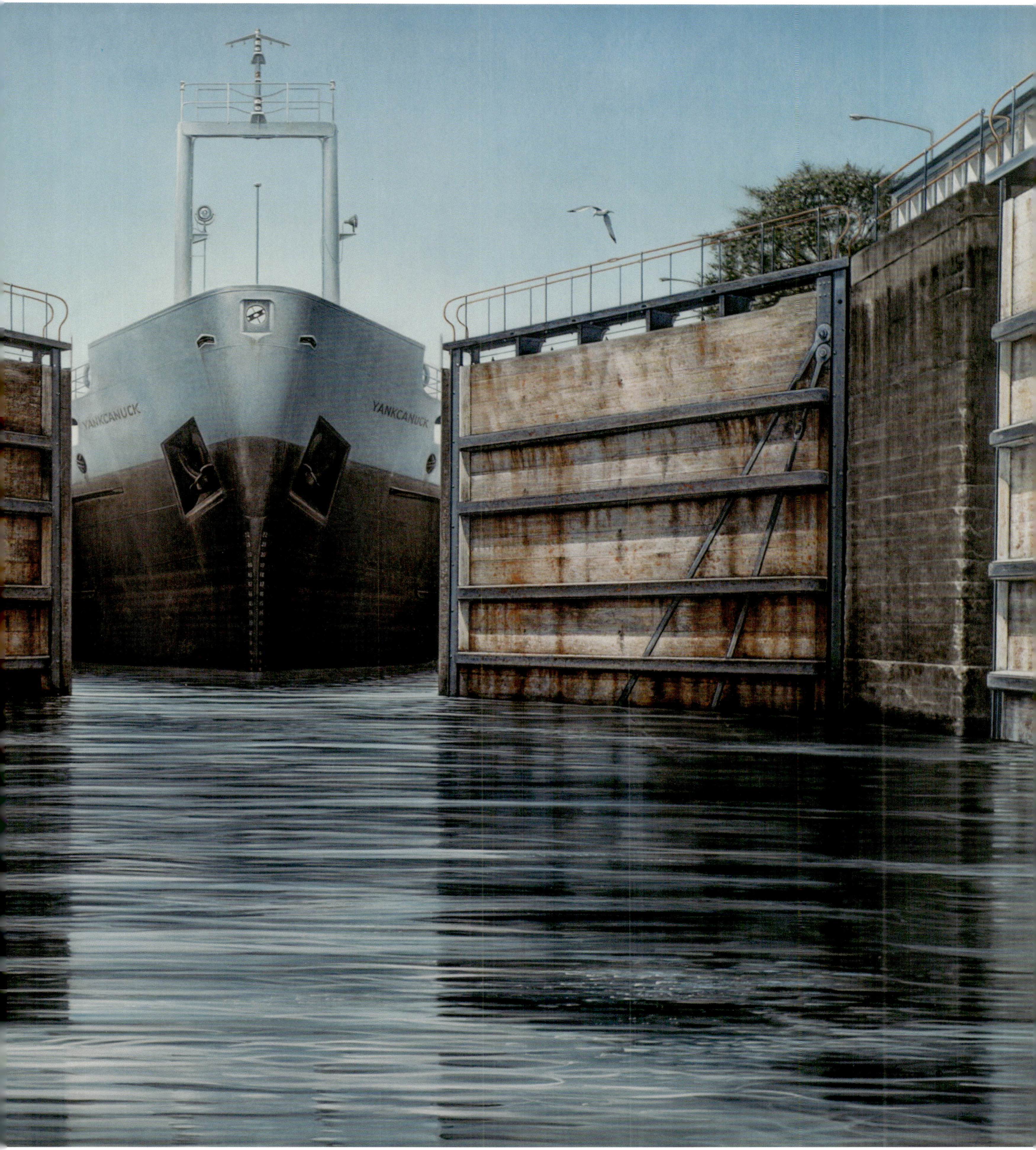
YANKCANUCK
YANKCANUCK

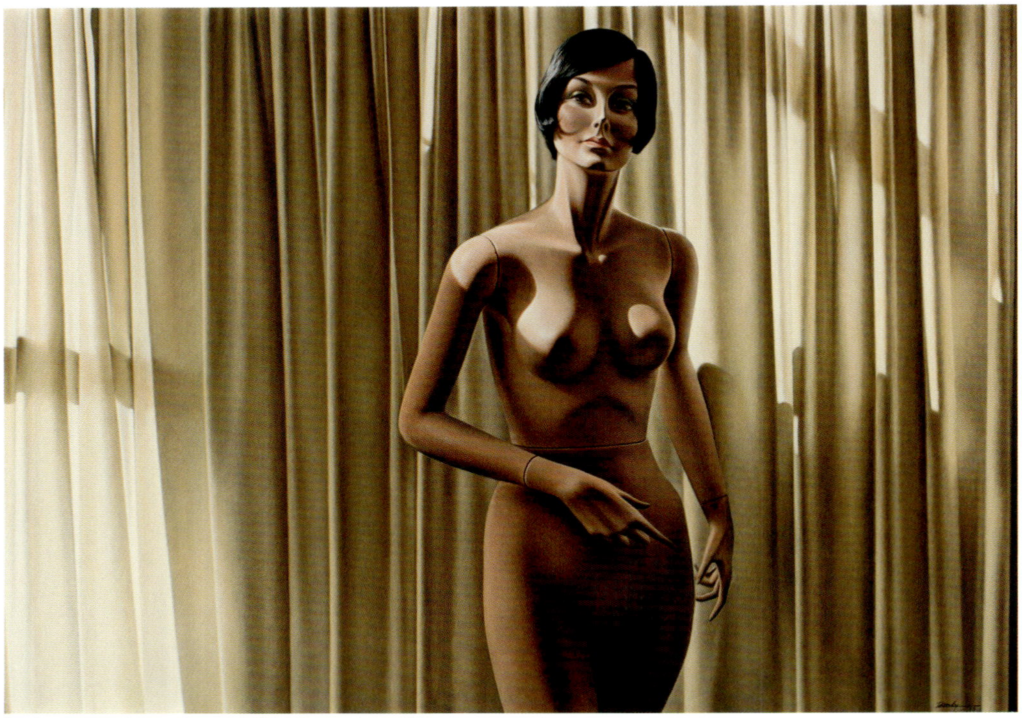

Mannequin, 1973

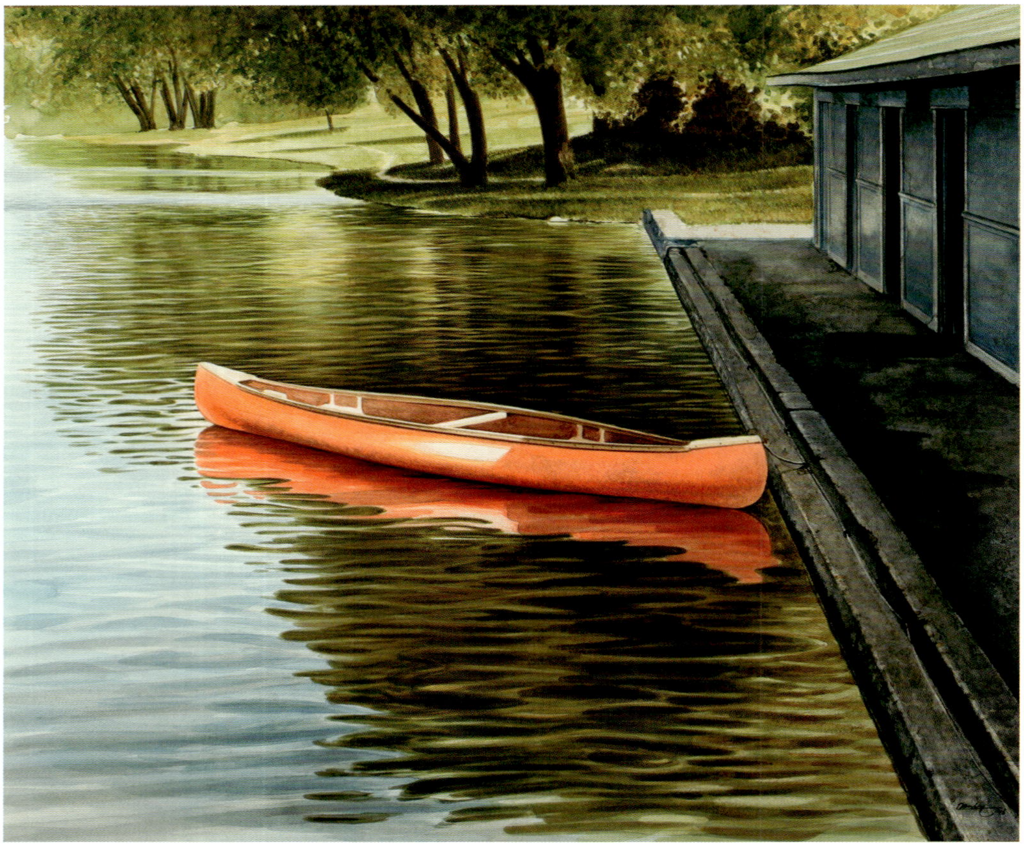

 Tethered, 1976

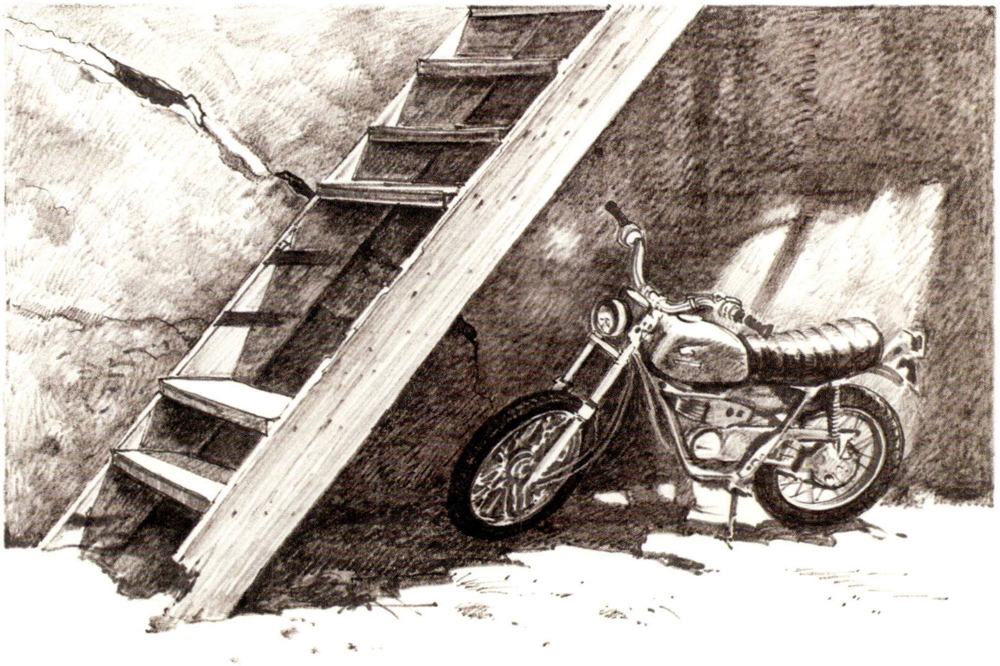

Motorcycle under Stairs, ca. 1975

. . .

As an individual, I experience life. I have everyday encounters and, occasionally, adventures. As an artist, I respond to these in my paintings. I create works of art that reflect my fascination with the multitude of themes and subjects that appeal to me, whether they are landscapes, seascapes, portraits, figure paintings, still lifes, or whatever — including sport. I respond to them all. For me, to specialize in one particular genre would be boring, if not debilitating. One can certainly equate specializing with limiting one's focus toward results that prove to be popular, but I have always avoided this temptation, preferring first and foremost to be true to myself. Whenever I have been asked to identify my best work, or my favourite, my answer has always been the same — "my next one!" (No matter what the subject may be.) That is my challenge.

While emphasizing this point in hopes of clarifying what I do and have been doing for many years, I want to add that the reason I include sport as a subject in my work is simply because it is a part of my life, and always has been. But it is hardly the major focus of my work.

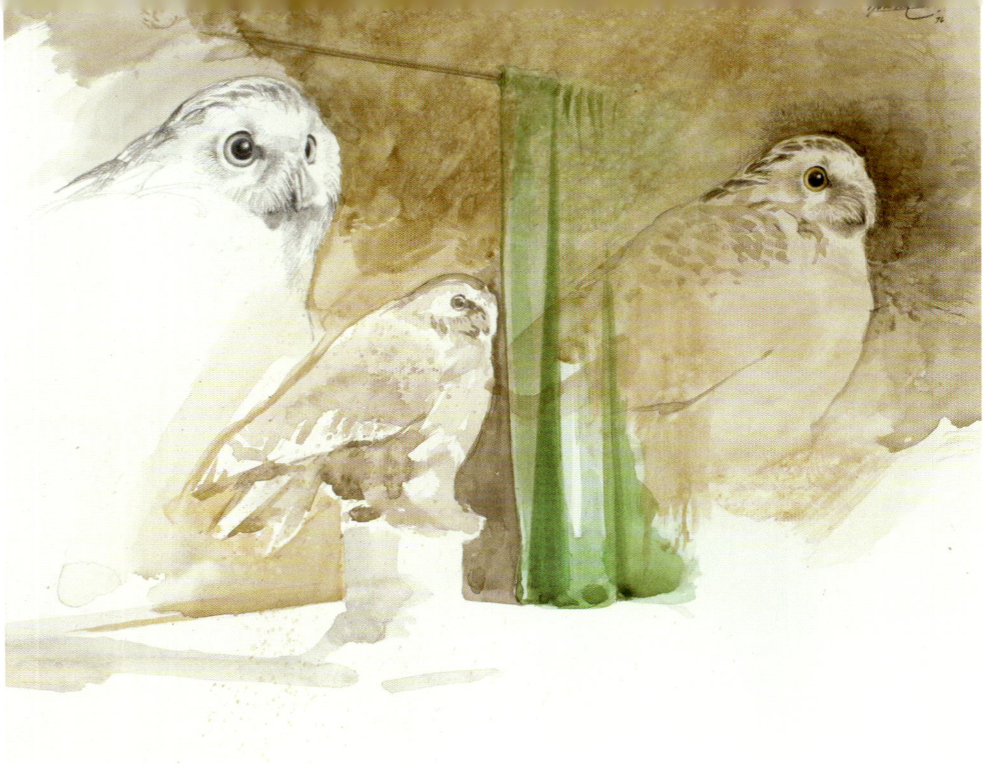

Study for Taxi Window, 1976

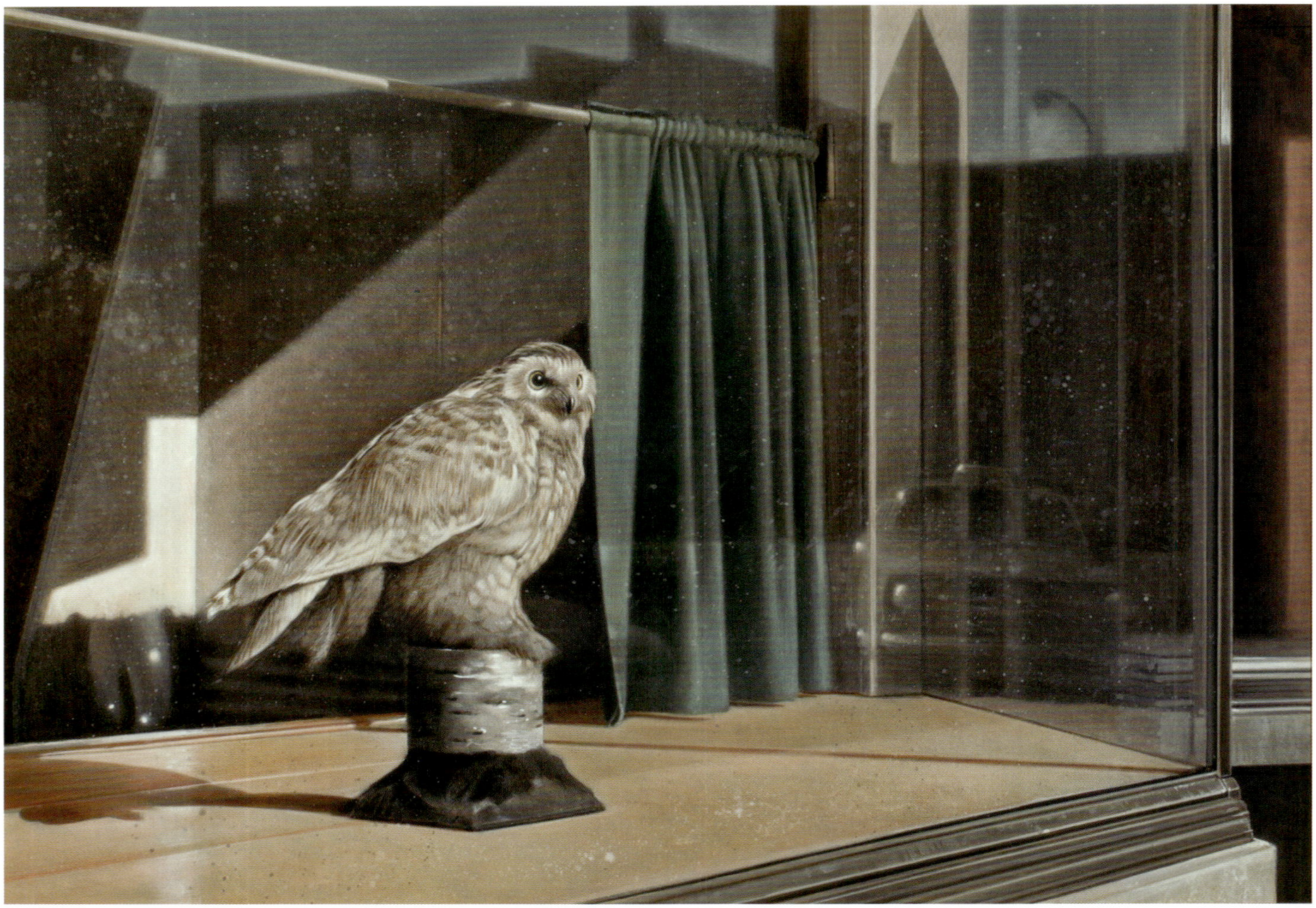

 Taxi Window, 1978

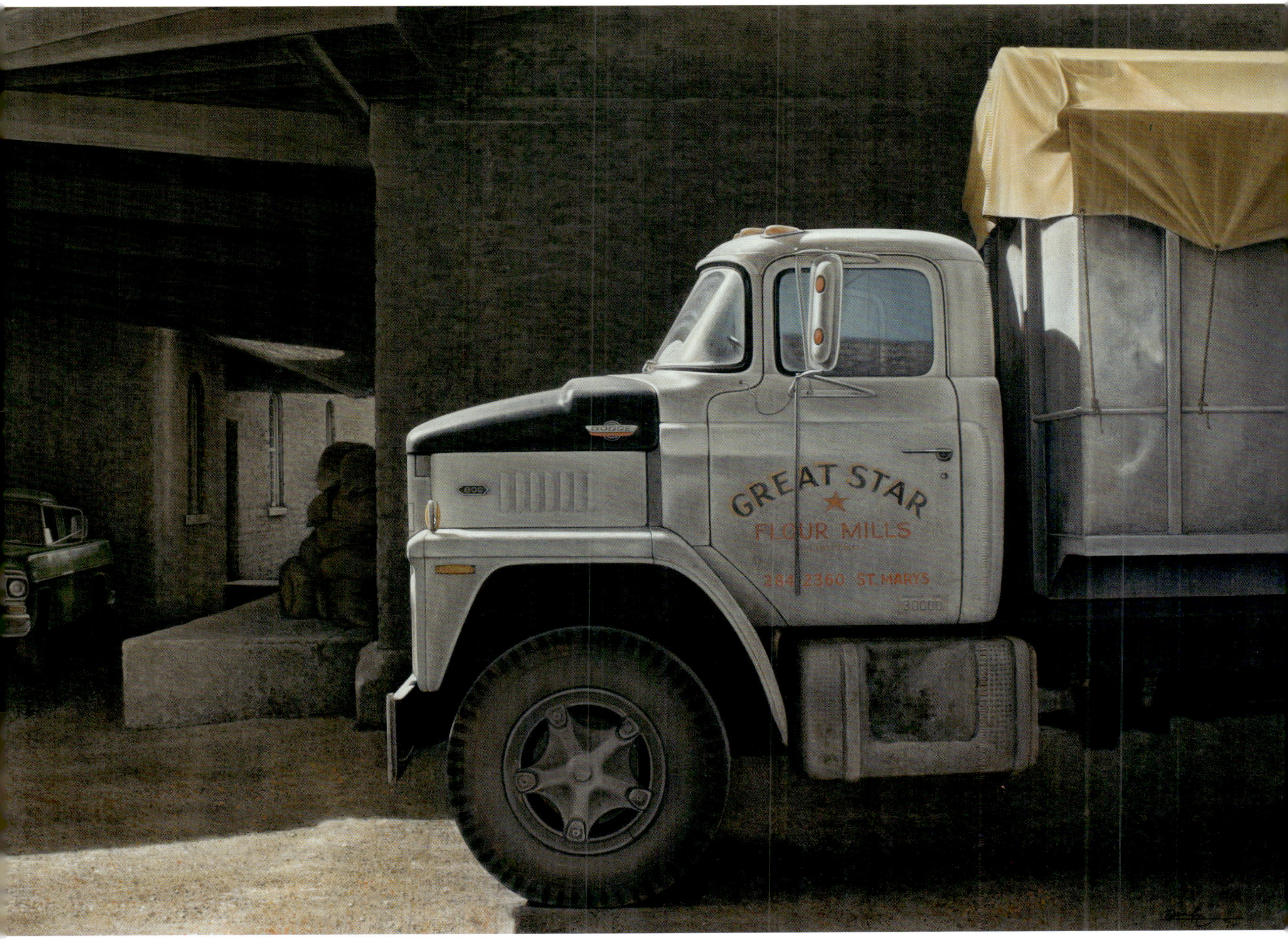

Great Star, 1974

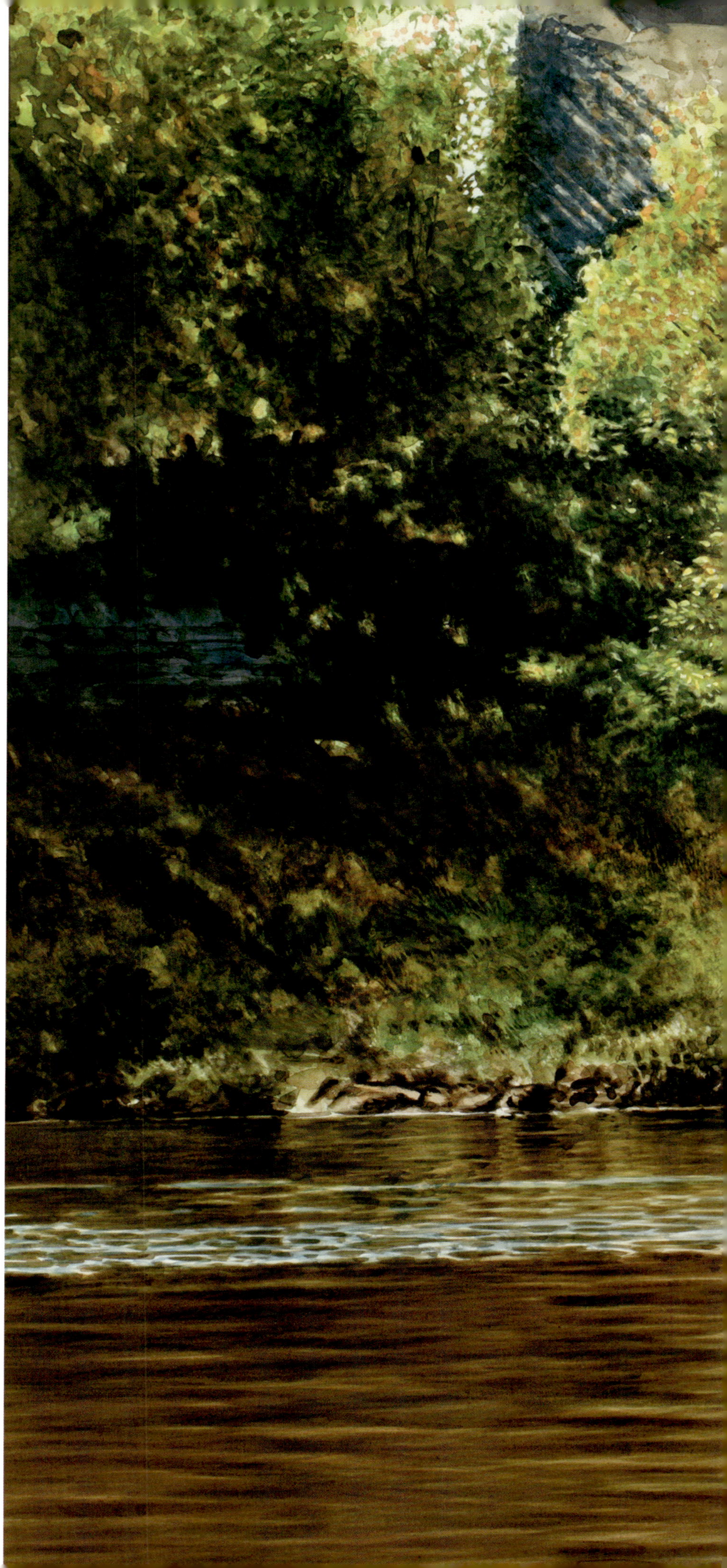

Secluded Tailrace, 1979

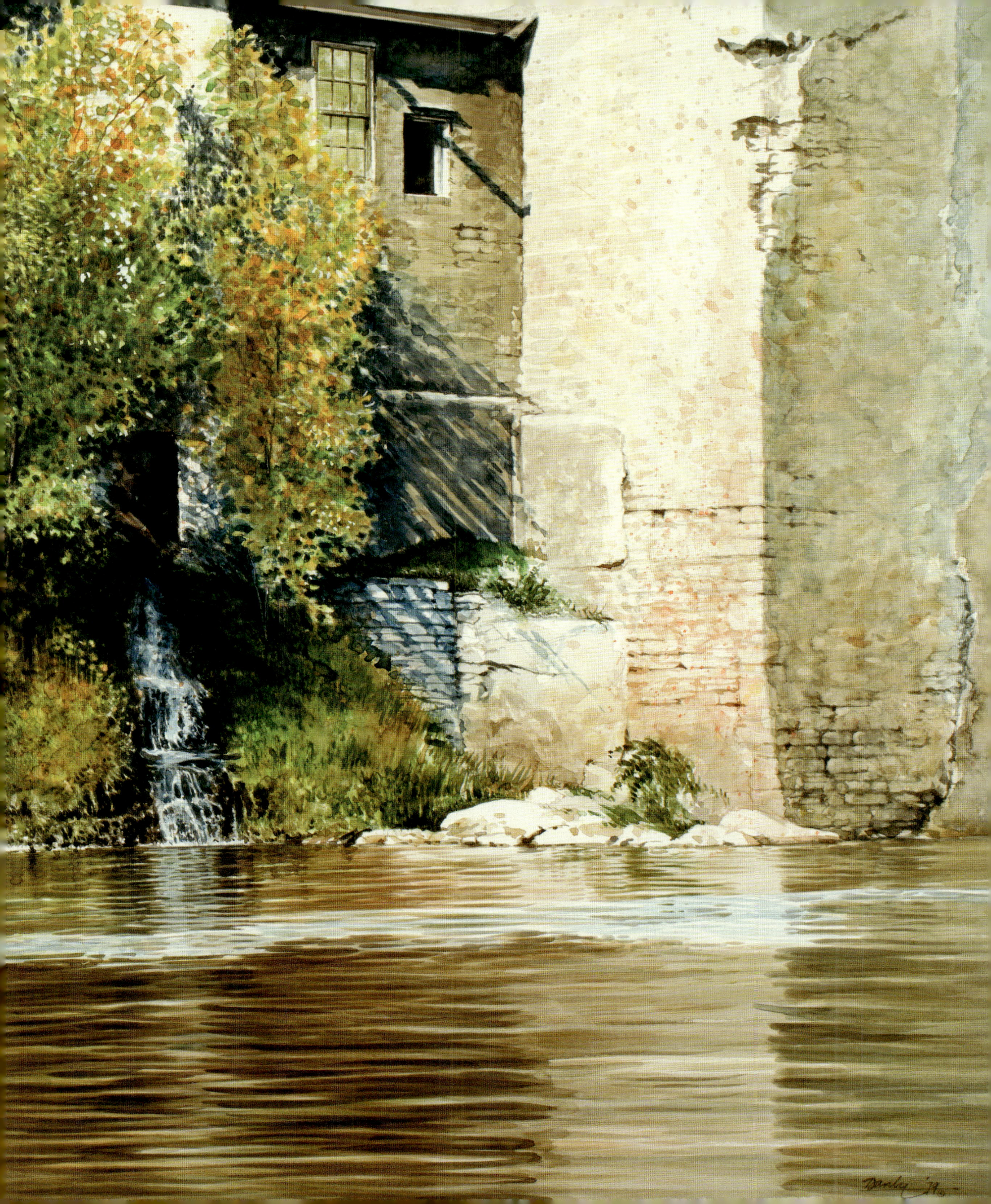

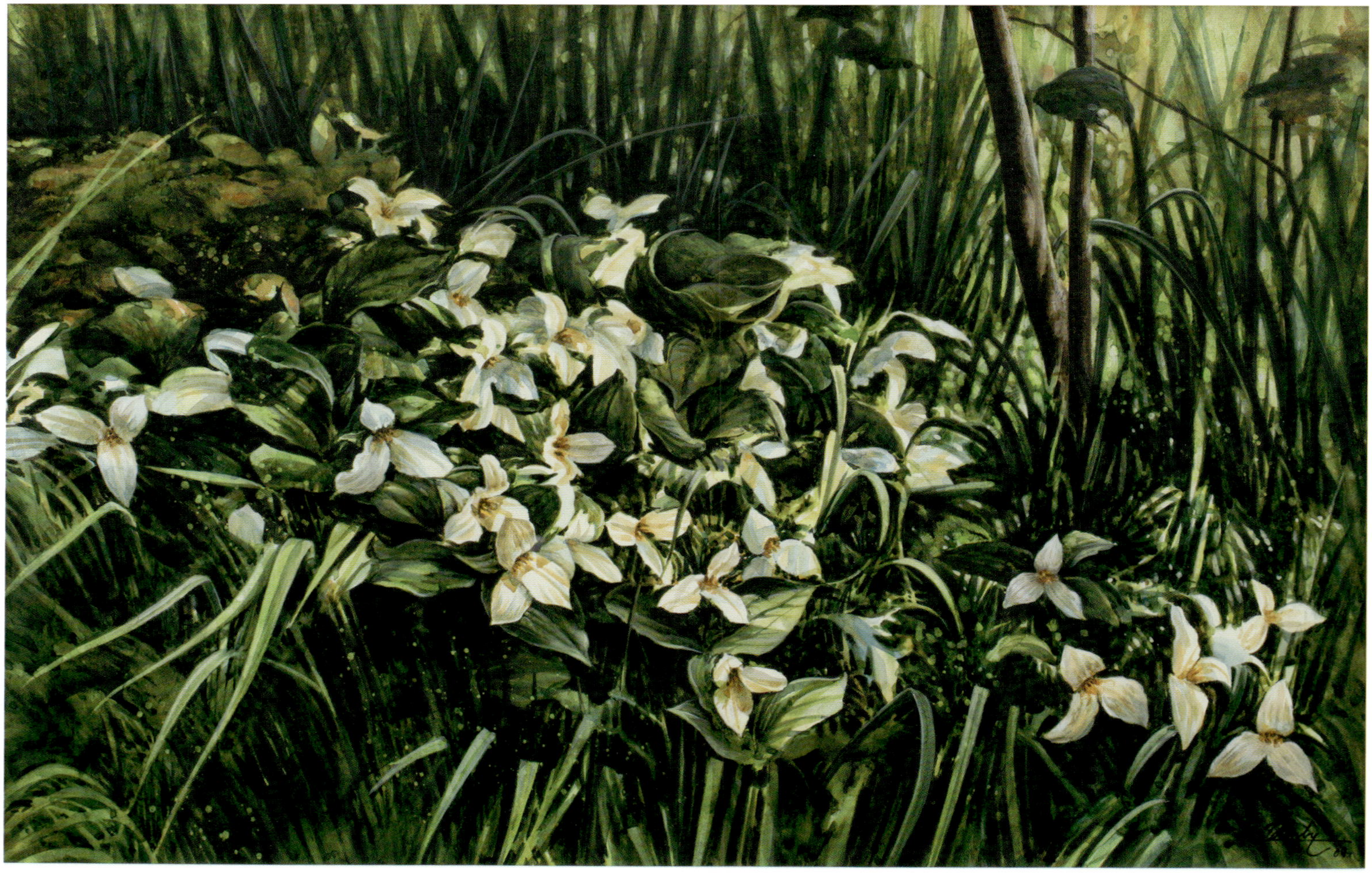

 Trilliums, 1980

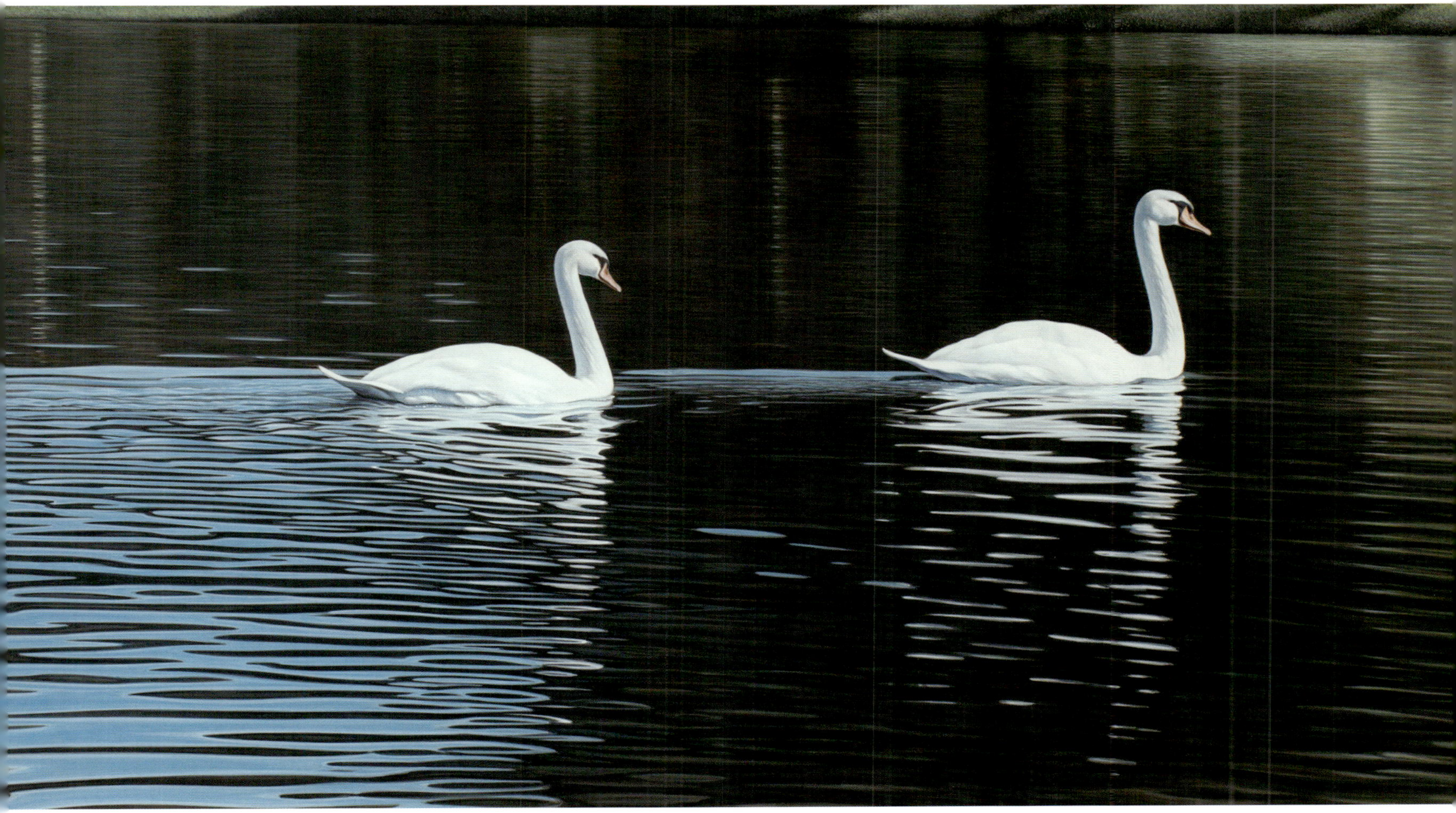

Stratford Swans, 1983

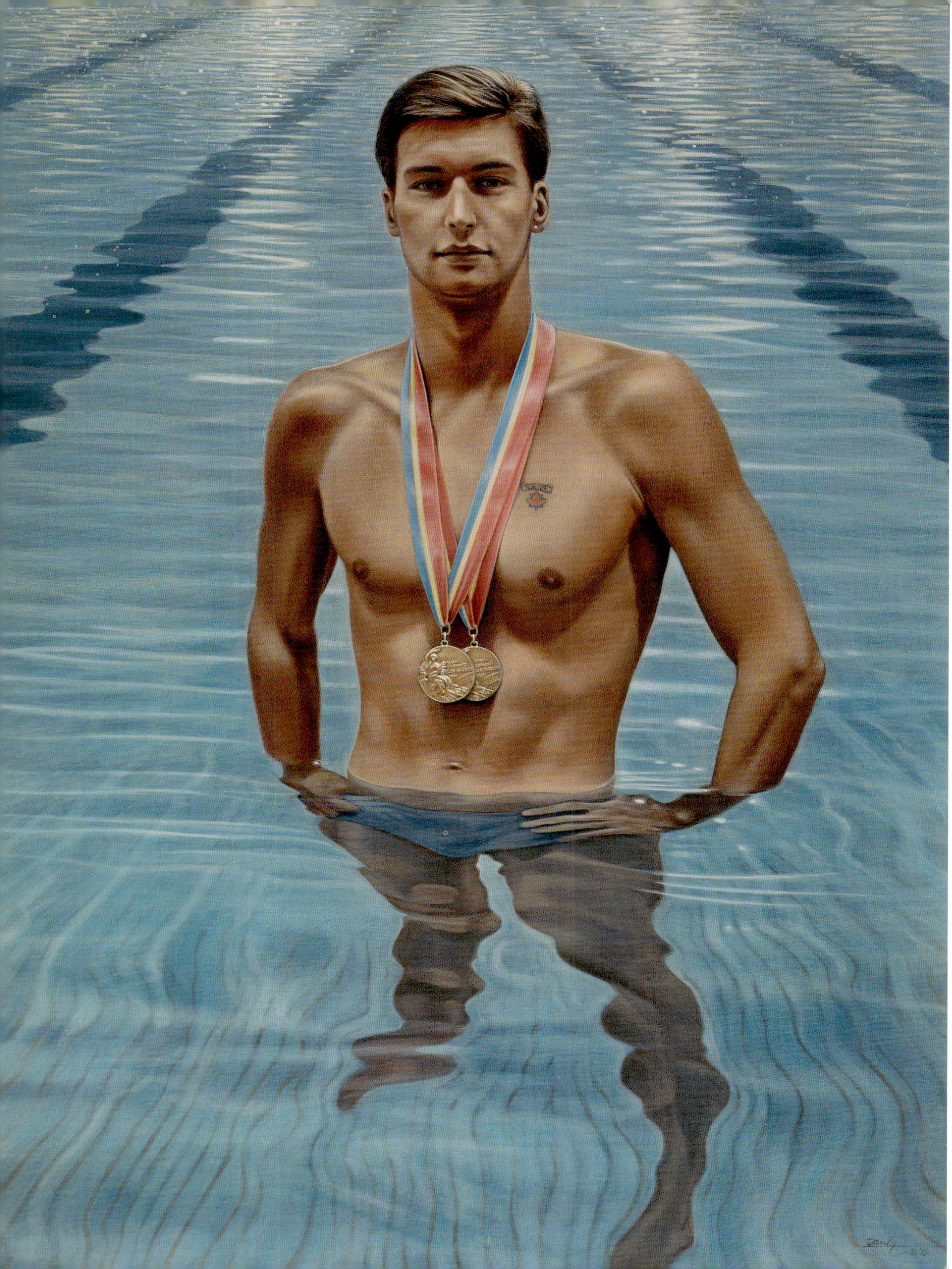

1980s

Refining a Style

Early in 1985 I had agreed to paint a portrait of Alex Baumann, Canada's double-gold swimming medalist at the 1984 Los Angeles Summer Olympics. The project was intended to commemorate Alex's medal-winning performances, as well as raise funds for the Canadian Amateur Swimming Association, through the sale of limited-edition prints and special posters. It would be sponsored by the Canadian Egg Marketing Agency (CEMA), with whom Alex was associated as a spokesperson. CEMA was delighted with the idea that my major medium was egg tempera and they insisted, without needing to, that the portrait should be painted in this medium.

Once I was able to schedule this work to begin in May, the challenge became how to identify a concept that pleased all parties concerned, including Alex and me. The only way to assess this was to try on a number of them and see what worked best.

Alex and I met in May and June, in Sudbury, at the Laurentian University pool where he trained. Both he and his coach, Dr. Tihanyi, instructed me in the finer points of his events, and I watched as he practiced his disciplines. He performed again and again for me, while I photographed him in action from different angles around the pool, gathering my raw material. He even showed me the exercise room and demonstrated various weight lifting routines to explain his training methods. I returned home and began to explore potential concepts in a number of sketches and watercolours.

I was surprised when I finally realized what I wanted and returned a final time to ask Alex to simply stand in the pool — wearing his two gold medals. This is how I painted the portrait, an unusual image of a superb (and patient) champion. It was completed in September, in my studio. It now resides in Canada's Sports Hall of Fame.

While in Paris, a very unusual mask caught my attention, in the window of a small bookstore. I inquired about it and was advised that it was the only one they had, and that it was for decoration, not for sale. After a brief negotiation, it was agreed that I could purchase it. I had no idea why it appealed to me, but I bought it anyway. It would prove to have more meaning as the year progressed.

Alex Baumann, 1985

I mounted the unusual mask on a post in my studio, not knowing what I would do with it, but nevertheless intrigued by it and conscious of its presence. One day, I saw an article in the local newspaper announcing that one of Canada's foremost interpreters of modern dance, Robert Desrosiers, would be performing in Guelph.

A light seemed to switch on in my mind. I realized that the marvelous theatricality of Robert Desrosiers would offer a terrific opportunity to use my mask. I had attended his phenomenal dance production *Blue Snake* in Toronto a few years earlier, and came away inspired by his creative choreography. I thought, perhaps I might persuade him to assist me with a painting.

Robert's hair style was very distinctive, large and fuzzy. It was unlikely that he would not be recognizable to anyone (who knew him) by placing a mask over his face. For some reason, I began to see considerable humour in this, and the more I thought about it, the more it appealed to me.

Finally, in advance of Robert's engagement in Guelph, I telephoned him and we ended up having a great conversation about my ideas over coffee. He was receptive and agreed to assist me. We scheduled a couple of sessions at his dance studio in Toronto in the weeks ahead, and I brought my mask.

Robert confirmed my hunch. He was perfect. The theatricality that I instinctively knew was needed, he delivered. He tried a variety of dramatic poses with the mask, in various improvised costumes, and I offered minimum direction. The results materialized in two large paintings, created over the following eighteen months. One was simply titled *Mask*, and the other, *The Dancer*. In the end, I decided against covering his face with the mask. I liked the idea of him moving it to the side and peeking out from behind.

On August 18, 1986, Gillian [Elmitt, whom Danby, since divorced from Judith, married in 1988] and I attended the Ian & Sylvia Reunion Concert at Kingswood, north of Toronto — a concert I didn't want to miss. They were superb and treated the audience to many of their classics throughout the first half of the show.

Following the intermission, the curtain parted, exposing an empty stage in total darkness, except for a single spotlight illuminating a small area around the microphone.

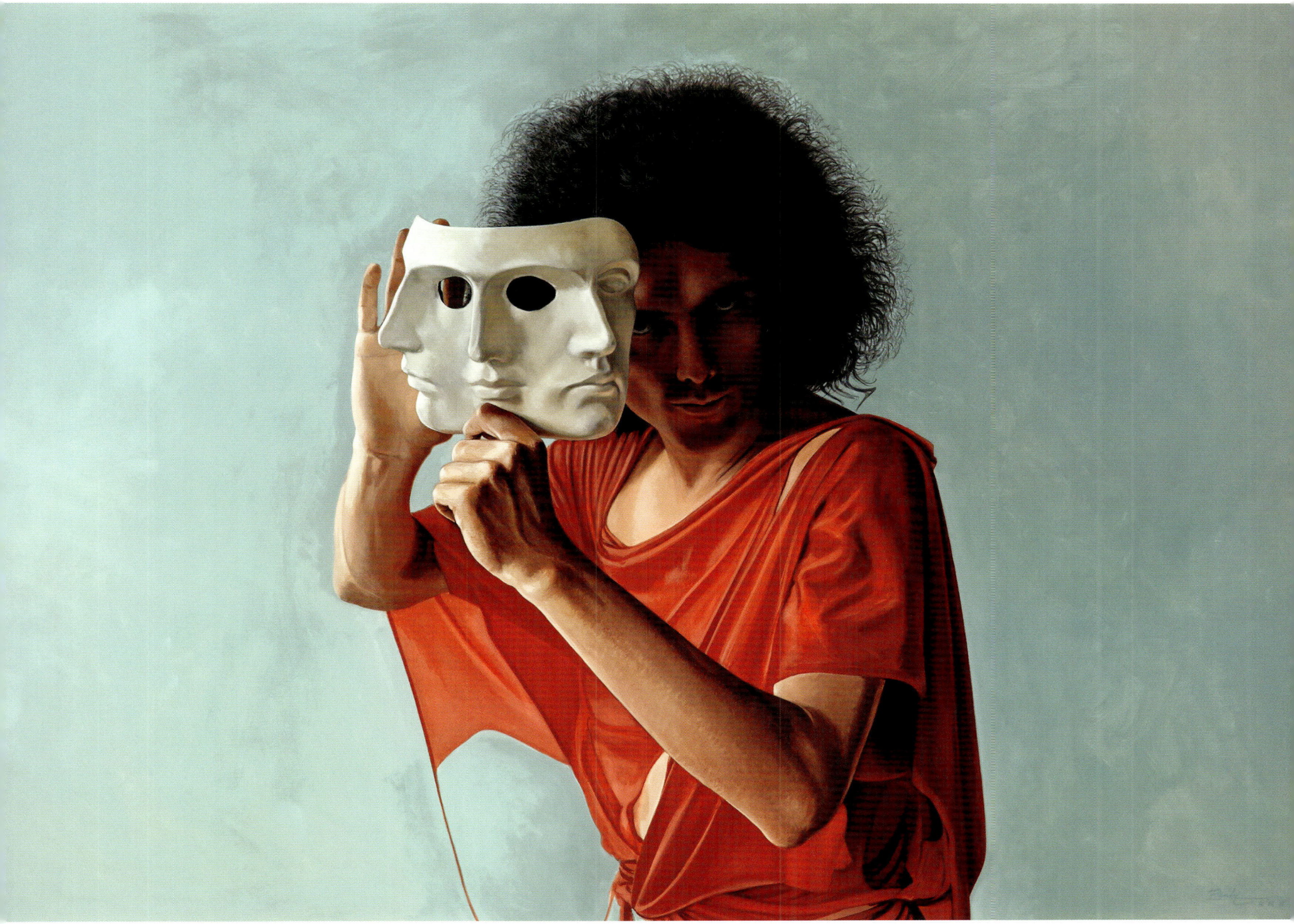

Mask, 1986-88

The audience grew silent in anticipation, not knowing what to expect, and it seemed forever before a single figure appeared from behind the curtain and walked into the spotlight — with no introduction.

Instantly, the audience erupted as it recognized Gordon Lightfoot. The place went nuts! We all jumped to our feet, cheering and clapping. I could feel the hair tingling at the back of my neck. After the longest ovation, we all sat back to enjoy Gord's gold.

Dressed in a white suit and a black tuxedo style shirt, he looked terrific! This was his first public performance in a few years, and we were all thrilled by his return. His performance was exceptional. Like everyone else in the audience, I'm sure, I was happily thinking to myself, "Gord's back!" As I watched and listened to him, I was particularly taken by his visual rejuvenation, combined with his dramatically staged appearance, and for some reason I began to think about a portrait.

After the concert, Gord and I had a good chat, during which I threw in my idea of a portrait. I suggested that he think about it for a time and give me a call if interested. He agreed. Days later, he telephoned and asked if I was still serious about the idea. I said, "Yes," and he said, "Then, let's do it." Over the following months, he would drive out to my studio for a number of posing sessions. I had the idea that casual attire in jeans and shirt might be preferable, for a more relaxed flavour, but I wasn't sure. However, I was firmly convinced that I wanted Gord to be in a natural setting.

He brought a couple of outfits with him, as I had requested (including his white suit), and we tried various poses that I felt were worthwhile. Then we would just sit and talk. After a time, he picked up his guitar and began picking a tune. Totally relaxed and smiling, he exuded the spirit that I had been watching for. Later, I asked him to change into the suit and black shirt and positioned him closer to the river with the large willow trees behind. In this pose, I felt I was connecting with his strong interest toward protecting the environment, as well as truly reflecting the impression he made on me when he walked onto the stage at Kingswood. But this time the stage lighting was by Mother Nature.

After completing a couple of studies in watercolour, I decided to pursue both of these images as major portraits, since I felt that each one conveyed such a unique depiction of an old friend, now a legend. Both paintings, titled *Gordon Lightfoot* and *Lightfoot: A Study*, were included in my New York exhibition in 1989.

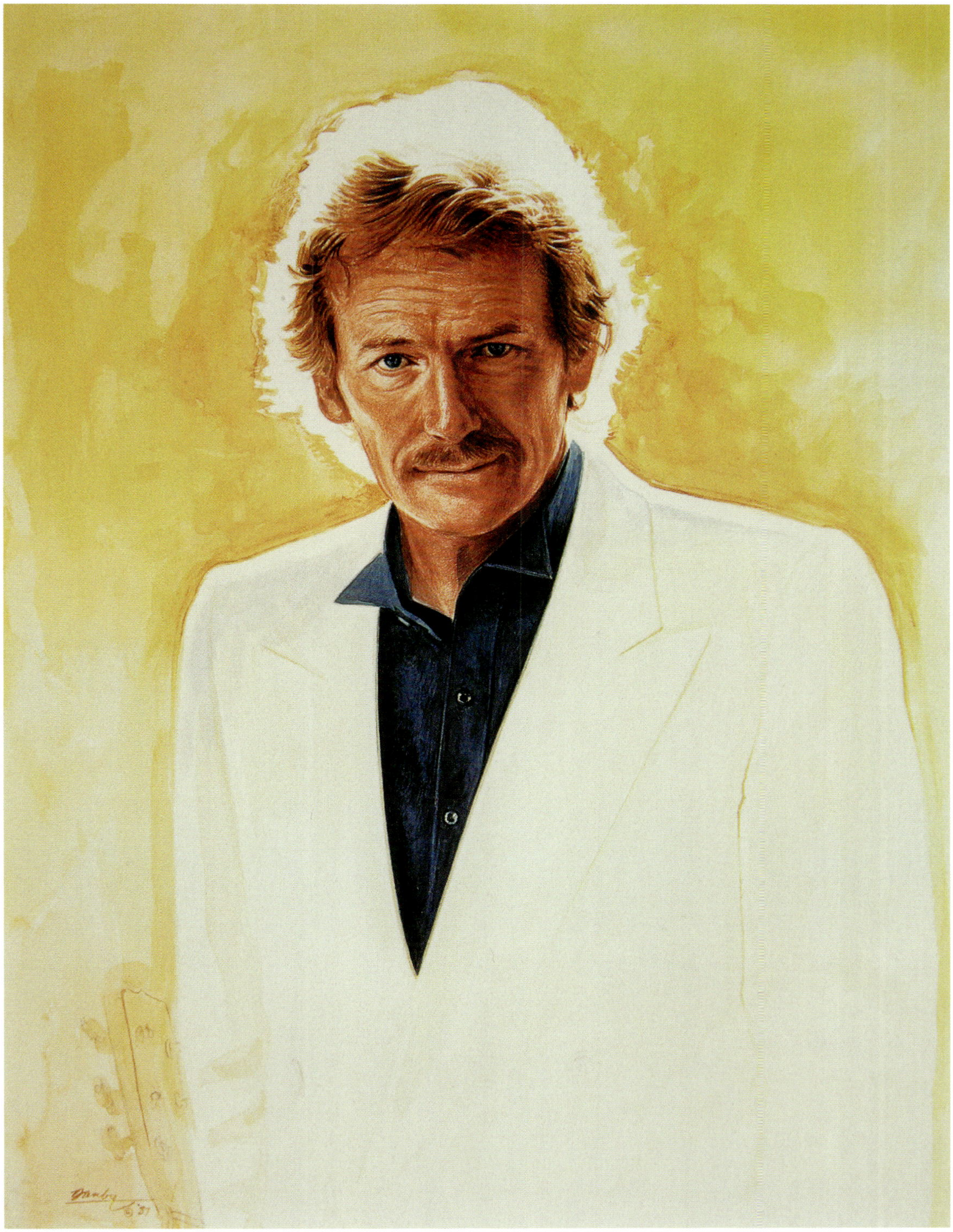

Lightfoot: A Study, 1987

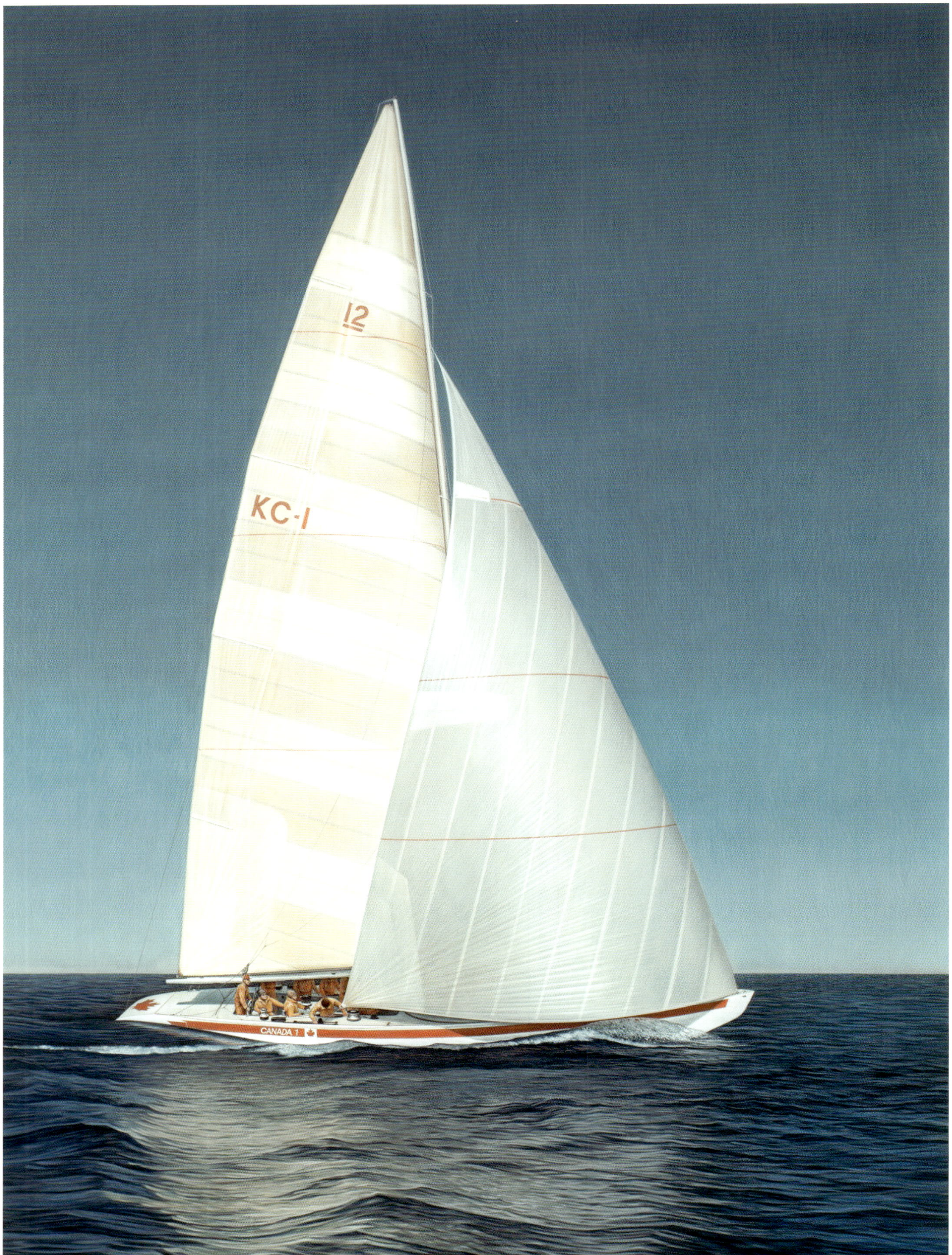
12
KC-1
CANADA 1

. . .

One of the results of my experiences in the 1980s, through our travels, was the development of a profound appreciation of the sheer scale of the ocean — the enormity of it. This is the reason why, after painting in egg tempera for many years, I decided to return to using oil, as well. Oil on canvas expands one's ability to address images on a large scale. Egg tempera is less suited for this because it requires heavy gesso panels and dries very quickly, denying any retention of fluidness in the paint. Each medium has its particular characteristics that I like to take advantage of when I approach an idea. But it was my urge to convey the vastness of the ocean that prompted me to greatly increase the scale of my working methods.

However, one drawback to this desire was my realization that the physical handling of a large stretched canvas can also be difficult. I needed to acquire a very large easel. After a considerable amount of research, I concluded that what I was looking for didn't exist in the marketplace — so I decided to design and create my own version. Weeks of analytical drawings and many more weeks of custom fabrication eventually succeeded in the completion of a marvellously versatile (and substantial) easel. It telescopes to accommodate any size of canvas, tilts through any angle desired, raises and lowers instantly with touch-control braking, and it allows me to swivel a painting 360 degrees at the same time. Now that's an easel!

Over the years, I have developed the habit of turning a painting upside down, or occasionally sideways, to alter my vision of it as I paint, or simply to enable me to work on an area more comfortably. This easel allows such movements to happen very quickly and with little effort, thereby encouraging my ability to employ this working idiosyncrasy, even with a very large painting.

Canada 1, 1983

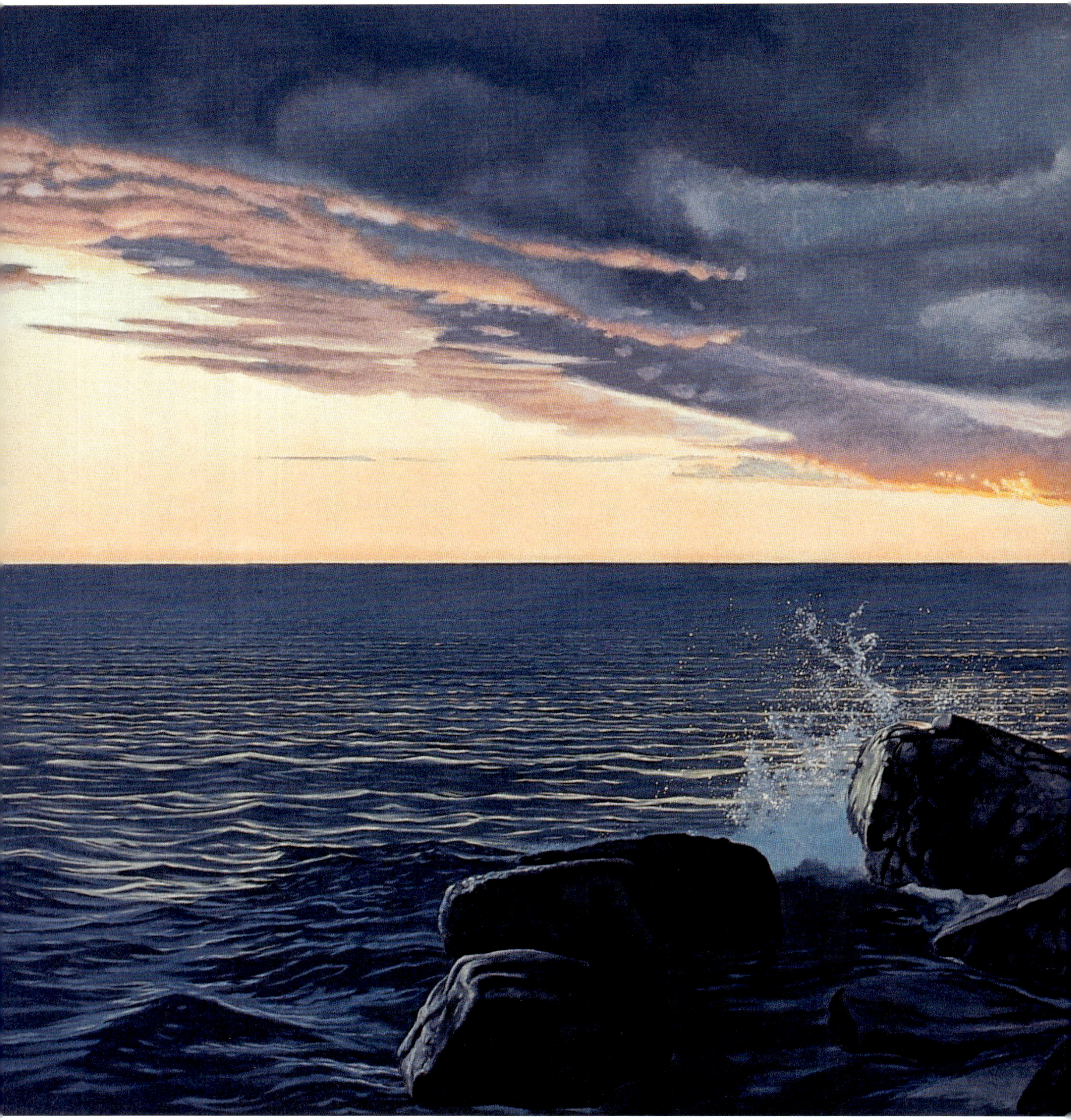

Rolling Thunder, 2002

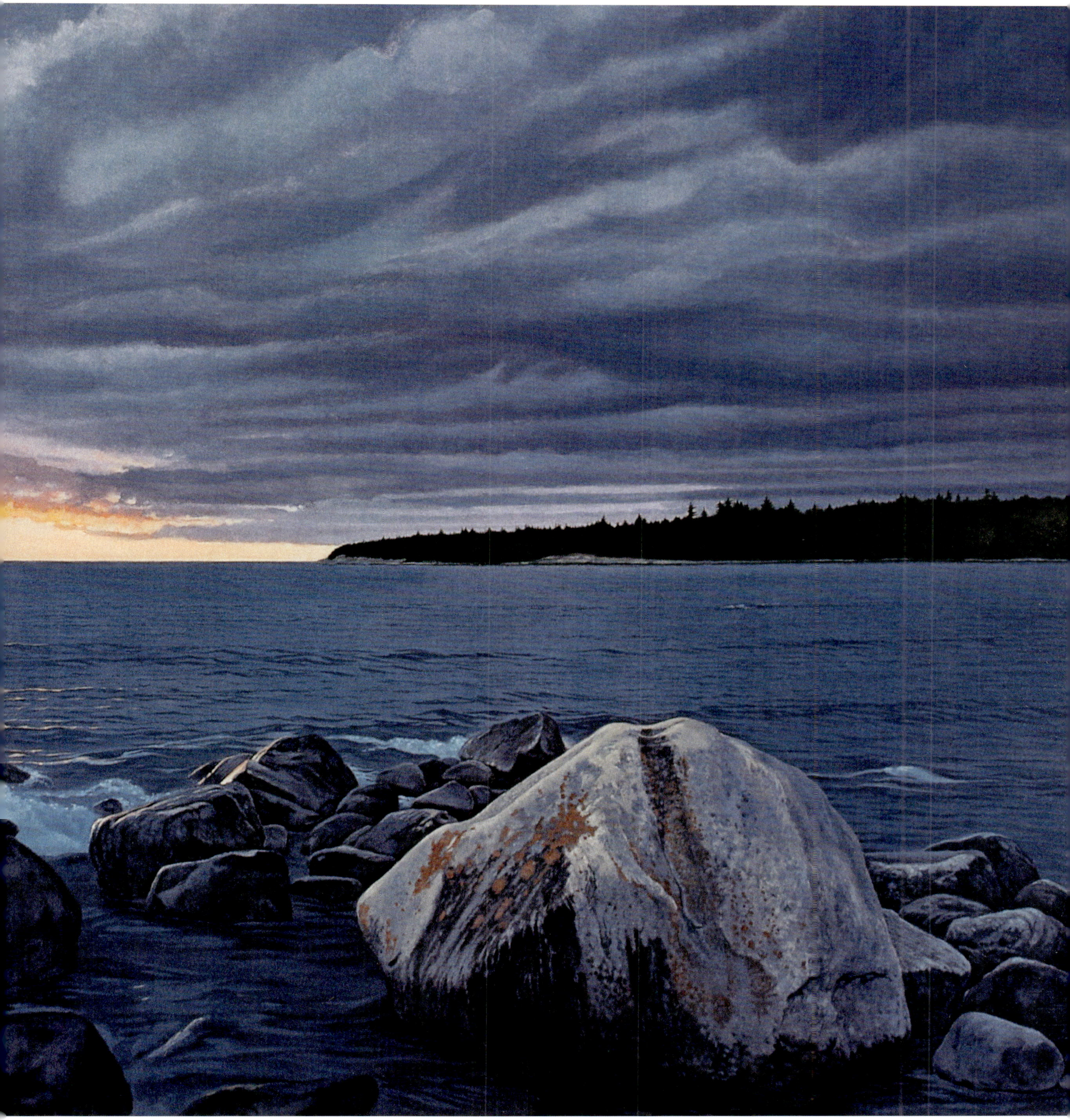

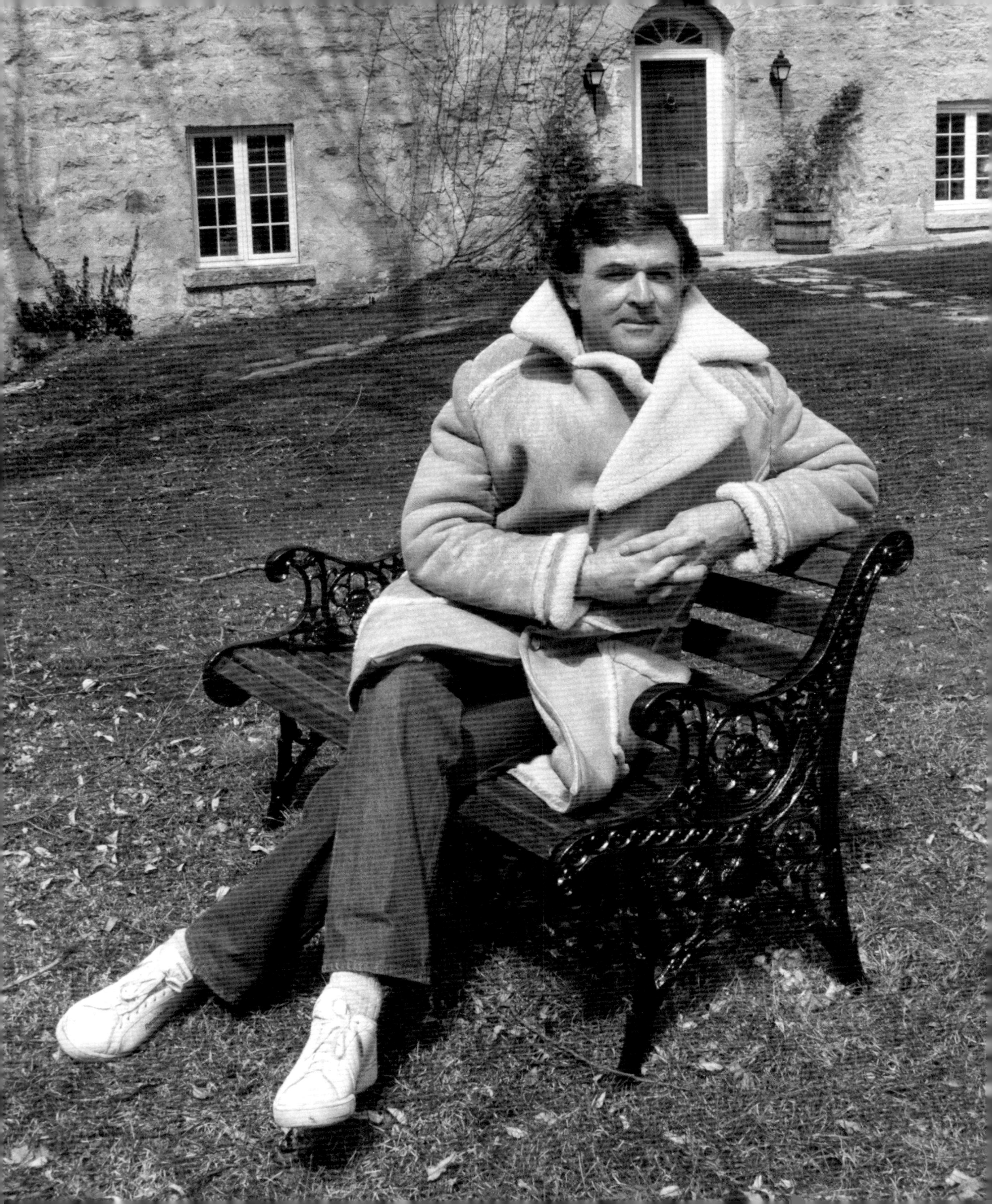

1990s

Closing the Millennium

I prefer to have a number of paintings in progress at any given time; it's my nature to let a painting lead me now and then, so that there is a process of give and take before I'm ready to confirm the decisions to rein it in. An image is rarely resolved in my mind before I tackle it. Even the concept can change dramatically while it's in progress. Therefore, when attempting to schedule the completion of a number of works, I always try to remind myself of this, so that there is never any inclination to compromise, which is not my habit. Many times, I found that a painting that I had set aside didn't get resolved until two or three years later, sometimes many more.

I anticipate that this revelation then begs the question, how can I return to work on a painting whose subject is so far removed from when I first explored it? The answer is twofold. First, the idea, the basis for wanting to explore it in the first place, has already been well established in my mind, in my response to the experience, which for me is always firsthand. Secondly, I use a camera to acquire as much visual information as I can, so that I have an abundance of imagery to refer to in the course of exploring an image. I may also return to the subject to improve my analysis, relative to circumstances. With this raw material on hand, I can delay the actual interaction with the paint and canvas until I can accommodate being able to do so effectively, with minimal interruption.

Photography has been utilized by artists since it was first invented. However, it is critical that one first sees with the eyes, rather than relying on the camera's lens to make judgments. In the course of creating my painting, I am not interested in replicating a photograph. I am not a photorealist. In fact, I rarely take a photograph that is interesting enough to replicate. My interest lies in synthesizing all of the various visual information that will ultimately create the picture the way I want it to be, which is not necessarily the way I experienced it. And the camera simply assists me in accumulating that information.

Often I hear the comment, "Oh, it looks just like a photograph," which is a well-intended but misinterpreted response to the work (I take it as a compliment anyway). However, the reality is that my painting doesn't represent the image that I saw. It represents the image that I want the viewer to see, which is a very significant difference.

Ken Danby in front of the Mill, ca. 1995
(photographer unknown)

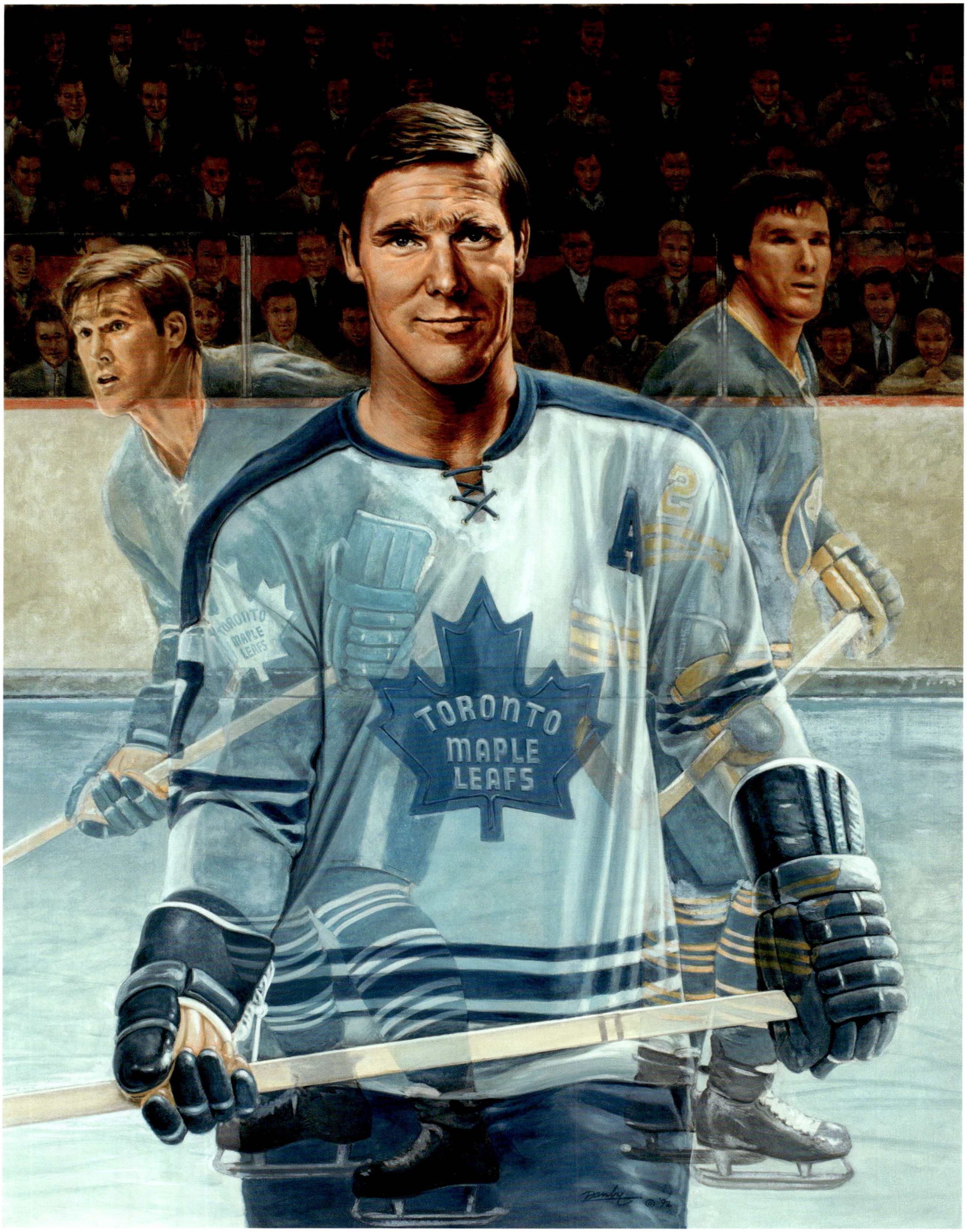

 Tim Horton, 1992

What is important is what I leave in and what I take out — what I emphasize and what I diminish. I control and orchestrate the image as it develops.

Regardless of the mechanics involved, or how an image materializes, it is the vision, imagination, and skill that direct the creation of a work of art, from the initial inspiration to ultimate creation. In my opinion, it doesn't much matter how a work of art is created. What's important is how effectively it communicates from the artist to the viewer.

I was working on a special project for the Tim Horton Children's Foundation — a commemorative portrait of Tim Horton, the late all-star defenseman for the Toronto Maple Leafs and the Buffalo Sabres, and co-founder of the Tim Hortons doughnut chain. This included limited-edition prints and posters as a fundraising project for the foundation. Once again, I was drawn back to hockey as a subject in my work (and would soon be again, as it happened).

The background of the painting consisted of many faces in the crowd. All are anonymous, except one. On a whim, as I worked to complete this, I painted in the image of my father, who was a dedicated hockey fan. When the poster was eventually created and displayed in each of the Tim Hortons coffee shops across the country, he took delight in pointing himself out to friends.

The Conestogo River winds through the village of Hawkesville, about a half-hour's drive from my studio. On a brisk winter afternoon, I drove across the bridge upriver and noticed a group of boys playing hockey on the ice below. I stopped and walked back to watch. Within seconds, I spotted a couple of horses and buggies parked on the adjacent field and realized that these were Mennonite boys. But if I hadn't noticed their mode of transportation, I wouldn't have known.

Later that night, the image kept recurring in my mind, and I felt a real excitement to explore it further. As it happened, I was fortunate to find them there again the next day — along with a beautiful crisp blue sky. As the afternoon advanced, long dramatic

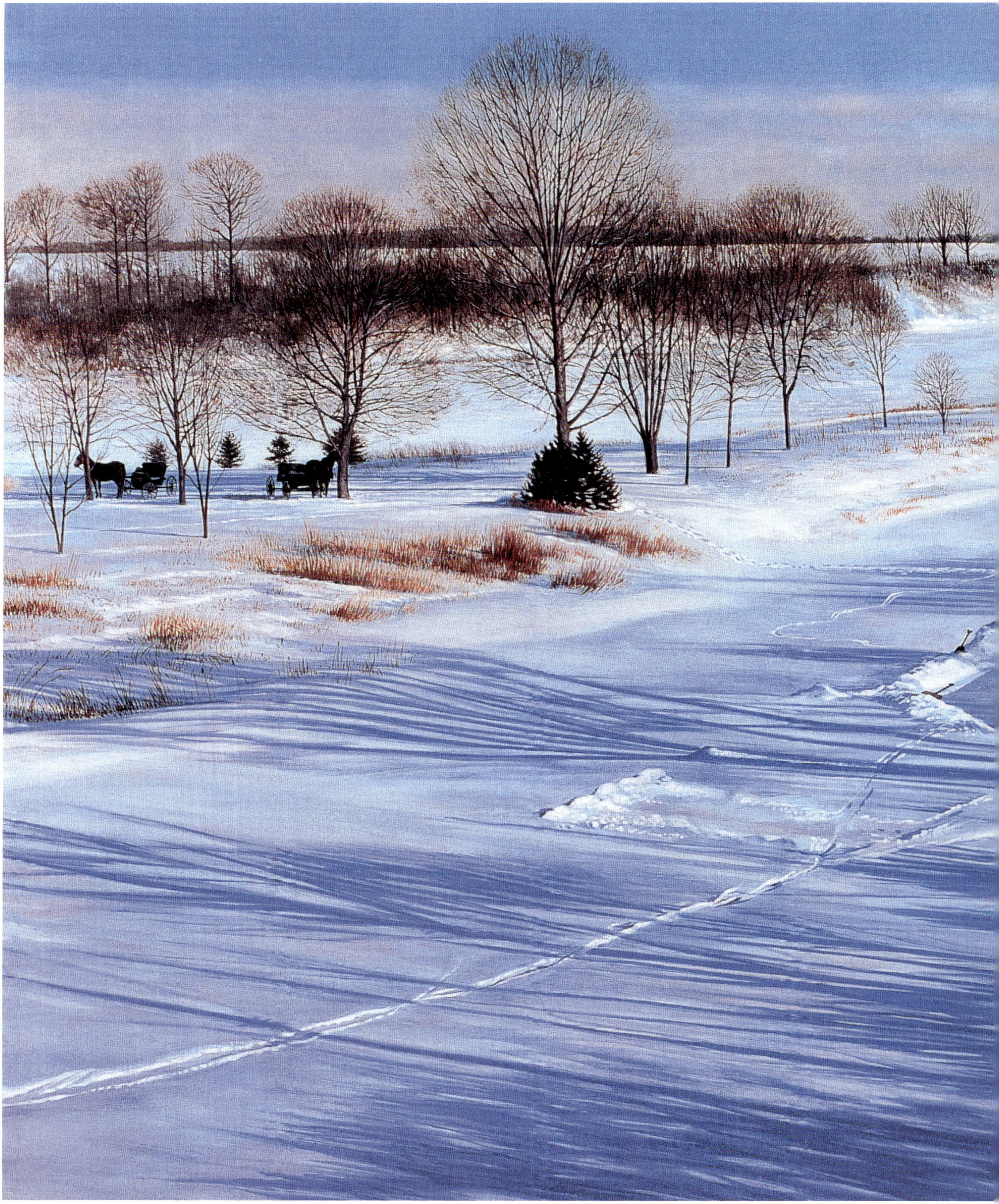

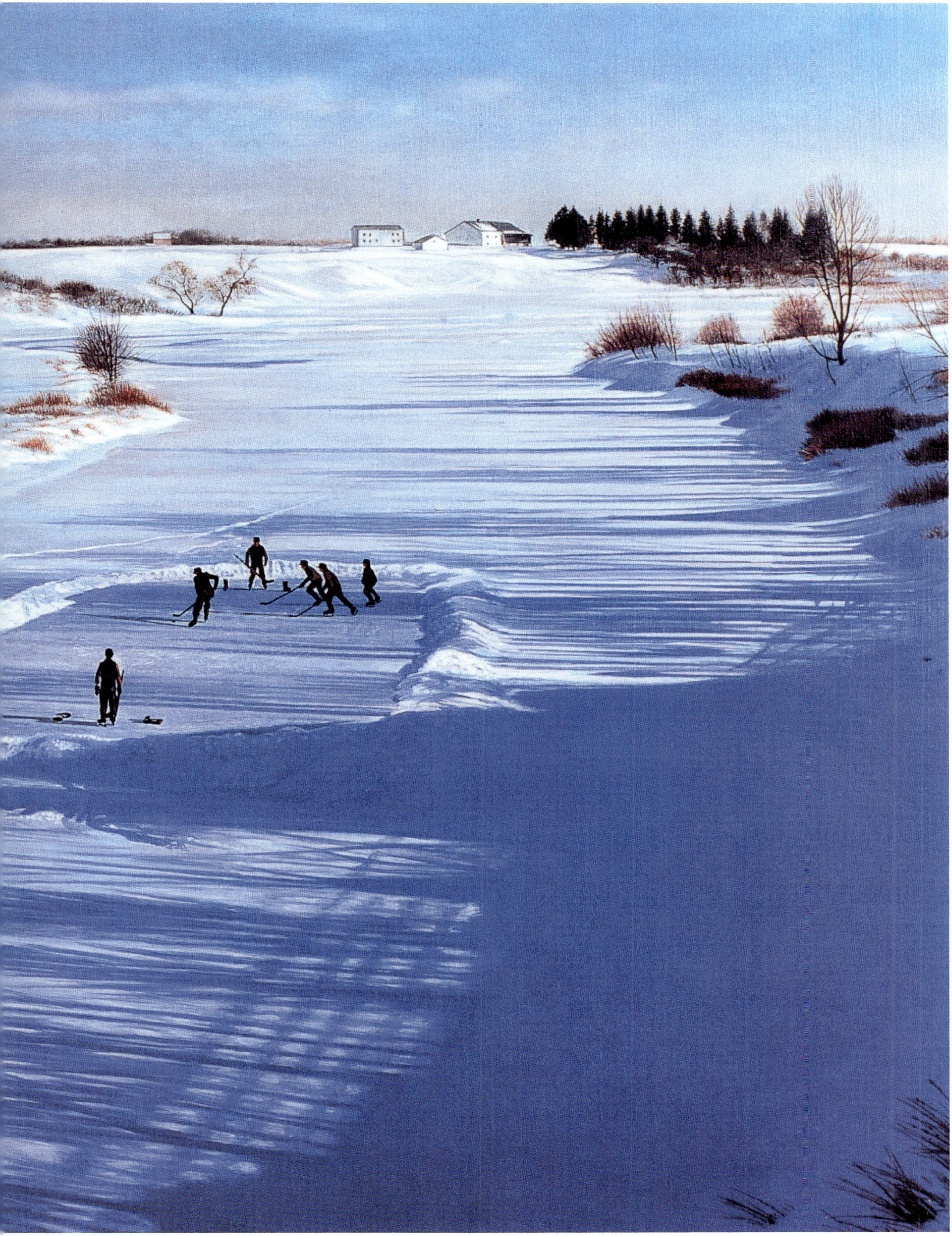

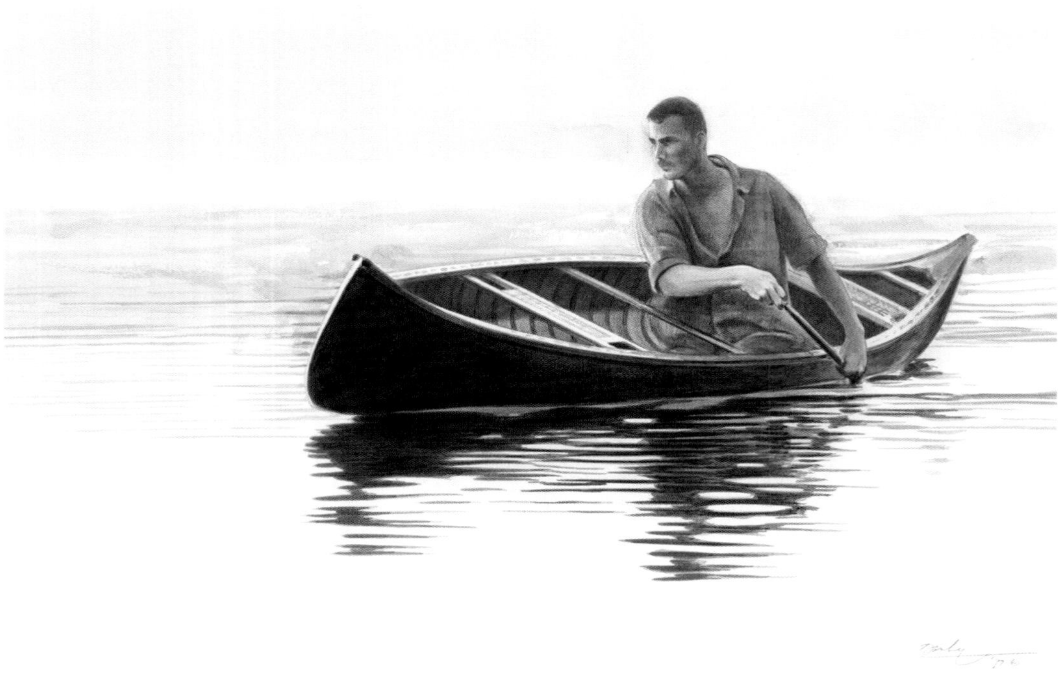

shadows extended across the snow and ice, creating marvelous abstractions in contrast to the literal images that first inspired me. Although my encounter and enthusiasm originated in early 1991, I couldn't get around to completing this work until three years later.

One of the influences that resulted from painting *Northland* and, later, *Tanamakoon* was a strong interest in revisiting the landscape of Northern Ontario — my roots. The wilderness of Algonquin Park also beckoned. During the summer, I made extended visits to both areas to research my ideas.

As a young artist, one of my heroes was Tom Thomson, the brilliant Canadian landscape painter who so influenced the Group of Seven, and who died prematurely and mysteriously, in Algonquin Park. I returned to the park, at Cache Lake, not far from where he died, to research a setting for what I intended to be a subtle tribute. My friends at Camp Tanamakoon, Kim and Marilyn Smith, assisted me in doing so. They provided their expert canoeist, Dean Wylie, who posed repeatedly for me out on the lake, as I explored my concept for the painting that became *Algonquin (in homage to Tom Thomson).*

 Completing the Stroke, 1997

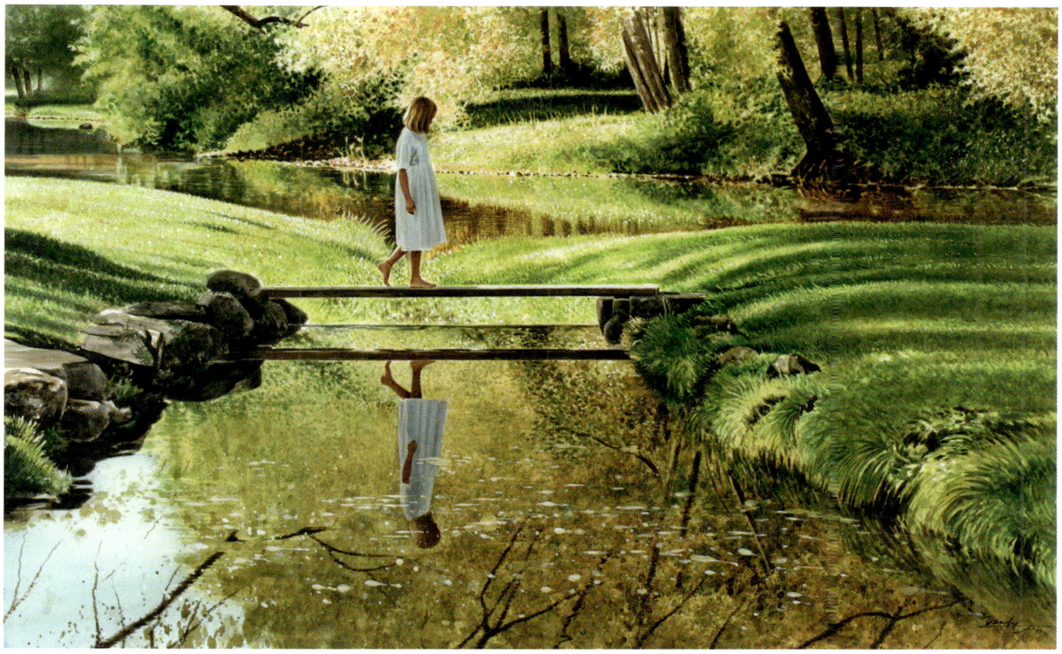

I envisioned the image of a canoeist passing across a glorious sunset, into the dark shadows of a reflected shoreline, as a kind of metaphor for Thomson's life. In the process of developing this work, a number of studies materialized, including *Crossing the Sun*, *Blaze of Glory*, and *Canoe Run*, all watercolours.

Sometime later, I travelled to Lake Temagami to explore its more northerly setting, which resulted in two large watercolours, *Pond Reflections*, and *Temagami*. A third response later became an original thirty-colour serigraph, called *True North*. Its title revealed itself when I realized that the image of my canoe kept reminding me of a compass needle, almost as if it was guiding me home.

One of the works that I painted depicts a young girl on a swing, titled *Her World*. The model was our nine-year-old granddaughter, Cheyne Reid, and the swing is one that we had made for her, hung from an old apple tree on our property. While exploring ideas with Cheyne for this project, I also asked her to change into her white cotton dress and try a pose or two near the river nearby. At the end of our millrace, we have a large, heavy plank, which allows one to cross over the water. She leisurely walked across the plank and instantly offered a double image with her reflection in the water below. I was impressed with the ease with which this simple act complemented the scene and asked Cheyne to

Cheyne's Walk, 1996

overleaf: **Algonquin (in homage to Tom Thomson)**, 1997

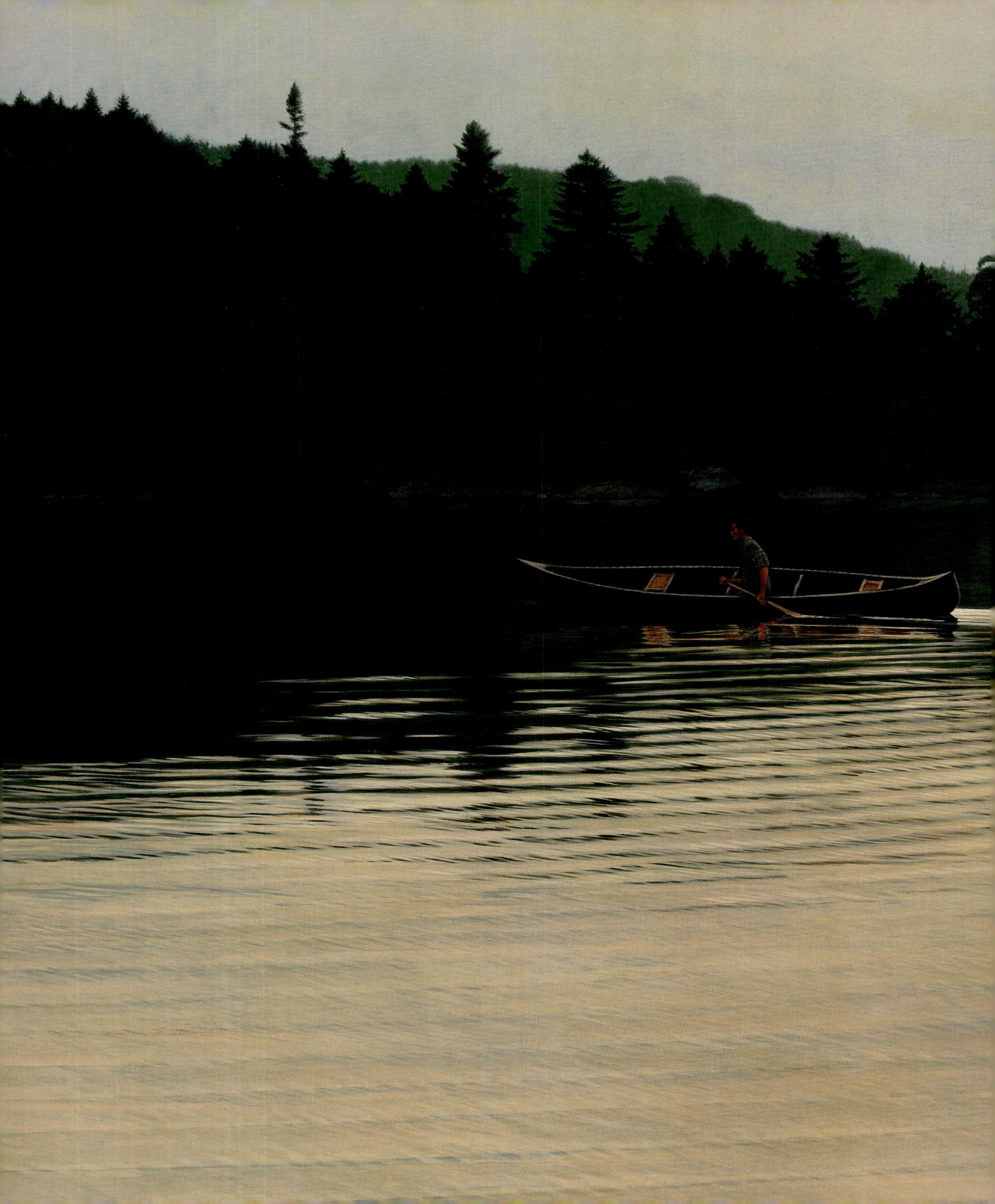

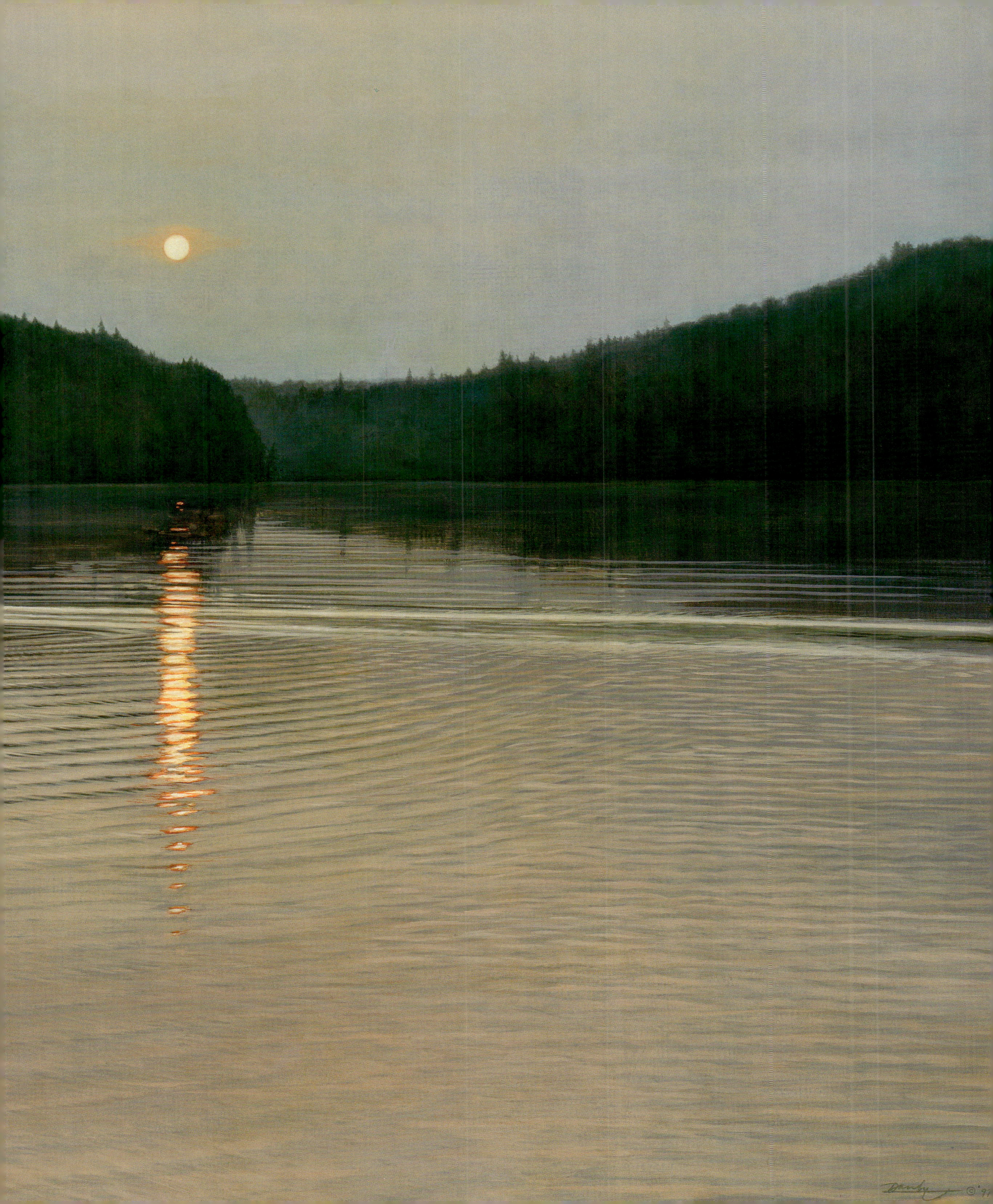

pose for me there. This later became a watercolour called *Cheyne's Walk*, which is rather self-explanatory. However, the twist is that Cheyne was born in London, England, and began her life with her parents, Julie and Don, in residence on their rather famous street, which became her namesake, Cheyne Walk.

I enlisted the assistance of my Guelph Goodtimers teammates to pose for a particular image that I had been contemplating for some time. A number of them had posed a year or two earlier for the same concept, but I still hadn't resolved it satisfactorily. I wanted to have another look, as my ideas became more focused.

The title, *Face Off*, aptly defines the action that I wanted to depict, but the drama, tension, and symmetry of this ritual at centre ice became quite a challenge to achieve. None of the foreground figures are identifiable, as it was not my intention to depict actual players or uniforms. But I needed experienced players and a veteran referee to provide the credibility for the action. While the anonymity of the main figures pleased me, my early attempts at the background faces lacked interest, so I responded by painting the entire audience to consist of family and friends (105 portraits)!

The act of creating art is an endeavour that engages a singular and rather selfish focus, especially for a painter. For me, art must be so, to be true to itself and its purpose. It isn't a collective or a cooperative effort. My visions are in my head. To see them realized requires extensive concentration and long periods of isolation, as I wrestle my concepts into being. I don't allow anyone to see works in progress for fear that their reaction might influence the direction I am taking. I won't even discuss it. I hate being asked, "What are you working on?" I have become adept at responding with a very general reply to avoid compromising my latest obsession on the easel.

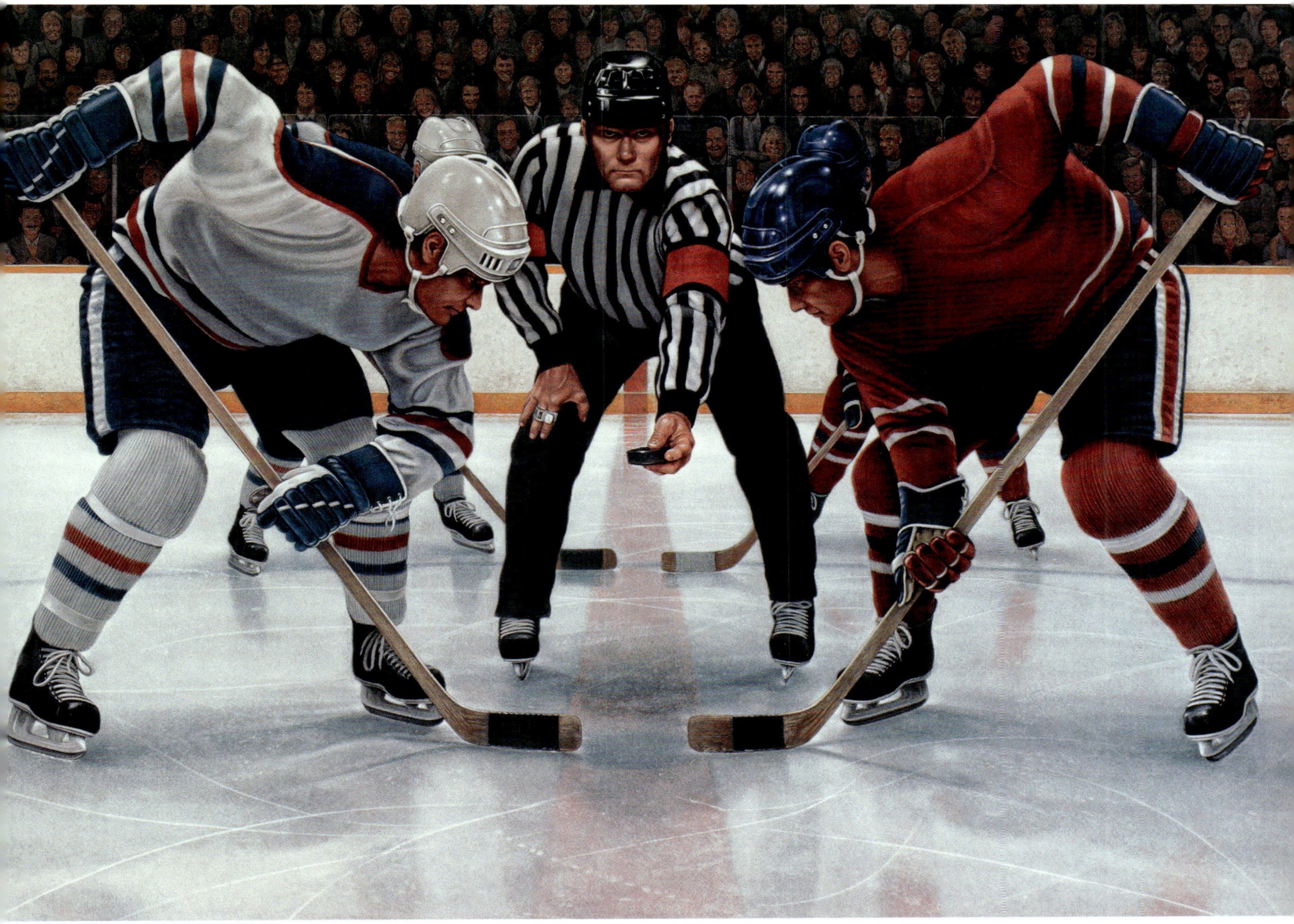

Face Off, 1997

. . .

One weekend in April 1999, I sat down to watch a New York–Pittsburgh hockey game on television. It had been speculated over the previous two days in the media that this would be Wayne Gretzky's last game — that he was retiring! I had known Wayne since 1984, when, as a guest presenter at the annual NHL Awards' Dinner, I presented him with his second Hart Trophy. I had also become a regular guest at his annual charity events in Brantford over the years. But more than this, I was a dedicated fan of the Great One and couldn't accept this rumour of his pending retirement. "Surely not, it's too soon," I kept thinking.

Not only did I watch the game, but I videotaped it as well (thankfully, as it proved to be a valuable reference in the future). For me, the game became one of the most profound hockey events in recent memory. It also became a love-in, a display of affection from the many fans, friends, and teammates in Wayne's honour. Between periods there were presentations, speeches, and accolades from various dignitaries, while video clips from highlights of his twenty-year NHL career were shown. At times, Wayne was close to tears, especially when his family members were brought forward, but he managed to retain his composure throughout.

Following the game, the fans wouldn't let Wayne depart. They applauded continuously as he skated around and around the ice, waving his goodbyes. When he left the ice, they continued applauding until he returned and again circled the ice, reaching out to them. This was repeated over and over until Wayne eventually left the ice for the last time, with a final grateful wave. This mutual display of reverence and gratitude between the superstar and his fans was truly an experience to behold. It stayed in my mind for weeks afterwards.

I began to accept that perhaps this was final, and it was then that I began to think about the idea of a painting — to offer my celebration for this exceptional athlete who also happened to be a friend. I decided to contact Wayne and propose the idea of a major portrait, together with a special publication of prints for his fans to acquire. The response from both Wayne and his agent, Mike Barnett, was, "We'd love to see this happen."

While one might expect such a painting to depict Wayne in action, playing the game, for me the defining visual moment of his career was that of him saying goodbye, standing alone on the ice, waving to the audience. It spoke volumes about the man's appreciation for his fans, and theirs for him. And it was an image that I couldn't get out of my mind after experiencing the telecast. The challenge was how to create it — after all, I wasn't at the game.

My first concern was to gain an opportunity for Wayne to pose for me. I learned when he would next be in Toronto, and we arranged to meet at his hotel, where he provided a couple of posing sessions. The results materialized as four head studies, one in pencil and three in watercolour. While none of these were intended to be models for the portrait, they offered me a first-hand analysis of Wayne's facial characteristics for future reference.

The next requirement consumed weeks of research and many preliminary studies, as I attempted to identify the pose that worked best for my concept. I acquired dozens of photographs from a number of press photographers, through various agencies, along with the rights to use them for my project. All of them were taken at Wayne's final game. I also acquired an authentic Gretzky sweater and took it to the Hockey Hall of Fame, to compare it with the actual sweater that he wore at the end of the game. (I discovered subtle but important differences.)

Over the next six months and more, I created a total of twenty-four studies before I was content with identifying the definitive pose for Wayne's farewell wave to his fans. In almost every one, I made a point of depicting his eyes looking at the viewer, to reflect that feeling of personal communication that I felt was so evident at the game. While I was feeling confident that I had found the pose that was most appropriate, I still hadn't given much thought to a background. One day, I was working on a large pencil and watercolour version of my selected pose and decided to quickly achieve a tonal wash around the top half of the figure. I mixed up a generous dish of dark blue and splashed it about with a big brush and then left it to dry. When I returned, I suddenly had the idea of creating an evening sky behind Wayne's figure.

Through my interest in the research of ancient cultures, I learned that one can actually go back in time through the use of a computer program. Like a celestial clock, the

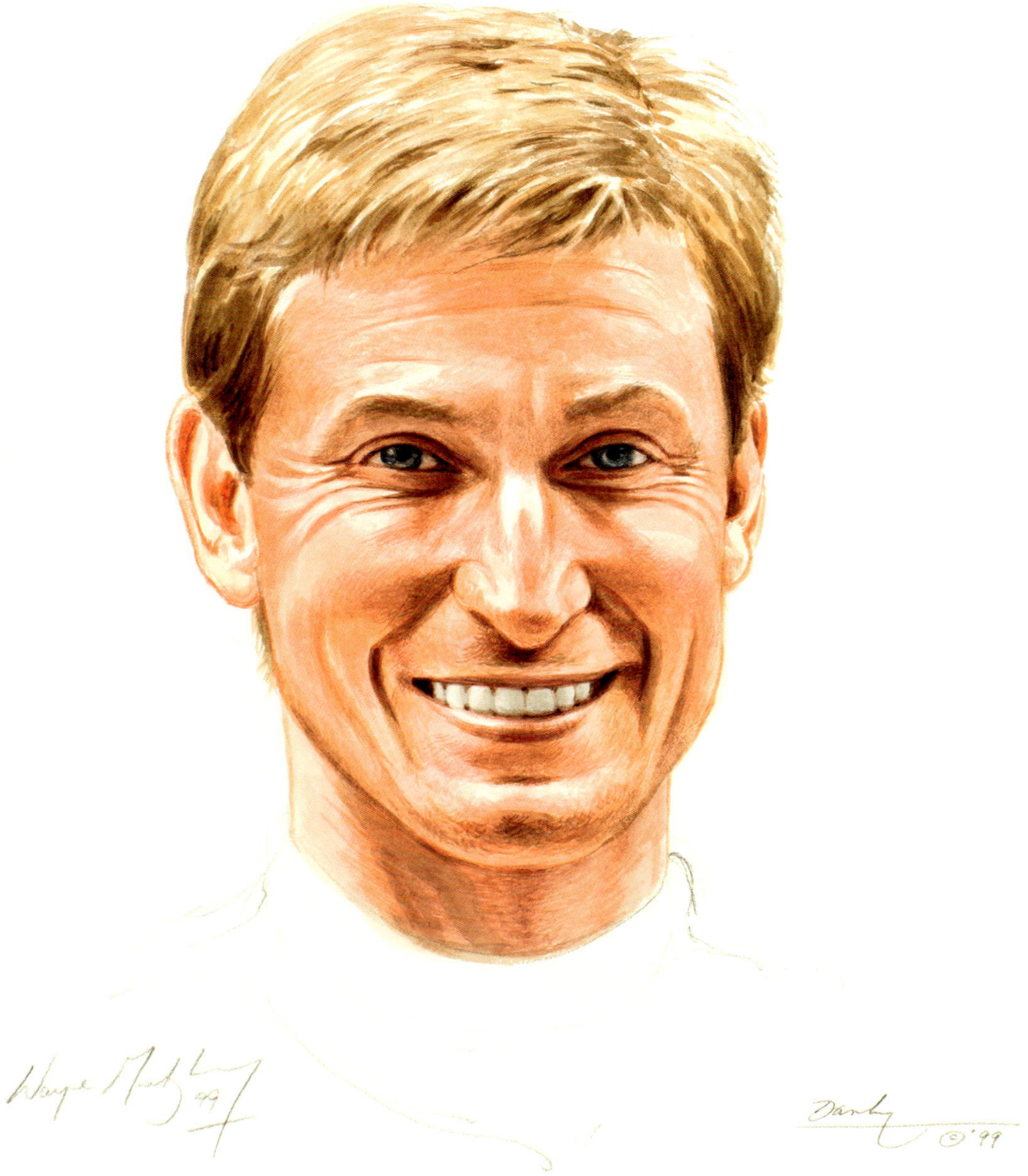

 Gretzky Head Study, 1999

placement of the stars and planets, relative to one's position on Earth, are unique at any given time. The computer allows one to recreate the night sky at any moment, from any location on the planet.

I chose Madison Square Garden in New York (by longitude and latitude), looking north at exactly 6:12:45 p.m. on April 18, 1999, precisely fifteen seconds before Wayne left the ice for the last time. The computer gave me a printout of this view. I then overlaid a similarly sized copy of the drawing for my selected pose and placed both of them against the window in order to see one through the other.

I was astonished by what I saw! The position of the horizon in the computer printout matched exactly my intended placement of the rink boards at Madison Square Garden. The image of the Milky Way across the entire sky corresponded uncannily with the alignment of Wayne's pose, from the tip of his outstretched hand, down through his figure, and to the other hand at his side. The positioning of the planets and stars were so appropriate, it was as if they were predetermined.

Once I had confirmed all of the combined elements — the pose, the facial characteristics, the background, and the uniform — the challenge remained to create the painting. I decided to paint it in acrylic on canvas. Acrylic is very durable and dries quickly, while still allowing the use of wet-into-wet, as well as glazing, techniques. It wasn't completed until the following year, due to my involvement with other projects and my refusal to rush it. All of the studies, along with the portrait itself, were unveiled at a special media event at Wayne's restaurant in Toronto, with both Wayne and myself on hand, in May 2001.

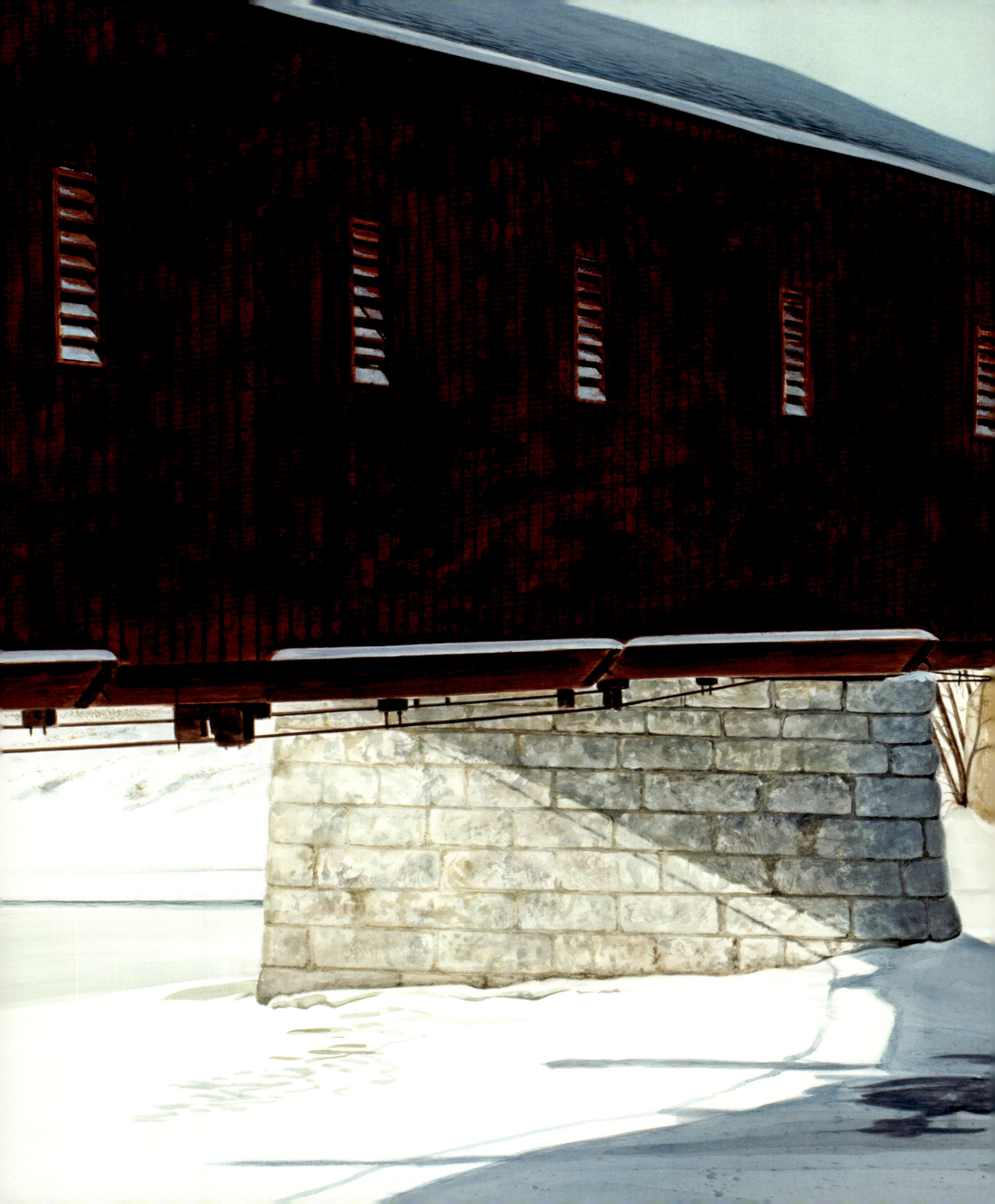

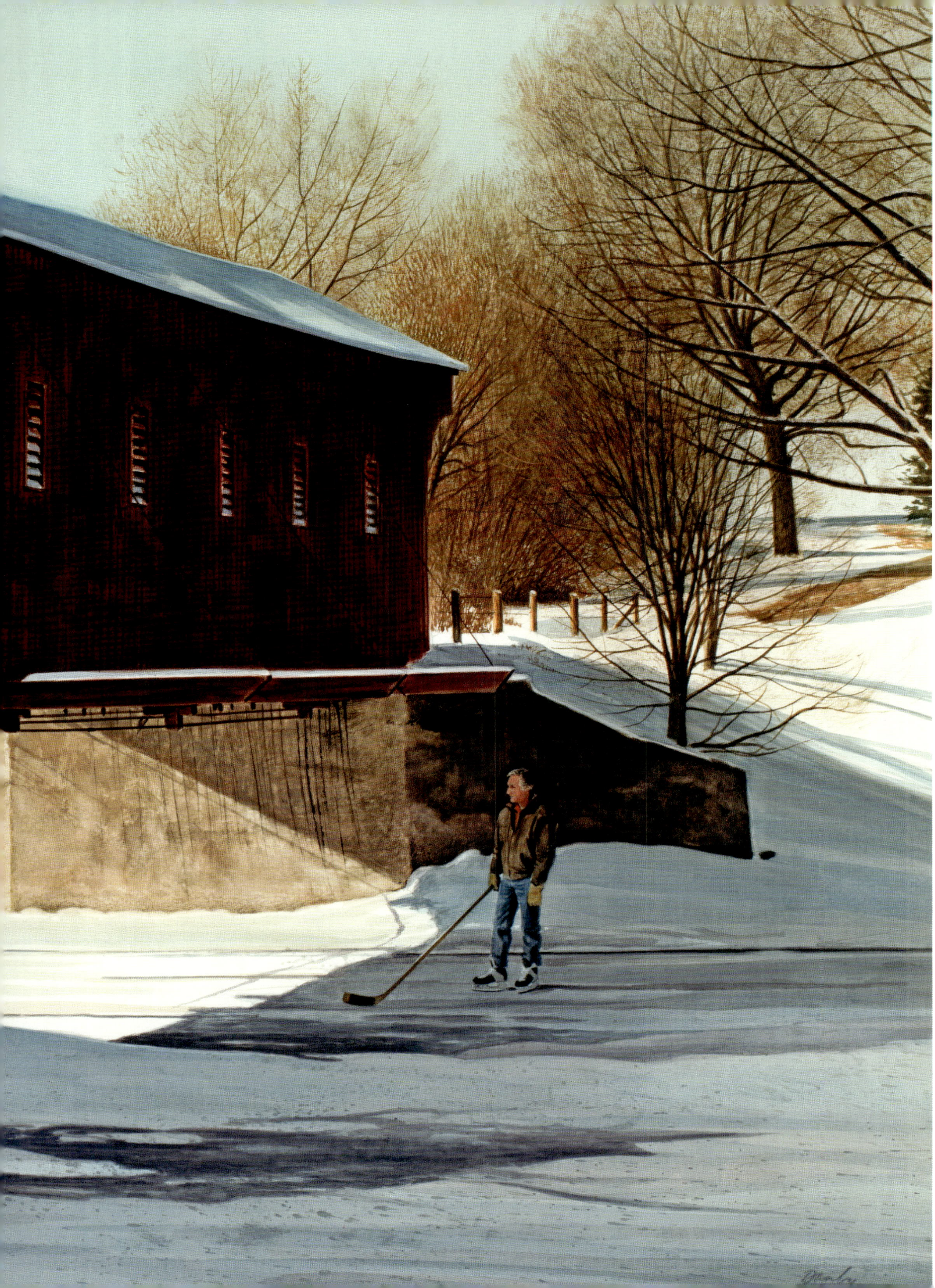

2000s

New Trails

While continuing to explore my Gretzky studies in early 2000, I received an overture that particularly intrigued me. I had attended the official opening of the Canadian Country Music Hall of Fame, at the Calgary Stampede the previous July, where I had met many of the Stampede executives while assisting Gary Buck with his event. I learned that they were planning a special millennium celebration, to be called *Trail 2000*, which would involve a dramatic horse drive, bringing the bucking stock overland from the northern Alberta ranches for the Calgary Stampede. The proposal I received in January posed the question, "Would you create a painting depicting the horse drive, and a limited-edition print publication which could assist fundraising for the Hall of Fame?"

The organizers offered to provide me with photographs of the last similar drive, which took place in 1987. I said, "No thanks. It's not simply the imagery that fuels my motivation, it's the experience." I explained that the only way I could respond to this project (as with any other) would be by absorbing some measure of the experience first-hand. Since it wasn't possible to do this and complete the painting, plus the prints, within the few days of the scheduled horse drive, I would not be able to do it. The reply was, "What if we gave you a dress rehearsal, in advance?" The more I thought about this, the more it seemed plausible.

I flew to Calgary on April 18, after waiting week after week for news of the snow's departure from the ranch lands. Following an afternoon of interviews, I joined up with Gary Buck and Michael Stinson (a representative of sponsor Kodak Canada) to drive four hours north to Hanna, Alberta, where we stayed overnight. Bob McKay, the superintendent, suggested that he could probably round up thirty or so horses for me to see when we came to the ranch but added that he couldn't be certain as "these things are pretty unpredictable." He had already arranged for a few cowboys to be there to help and we spent a short hour around the kitchen table, getting to know them over coffee. I explained what I hoped to achieve, and they felt that with a little luck, we could do something. As it happened, it was a beautiful sunny day, with a clear blue sky. So Mother Nature was helping out, as well.

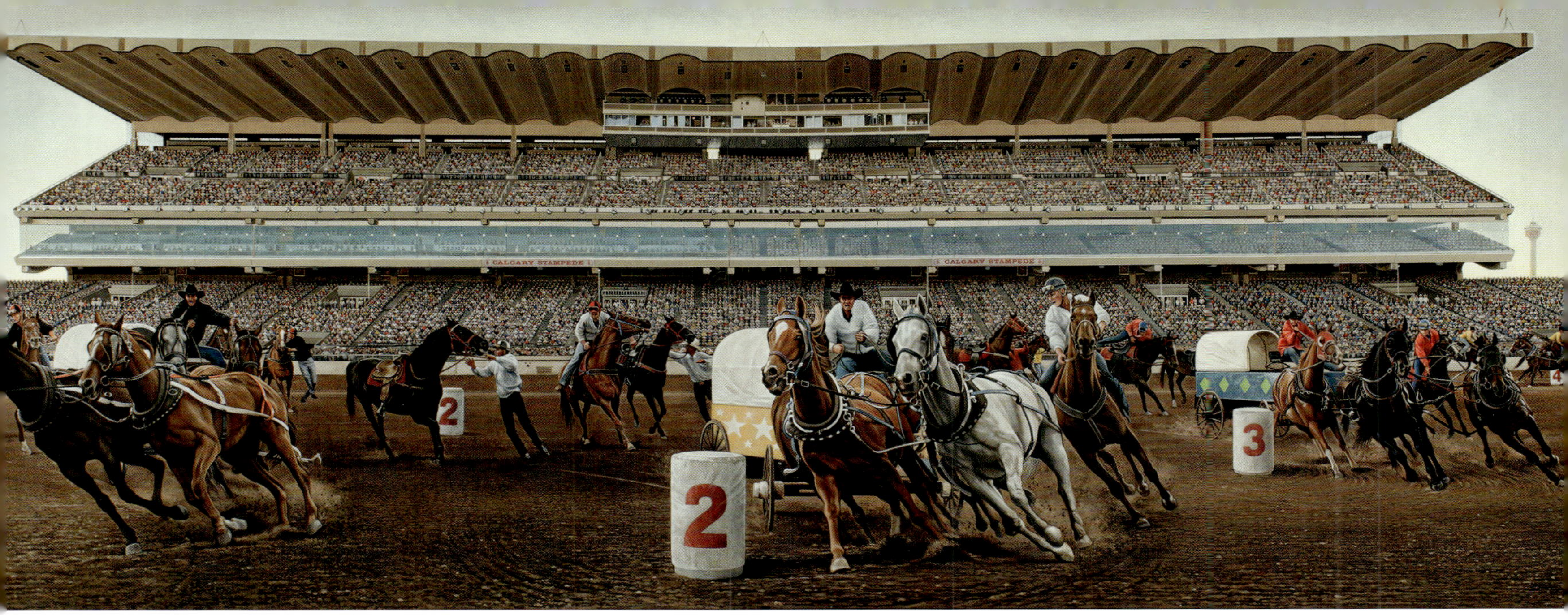

While the cowboys saddled up their horses, Bob and I drove off in a pickup truck to visit a few sites on the ranch that he felt could be useful, if they worked for me. I settled on two particular sites for specific reasons. The first was near a small creek at the base of a coulee, or ravine. A rough dirt road came straight down the hill, crossed the creek, and then continued up to the top of the next hill. The second site was at the base of another coulee, with a long, high ridge above, and a wider stretch of the creek in the foreground. If we could persuade the horses to run along the ridge, down the side, and turn at the creek, I would see them in a combination of directions.

Once we had settled on our plans, we proceeded to see if we could find some horses that would be willing to "pose" for me. I intended to capture the high-speed action with my camera, if the cowboys could choreograph my concepts.

Now it was time to cue the horses, but where were they? In my naivety, I assumed that the cowboys would ride off into a field and round up a few. Instead, one of the cowboys drove off in a pickup truck and disappeared over the horizon. About half an hour later, we saw the truck far off in the distance, driving very slowly across a field.

Within a few minutes, a group of horses appeared on the top of a distant knoll. Then minutes later, another group appeared, and then another. The truck kept driving along, slowly and deliberately. More horses came into sight. The whinnies of a few, combined with the sound of hoof beats, attracted ever increasing numbers, and soon they were all running toward where we waited for them.

Suddenly, another group of forty or fifty appeared over a rise and joined the growing herd. I couldn't believe my eyes! Within twenty minutes or so, a calm, empty field became the gathering place for approximately two hundred swirling and snorting bucking-stock horses. It was an incredible display of herd mentality, triggered simply by the appearance of the pickup truck in their grazing fields. Bob's hope of being able to locate thirty or so was mightily surpassed!

Once they had all calmed, but only slightly, the main gate was opened, and out they charged, funneling onto the ranch road, looking for room to run. Sonny and I were in the pickup truck. The other cowboys were on their horses. He asked me if I wanted to get to the first site in advance of the horses, which were already galloping down the road in its direction. I said, "Sure, let's try!" We accelerated, surrounded on all sides by horses. I could have reached out and touched them. We were all moving along quite rapidly, with horses racing in and out of the ditch beside us, as well as in front. It became impossible to get ahead of them so we just remained part of the herd and let them lead us — to where we wanted them to go.

When we had all entered our preplanned chute area, one of the cowboys closed the gate behind. The gate at other end, at the top of the far hill, was already closed. We positioned the pickup truck partway down the hill and got out. I stood in front of the right fender. When the horses were turned around on the far hill, they would come back across the creek, right at me, as I had planned. I signaled Bob to start them running. I knew they would swerve aside to avoid the truck, if not me, and of course they did — but only at the last minute. I could almost hear the pounding of my heart overwhelming the roar of thundering hoof beats, as two hundred bucking-stock horses galloped right past me!

After they turned around on the hill above, we waited a few minutes, and then the cowboys brought them back down and past me again. We repeated this back and forth gallop, up and down both sides of the ravine, three times, and I shot a lot of high speed film. Then I decided that we had succeeded with this site and should head for the second.

Sonny and I drove up the hill and back along the road that we had arrived on earlier, to rendezvous with the herd at the second coulee. Meanwhile, the cowboys were already guiding the horses toward it from the top of the far hill, perhaps a half-mile away. We arrived at our predetermined position and waited.

Before long, we saw them come into view along the other side of the creek and then being herded up to the high ridge. Only four cowboys were attempting to direct two hundred horses along the ridge and down the far end slope. Every few seconds, horses attempted to break rank, and, just in the nick of time, a cowboy would appear from nowhere to keep them together. Finally, they reached the end slope and turned downhill. Kicking dust and gathering speed, they careened down the hill and swerved at the creek — galloping past it, right in front of me, just as we had hoped!

Within a few seconds it was over. Bob turned and waved, as if to say, "I hope you got it!" I signaled back to him to try the maneuver again. He ignored me, as they all rode off to take the horses back to their grazing pastures. We laughed about it afterwards. He explained that he hadn't thought they would succeed the first time, never mind trying it again. He also said that it wouldn't have been possible at all if we hadn't tired the horses a bit by running the chute site first. We all met back at the ranch house for a late lunch of great chili. Thanks to their expert assistance, I had my raw material and sufficient first-hand experience to return to my studio and get to work.

This was certain to be one of those paintings to be completed over one straight stretch. Many long days and late nights were consumed in its creation. At first, my composition attempted to include both the ridge sequence and the face-on gallop, as I decided to turn the horses toward me in the painting and have them splashing across the creek in the left foreground. This is how the image developed. Weeks later, it began to trouble me. It seemed awkward, and I realized that I was trying to include too much.

With my deadline looming, I determined that I had to eliminate the entire left side of the painting. I took a big brush with a lot of white paint, gritted my teeth, and proceeded to paint over all of the oncoming horses, that I had spent weeks developing. Once they were gone, I felt a sense of relief. I had solved the problem created by allowing the work to develop complexities that it didn't need. The answer was to return it to a more elegant simplicity. There was still much to be done to resolve the left side, but when completed, I was pleased with the whole picture.

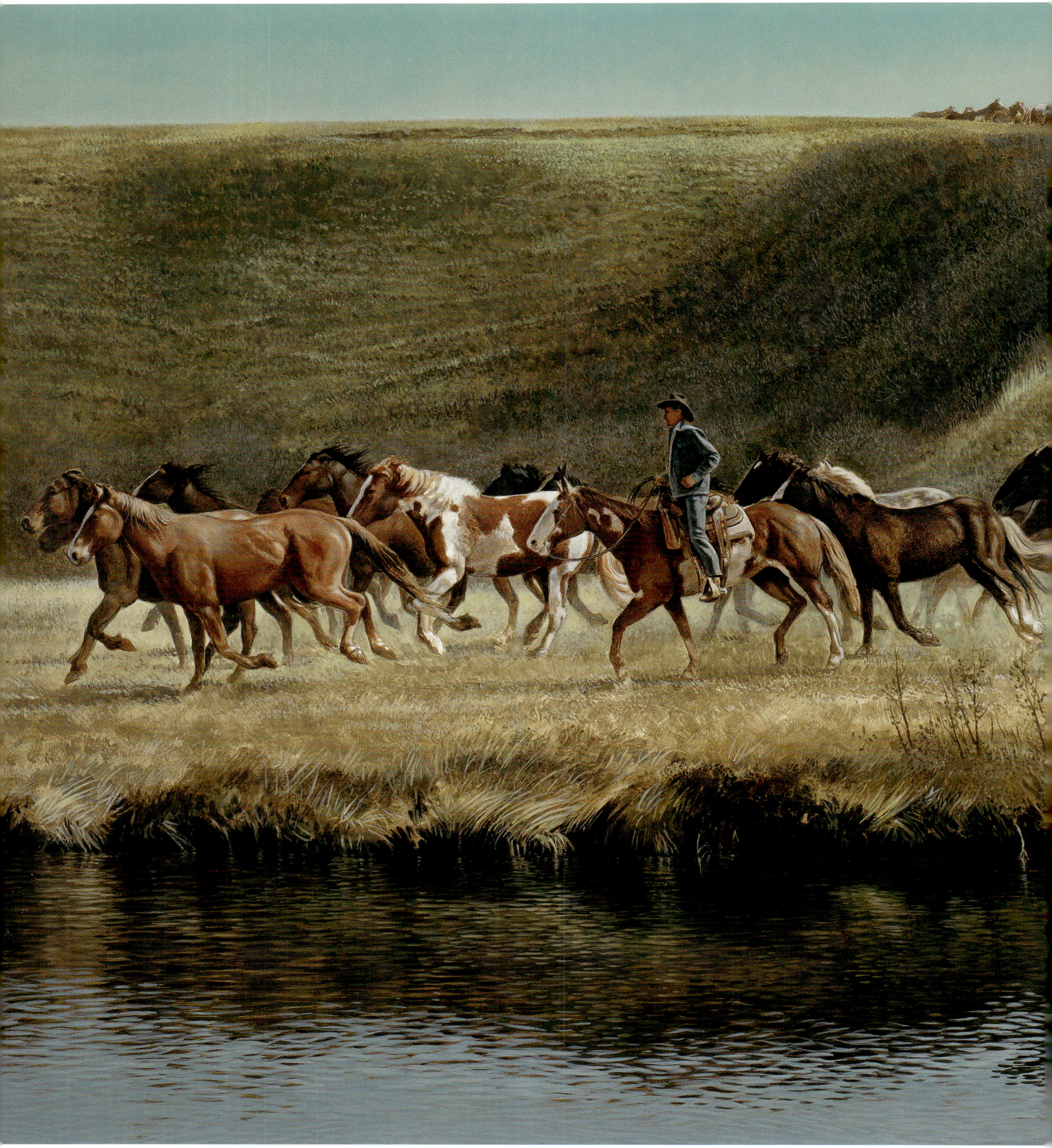

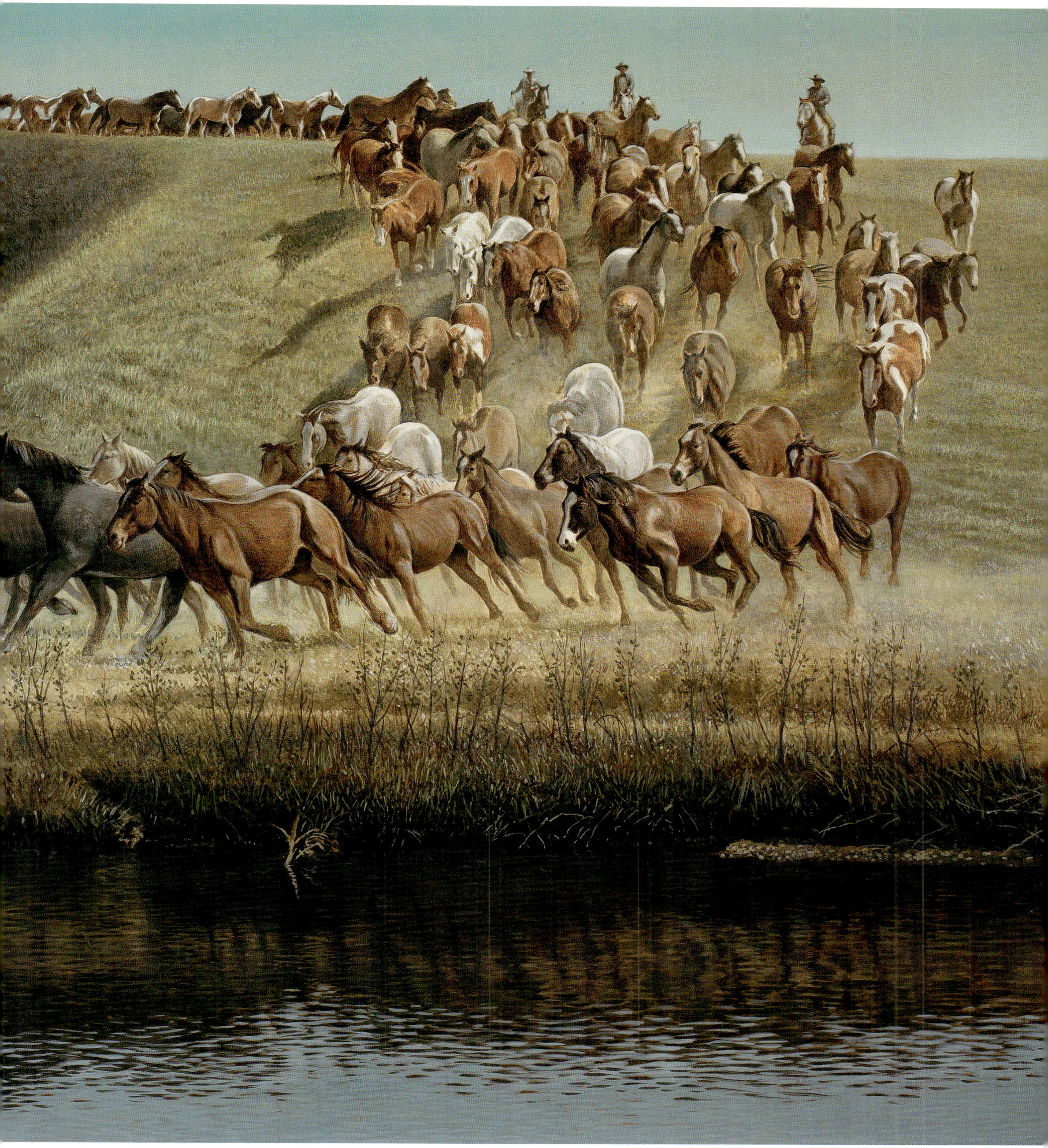

. . .

Not too long ago, I received a letter from a university student who was conducting research on the contribution of my art (with regards to subject matter, style, etc.), to a sense of Canadian national identity (!). She said she would appreciate any comments on this that I could offer. While I was quite surprised by the premise of her research, I answered as candidly as I could:

> If my work contributes to a sense of Canadian national identity, it is certainly not the result of any conscious intention on my part. Yet I am indeed grateful for the fact that it does seem to generate a significant response from the Canadian public.
>
> I have always subscribed to the principle of simply being true to myself, as I approach my work. The fact that I am a Canadian, living and working in Canada, and was born here (through a Canadian heritage of some eight generations) has, I'm sure, reflected itself in my work and will always remain a part of it.
>
> While I am simply responding to my life's encounters and experiences as I pursue my image making, I am always amazed when viewers identify with my images on such a subjective level. It reinforces just how subjective art really is. So if your focus is valid, and my work does contribute to a sense of Canadian national identity, it's a result of how it is perceived by others, not through any particular intent of my own.

I might have added that I don't particularly think of myself in terms of being a Canadian artist. I am an artist, period. My work certainly reflects what I am, and where I have been, but without any intentional geographic or nationalistic parameters. As far as I am concerned, anyone who encounters my art is my audience, no matter where they encounter it. My work embraces my experiences from wherever I may be in the world, at any given time. And over the past forty years it has been well received in many countries around the world.

It has often been said that Canadian art, generally, is of little interest to those outside of Canada. If this is so, perhaps it is a result of an overemphasis by the art community on the qualification of it being Canadian, which I believe is unnecessary. Certainly, my pride in my country does not program the directions of my work as an artist. As I have stated previously, there are ultimately only two kinds of art — good and bad — and it's up to the viewer to decide. No amount of profound pronouncements through art-speak by "experts" of what is in and what is out will change this — nor will nationalistic qualifications.

I am a descendant of ancestry that was in Canada long before Confederation and of ancestry that was in America long before the Revolution. My family lineage in Canada is mainly derived from Britain, with distant British and German heritage in America. Having an awareness of this gives me a keener sense of who I am. Having made the decision to devote my life to creating art when I was just ten years old gives me a strong sense of what I am.

There is a famous inscription carved above the entrance to the Temple of Apollo, at Delphi, Greece, the site of the ancient Olympic Games. It applies to all aspects of life, as well as sport. In translation it reads, "Know thyself." I believe this to be a critical component for achieving success in any endeavour.

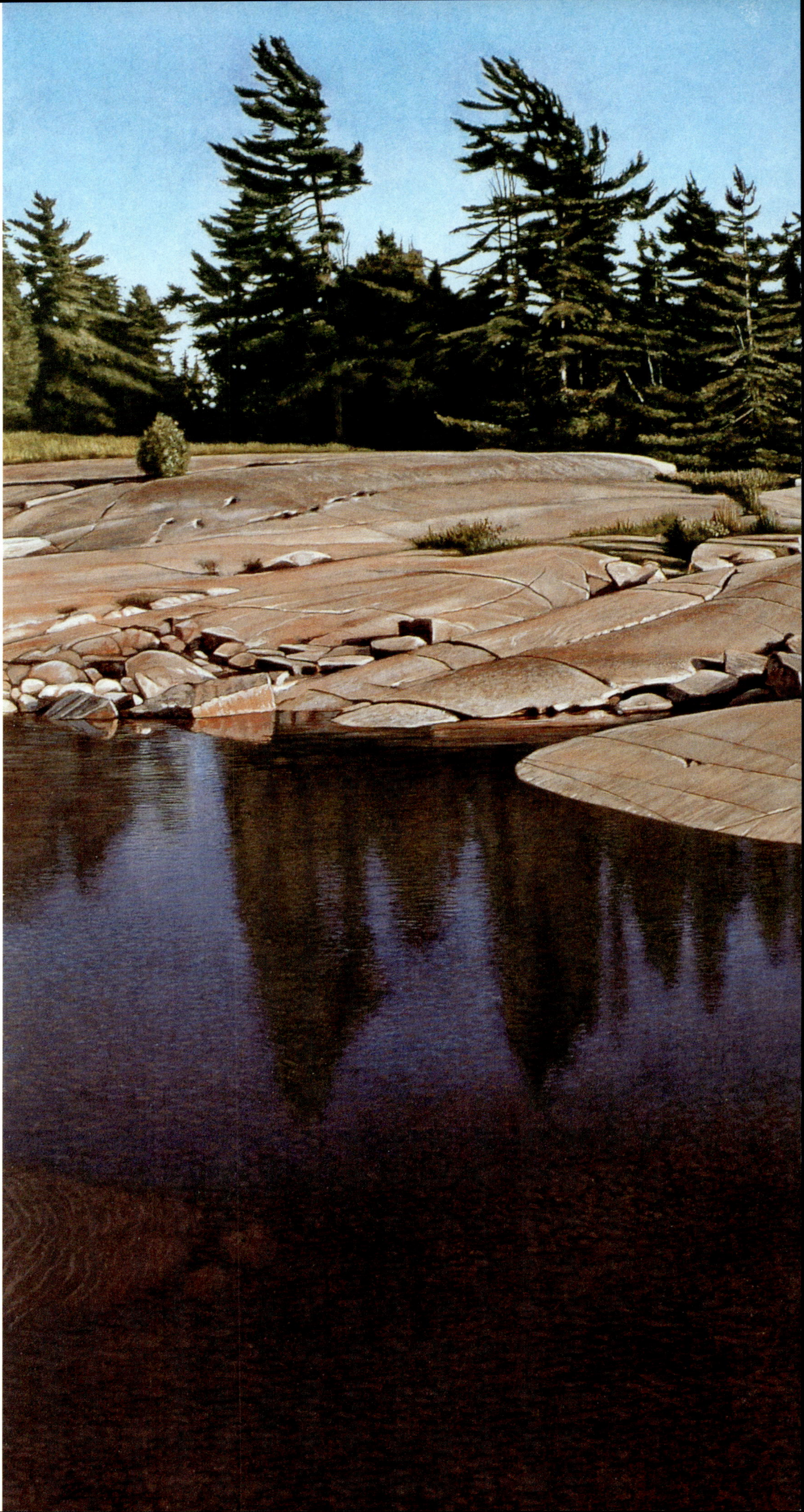

 Island Reach, 2003

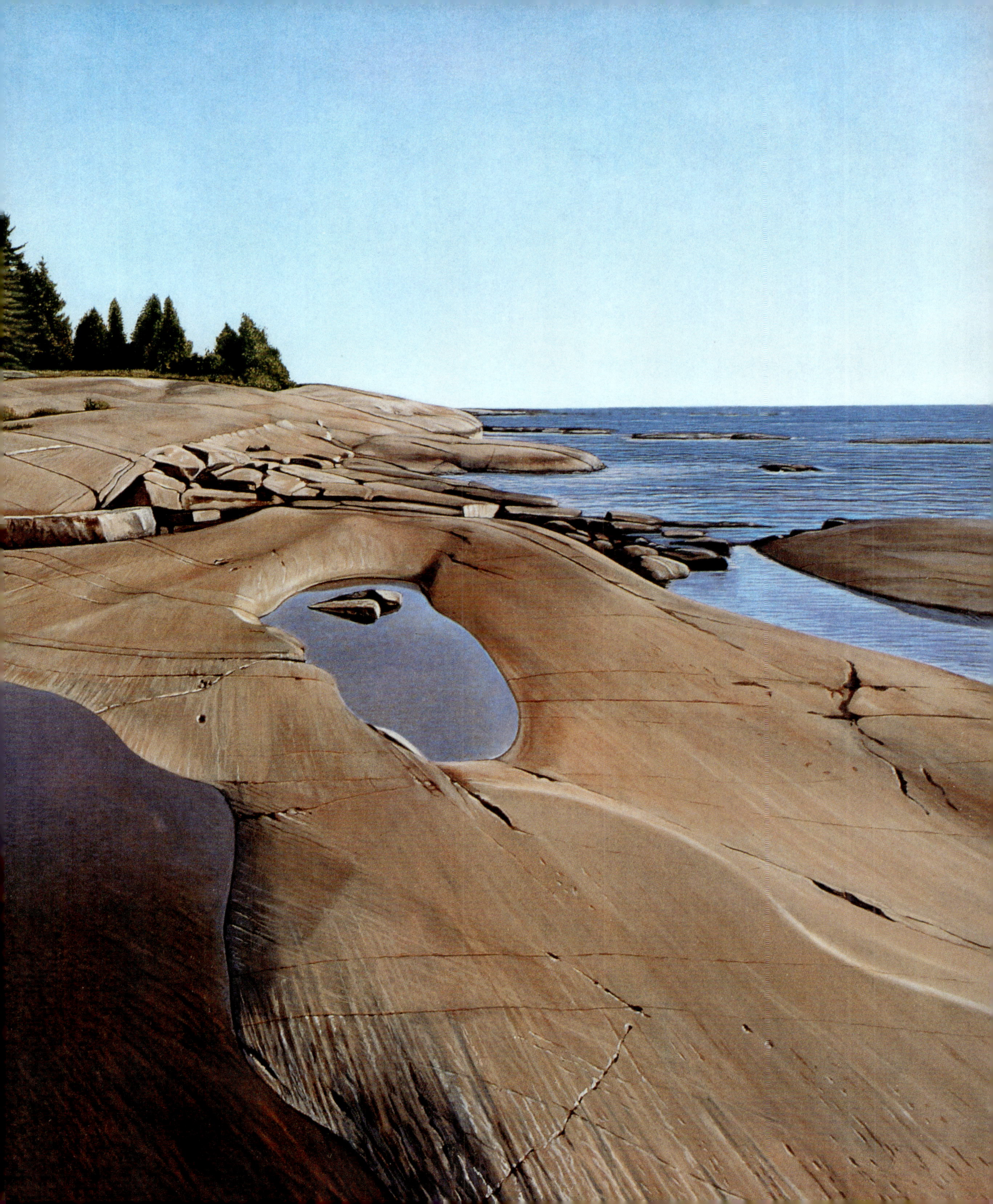

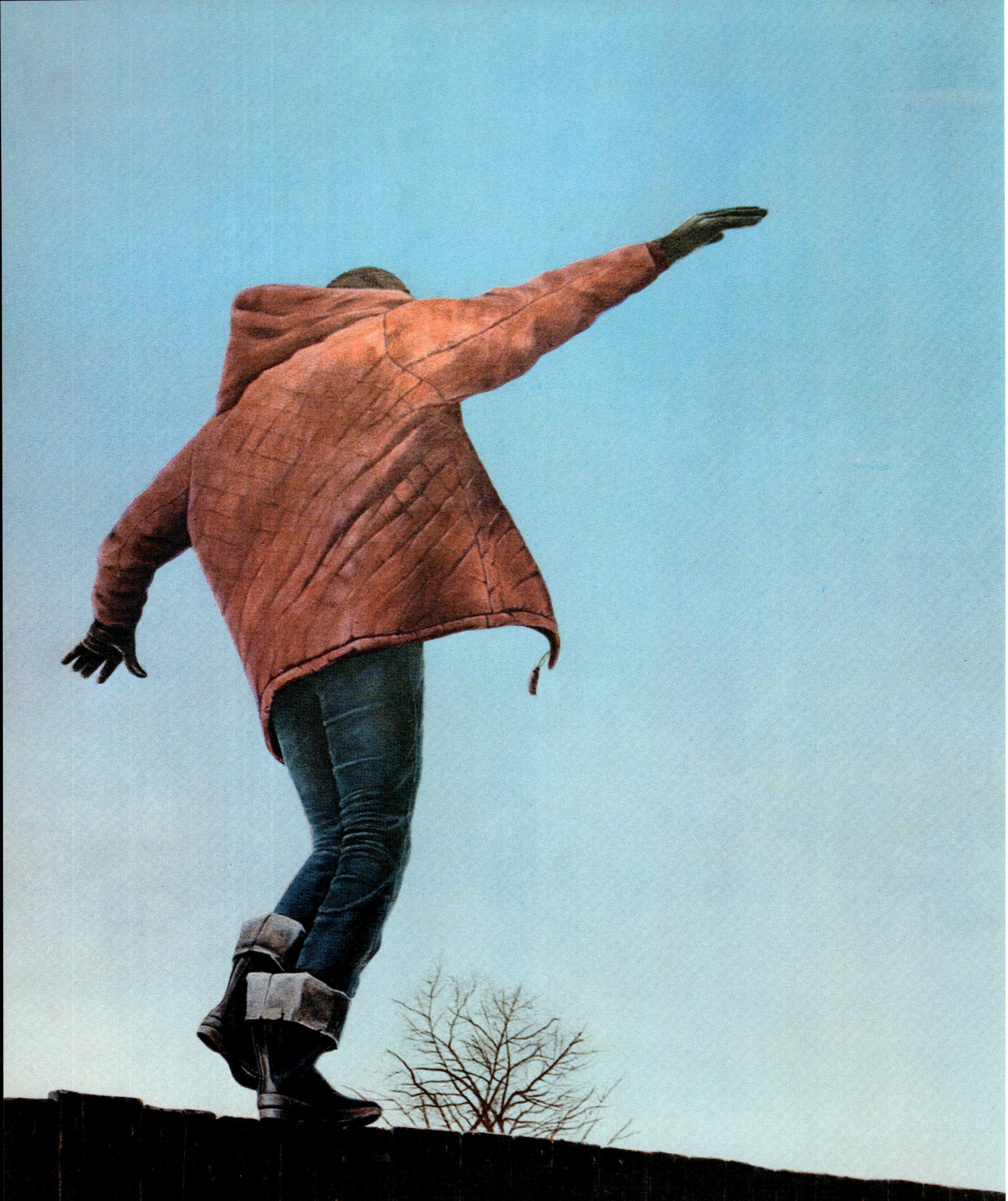

The Serigraphs

Greg McKee

I served as master printer and studio manager for Ken Danby Studios from 1979 until the studio's closing in 2011. Working closely with Danby, I assisted him in the production of serigraphs as well as assuming other tasks that keep artists from their easels: construction and preparation of canvases, arranging photography and framing, shipping, planning exhibitions and managing the collection.

Serigraphy played an important role in Danby's artistic production, as his many well-known prints bear witness to. To appreciate the art of serigraphy it is useful to distinguish between an original fine art print — specifically a serigraph — and a reproduction print, especially as both may be produced as limited editions. Reproduction prints are copies of original art — the equivalent of high quality photocopies, which are commercially printed and usually rely on photographing or scanning the original art. The original art may be created by the artist, but the reproduction really has little to do with the creative process. Original fine art prints are, on the other hand, created by an artist, or in some circumstances, by an atelier under the supervision of an artist. For a serigraph, each print is printed colour by colour, and is a work in progress until such time as the artist is satisfied with the result and signs each print. No reproduction of something else is involved.

Andy Warhol may have popularized serigraphy, but artists had been exploring the potential of the medium for some time. A.J. Casson published the possibilities of silk-screen reproduction in an article for *Canadian Art* in 1949. Alex Colville began using the process as early as 1955, followed by Christopher Pratt and Toni Onley. Danby was exposed to all forms of printmaking while a student at OCA. He explored drypoint etchings, purchasing a small press, copper plates, and paper in the early 1960s, but none of these prints ever made it to a gallery. They were stored until found after his death. Later, he abandoned the small format of etchings in favour of lithography. Instead of using unwieldy lithographic stones, Danby would draw with a wax-based lithographic pencil on a slightly textured paper, which was then given to a commercial printing house that transferred the drawings to an aluminum lithographic plate and printed under the artist's supervision. Frequently, but not always, these lithographs were either studies for, or at least related to, major tempera pieces featured in the exhibitions, and used as images on the show posters. Starting in 1965 with *Letting Go (Boy on Fence)* — inspired by an image he'd seen in the film *Mary Poppins*, — he continued to produce lithographs for the length of his career. So, having achieved success in printmaking with lithographs, why turn to serigraphy?

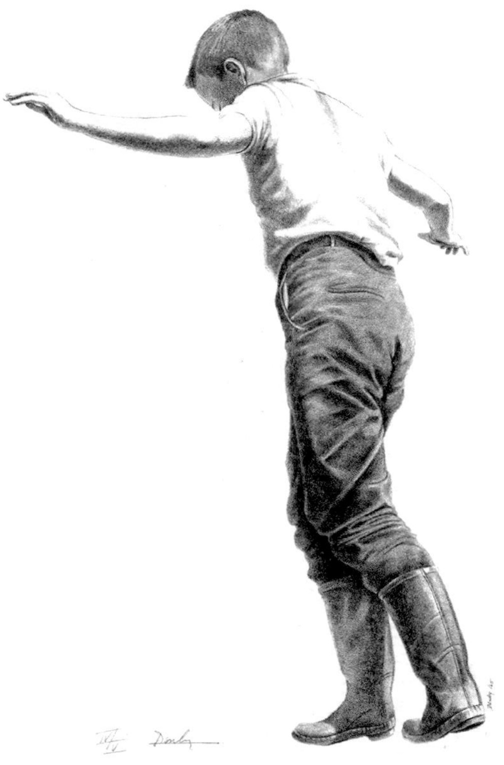

Serigraphs allowed colour, in contrast to the black-and-white aesthetic of lithography, and provided opportunity to explore images in depth — closer to the process of egg tempera. In fact, it was Danby's use of egg tempera that made him realize the potential of silkscreen printing. He had been painting with egg tempera since 1963, pushing this ancient medium to its full potential. Egg tempera is quick drying and tough when fully cured, but delicate and susceptible to damage when painted on gessoed panels. The medium is ideally suited for tight and detailed work, with best results achieved by using a layering procedure. Unlike oil paints which allow wet colour into colour blending, tempera dries quickly, so the colours are applied in layers on top of each other. The image is first painted on the bare gesso in black India ink with semi-transparent layers of local colour placed on top to block in the basic composition. The black drawing shows through enough to allow modeling with layers of whites, blacks, and more colours, building form and allowing underlying colours to glow through. Danby recognized the similarity in the layering procedure in the two mediums as early as 1966, and after years

Letting Go (Boy on Fence), 1965

of research, decided that with adaptations, serigraphy could offer rich, colourful, fully modeled images that were not identical but similar to egg tempera paintings. Although Jasper Johns was creating multi-coloured serigraphs reflective of the under-painted and dripping paint style of his signature "flag" series, it was Danby who pioneered the process of making multi-coloured prints based on the egg tempera process, and of that degree of realism.

Creating a serigraph is labour intensive. Danby's prints often contained between twenty-five and thirty-five colours. Each colour requires a drawing — which can take between an hour and several days to create, depending on the detail. Each drawing requires a screen stencil, which in turn requires preparing and setting up for printing. Each printing requires colour testing, ink preparation, and printing upwards of five hundred sheets of paper. An edition of one hundred prints requires 150 to 250 hours of drawing, thirty or more days of printing, and up to fifteen thousand individual pulls. Most painters who are printmakers can't afford the time away from their easels, so it was, and is, common practice for the actual printing process to be completed by an atelier, or by a trained printer who does the actual extensive physical work, while the artist creates the drawings and supervises colour choices. Danby's brother, Marvin, was the master printer during the 1970s, learning the craft with his brother; a baptism by fire resulting in some exceptional prints over those years. A hallmark of a Danby serigraph is the quality of printing, achieved to full effect through Marvin's efforts. I followed Marvin, starting in 1979, printing the editions until Danby's death in 2007.

The first serigraph, *The Wagon* (1970, edition of 180), was experimental, using thirteen colours. The subject was reminiscent of the earlier '60s imagery of open fields and absent of people, and while it proved his theory that serigraphy could result in colourful, realistic prints, it still lacked the depth he sought. That year saw the creation of five editions, each making progress and pushing the envelope a little farther. The creation of the fourth print, *Butterbowl*, (1970, edition of 75, twenty-one colours) marked a turning point. It employed more colours than any previous print, and the warm and glowing light reflected from the surfaces, together with the transparency of the reflections on

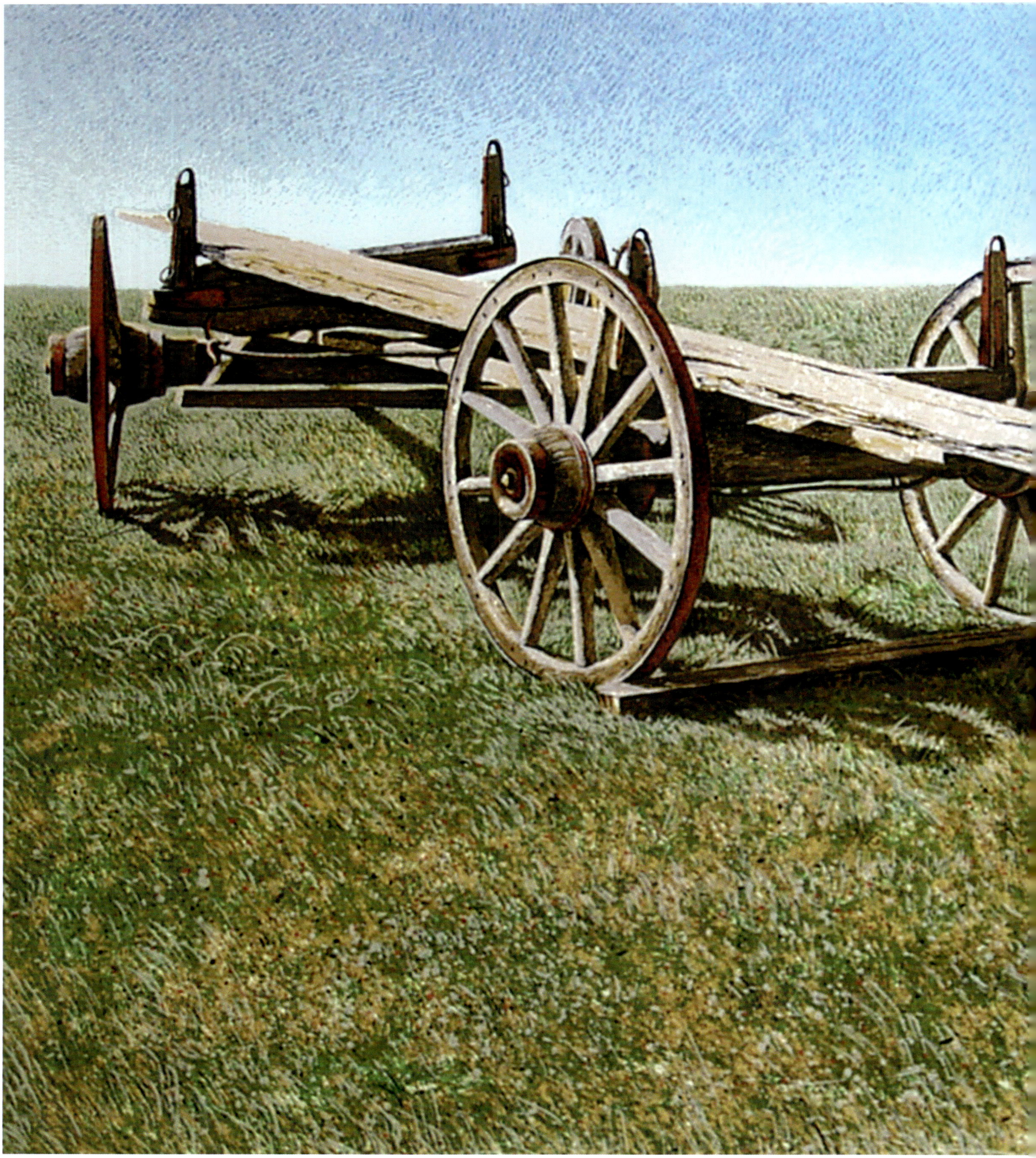

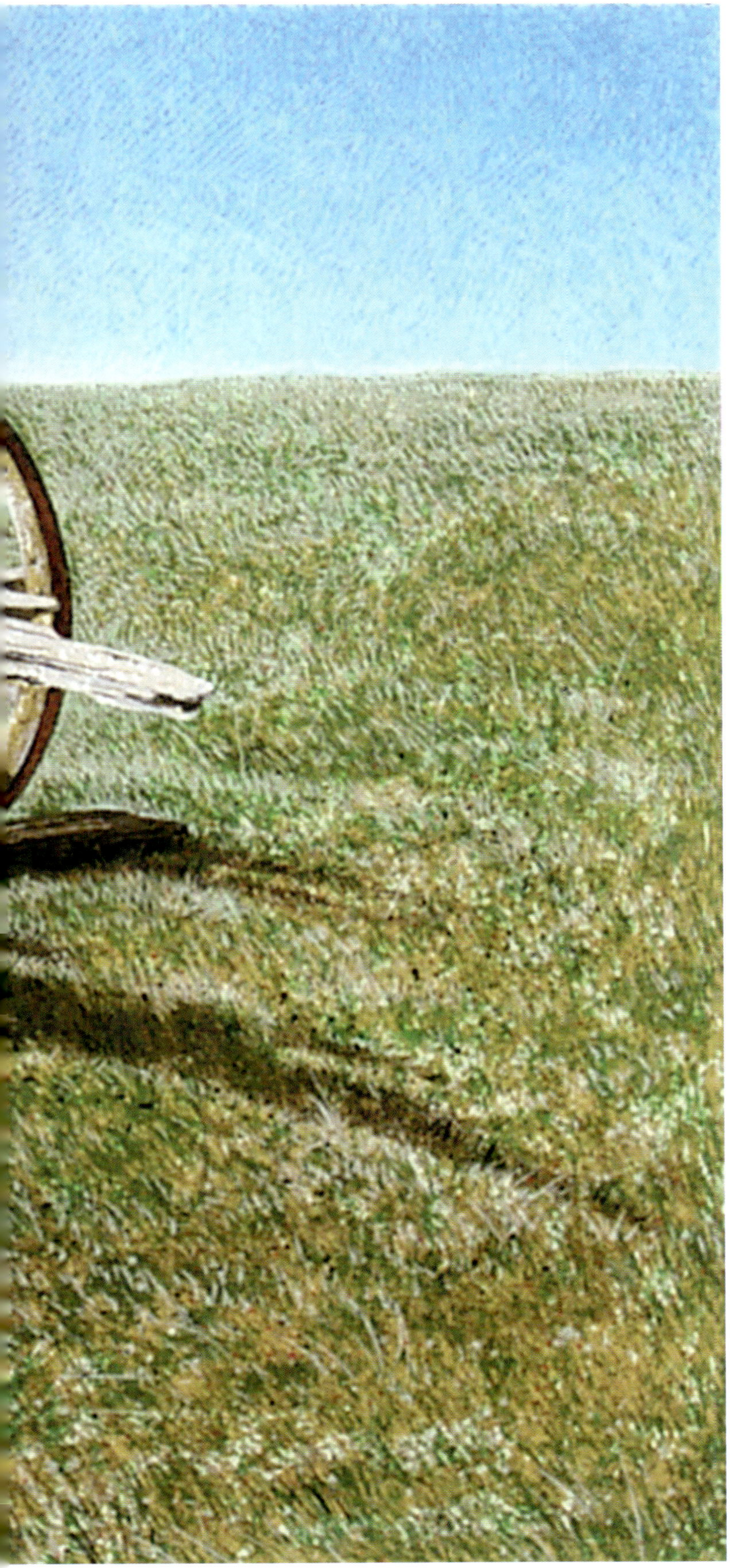

the window and the strong graphic element made it a winner. The process of constructing the print like an egg tempera painting produced a serigraph unlike any seen before. 1971 saw three more prints, two of them — *On the Gate* and *Early Autumn* — featuring his son Sean. *Early Autumn* (edition of one hundred, nineteen colours), depicting Sean lounging on a massive dead elm branch and gazing into the distance, was a tour de force. The textures, detail, colours, modelling, and strong design all combined to make the serigraph as close to making an egg tempera painting as Danby could have wanted. After fewer than two years, and with only eight editions, Danby had already achieved an amazing result. Apparently the Museum of Modern Art agreed, as they purchased a proof for their collection.

While Danby continued to work in watercolour, tempera, and lithography, his prints were becoming highly sought after, with the editions selling out quickly after their releases. *The Skates* (1972, edition of one hundred, twenty-two colours) was one of the first sports images that Danby became so famous for, and was created around the same time as the iconic *At the Crease*. Danby presented each member of the Canadian national hockey team with a print after their spectacular victory over the Soviets in the "Super Series" of 1972. While he was now comfortable with the process and satisfied with the results, Danby again pushed the boundaries with the production of his largest print — *Sunning* (1974, edition of one hundred, twenty-nine colours), a depiction of a young woman

The Wagon, 1970

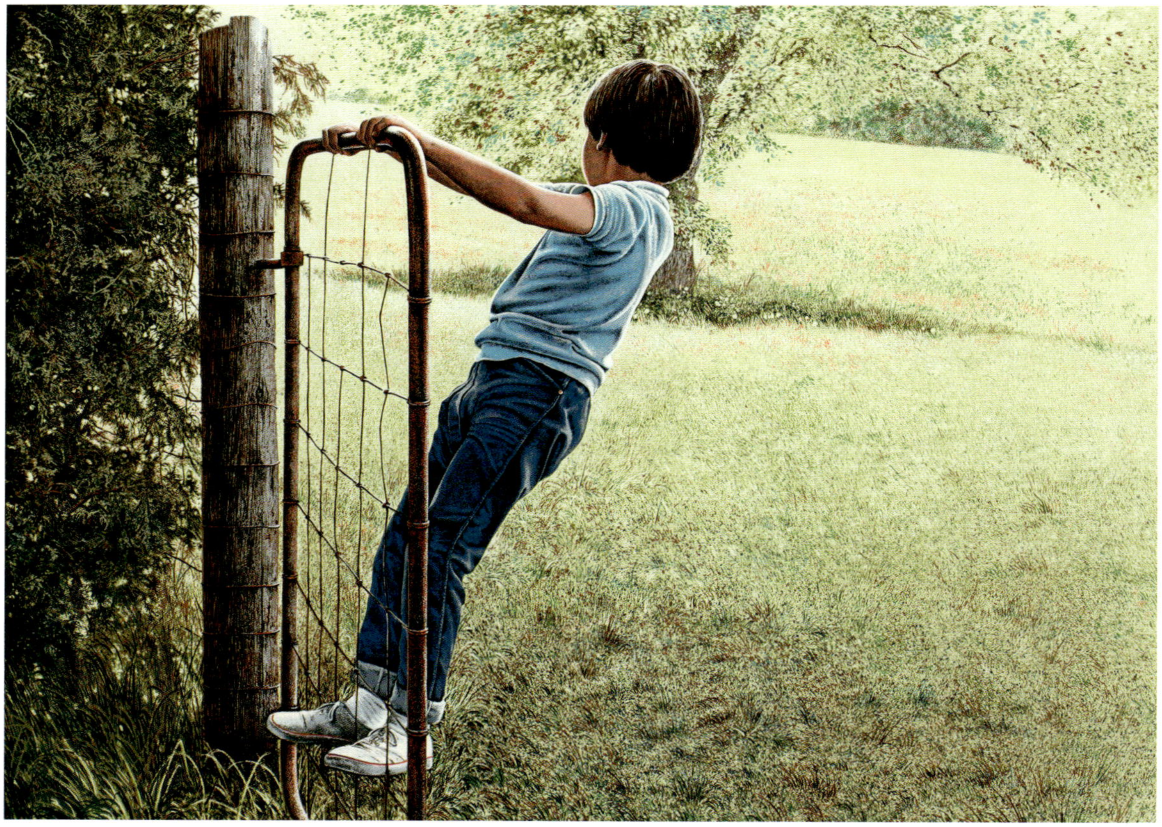

On the Gate, 1971

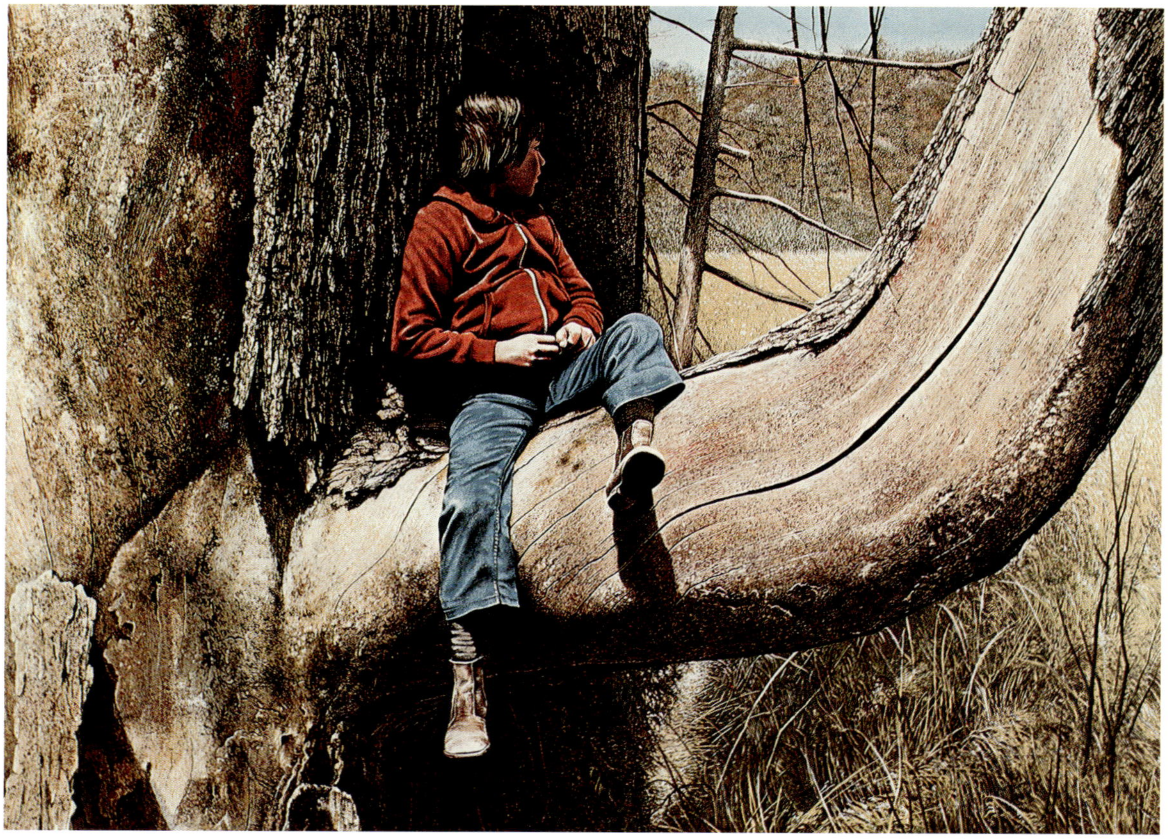

Early Autumn, 1971

sunning herself on a lawn chair. The earliest prints measured 31.8 by 42.4 cm, using eleven or twelve colours, the size increasing to 45.7 by 61 cm, with an average of about nineteen colours. *Sunning* measured 63.5 by 86.4 cm, and used twenty-nine colours. The upsized scale represented a massive amount of increased work, both in drawing and printing, and required new, larger screens. The details in *Sunning* are exceptionally fine, and the colours are gently gradated using multiple glazes. Each drawing would have required many hours, but the result set a new standard. The effort, however, may have proved too extreme, as subsequent works returned to the 45.7 by 61 cm size. The large size was never repeated. In 1976, Danby tried a different approach to imagery with the creation of a portfolio of four prints called the *Olympic Serigraphs* (*The Diver, The Hurdler, The Sculler, and The Vaulter,* 1976, editions of 150, five colours) in response to his experience at the Summer Olympics in Montreal. At 40.6 by 45.7 cm, these were smaller prints featuring athletes at the height of their sport. Each image was given a single background colour, and the figures were restricted to black and white — overall, a return to a more graphic approach. All of the modelling was done in a series of four drawings, ranging from deep black to light gray, and all highlight whites were restricted to the colour of the unprinted paper.

One of his last prints, *True North* (1998, edition of one hundred, thirty colours), depicting an empty canoe on a rocky shore, might well serve as a symbol of Danby and his artistic legacy. Ultimately a truly Canadian image (as was the artist), the canoe serves as a needle on a compass, pointing to the distance — the unknown — in a positive but reflective manner. The craft, a proven vessel weathering many trips, is at rest waiting for the next adventure. Ken's last adventure in Algonquin Park, September, 2007, took place in a similar canoe.

Danby continued to explore the potential of serigraphs until his last exhibition, with a career total of thirty-two serigraphs. When creating a silkscreen print, Danby never knew what the next stage would be — the first stages of establishing the position and composition with the black, and blocking in the local colours, went quickly, but still required forethought and intuition. The next stages usually responded to the previous stage, and Danby never knew what that stage might be until he saw how the print had progressed up to that point. No two images followed the same procedure; each was

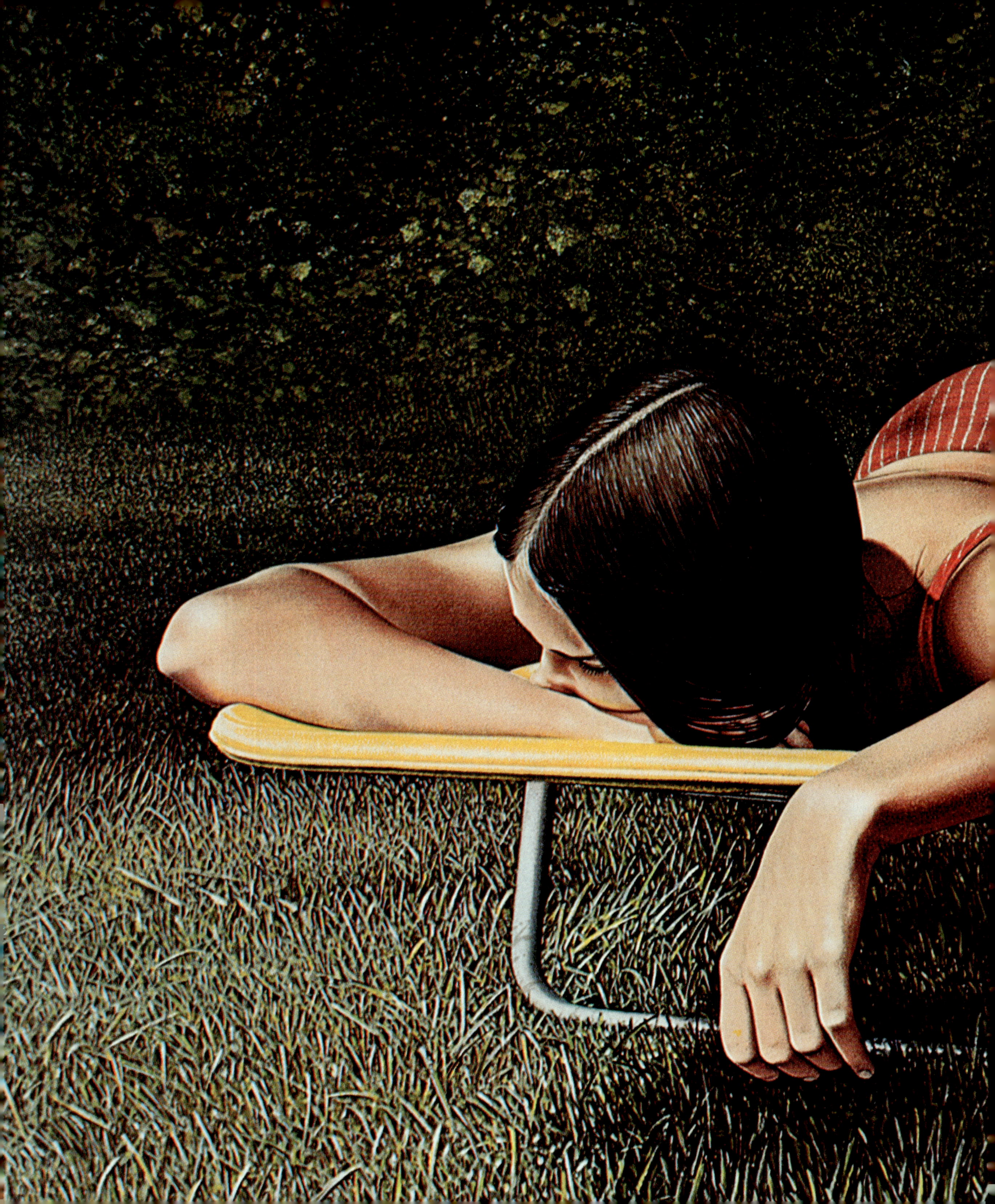

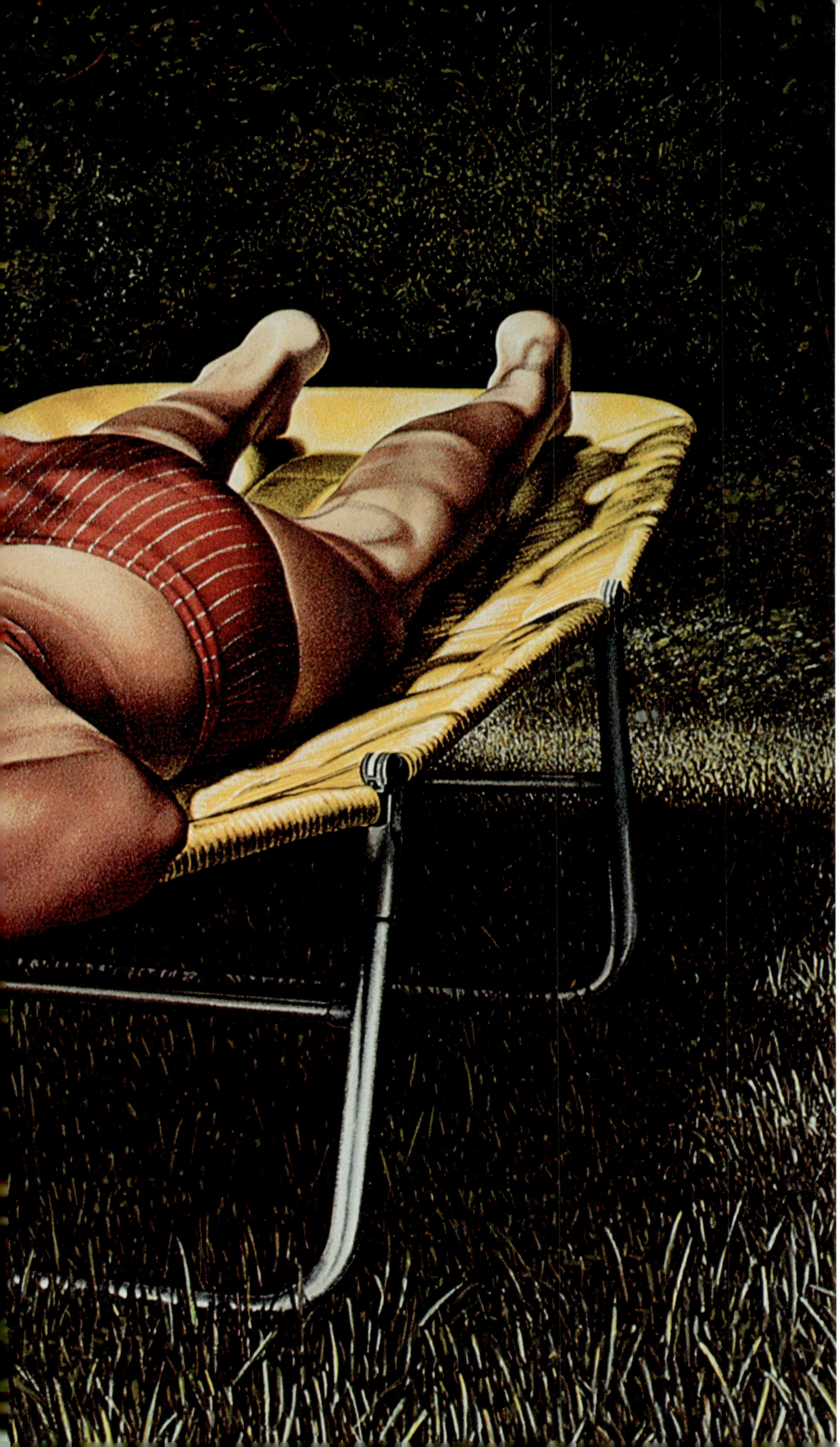

Sunning, 1974

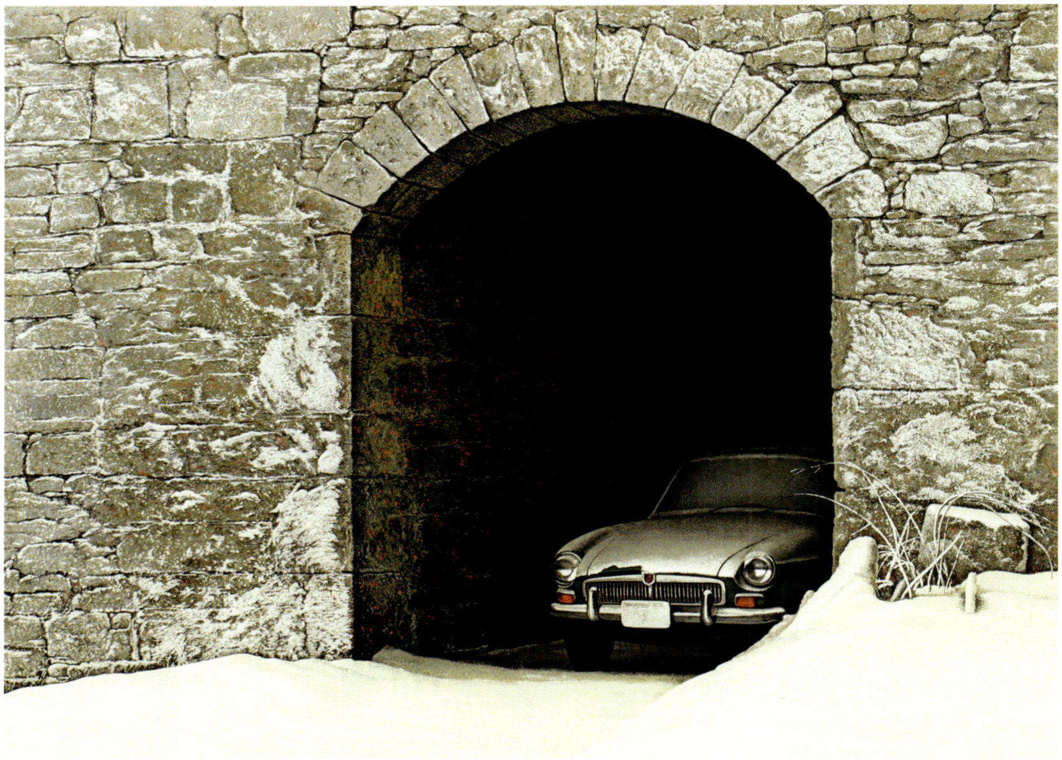

unique. Danby studied each stage scrupulously, often walking around the proof, turning it upside down, and observing it from all angles in an effort to determine what came next. (This usually involved a lot of eyebrow pulling — a personal quirk he had when deep in thought.) In Danby's own words, "the technique is an intuitive and creative one, combining silk-screen mechanics and tempera procedures of painting. There is really no limit to where the print may be taken, as with a painting. I take pride in the fact that this is an innovative technique, which I am told no other artist in the world is using to this extent. On the other hand, I regret that the complexity of it has caused people to misunderstand the result, thinking that photography or reproduction of an existing painting is involved, when it is not."

 Under the Arch, 1972

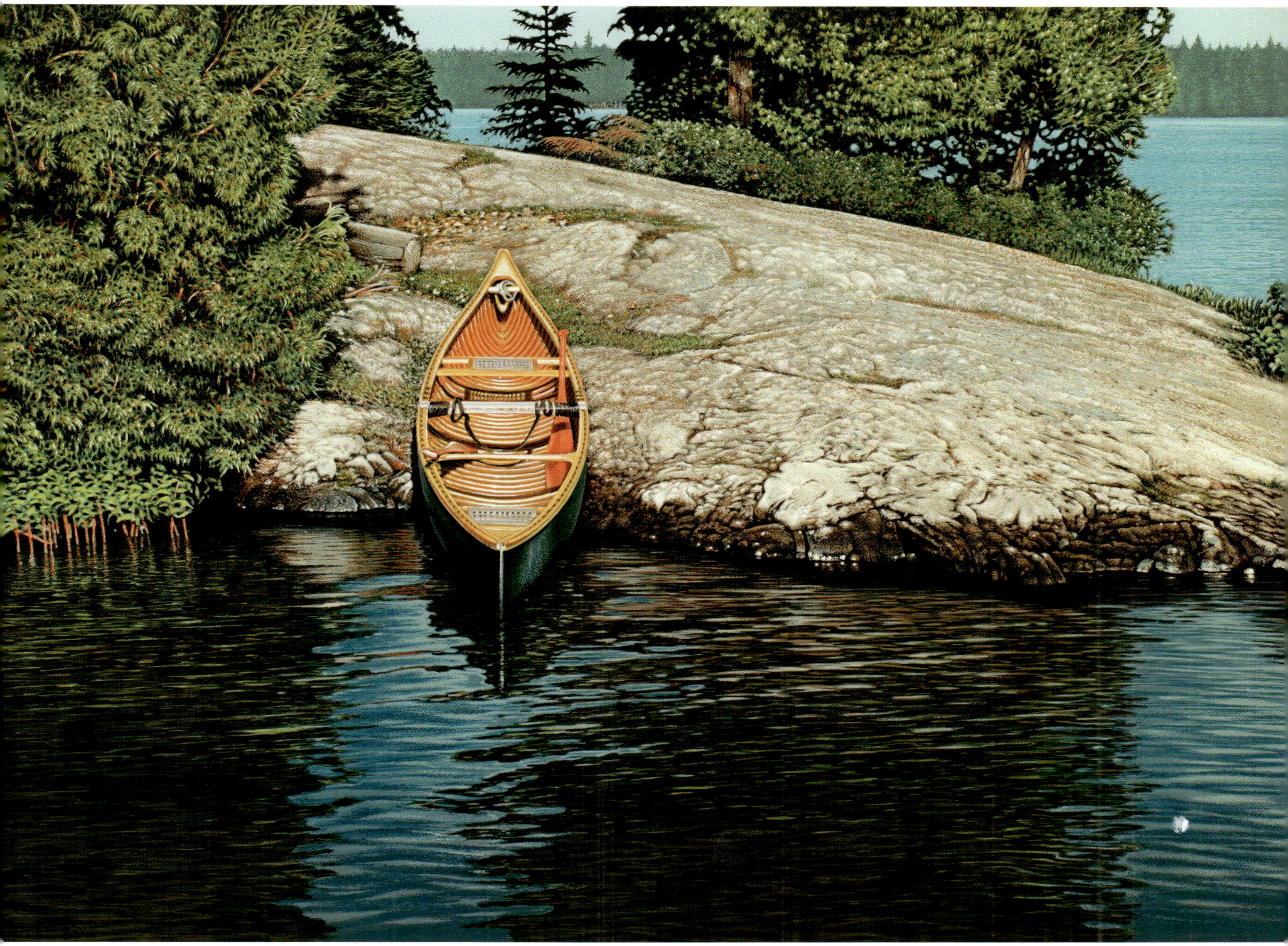

True North, 1998

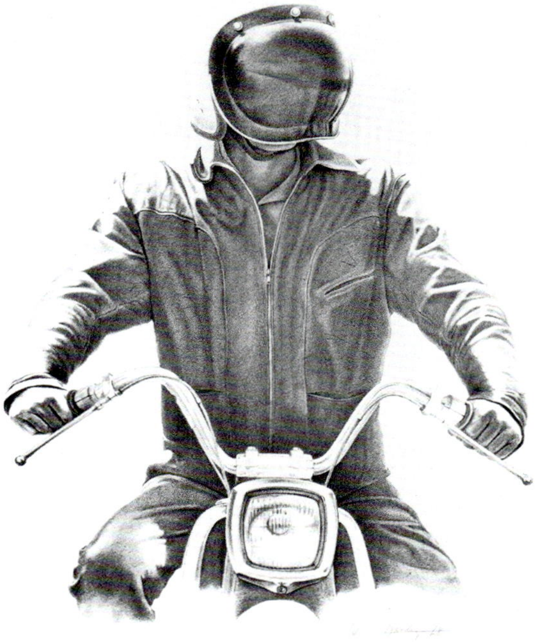

The Motorcyclist (Heading Out), 1968

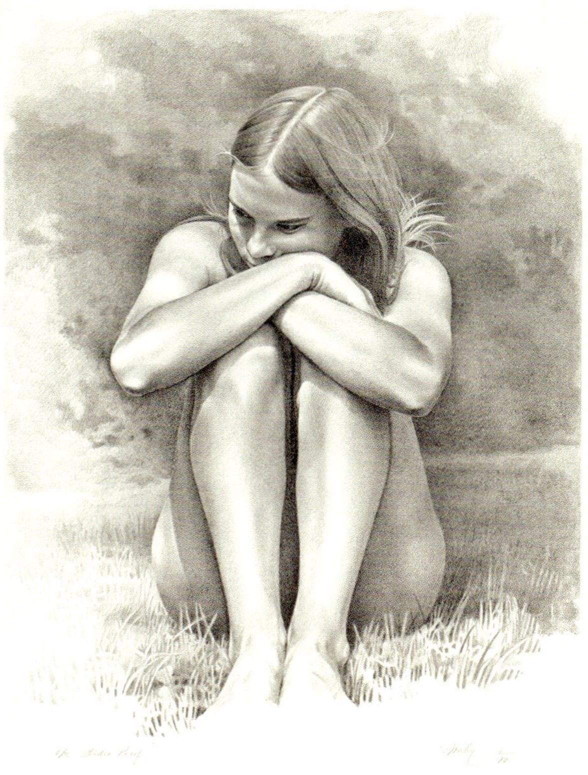

 The Dreamer, 1972

The Graphic Work

Excerpts from an April 11, 1980 conversation between
Ken Danby and Andrew J. Oko, curator, Art Gallery of Hamilton

Oko: How do you feel about a show devoted entirely to your prints?

Danby: Naturally, I am delighted at being exhibited. What artist wouldn't be? I'd like everyone to see what I do, and I would like no one to see what I do. It's that personal, because it's never ready. So, I'm always facing a dilemma. I'd love to show what I have just finished. But it's never right. It's constantly my battle, but it has taught me to move on to the next thing. I don't quarrel or quibble with that thing, because it's now past me. The new prints are going to be so much better than what I have done, that I would always want you to just wait. Postpone it two months, and then I would probably ask for another two months.

So, I recognize that there is enough work behind me that probably justifies a little broader look. On the other hand, I'm far more excited about what's coming.

Oko: Does this apply to your work in all media?

Danby: Anything I've done. Because there is nothing that I'm really ever satisfied with. With hindsight, everything I've done could have been far better. Sometimes I suspect that a lot of what I've done has been too literal. On the other hand, that's one of my needs that have to be satisfied. Sometimes I feel that I dwell too much in one area and overlook another. Everyone's hindsight is always 20/20. So, it's a case of being able to recognize these things, even if it's after the fact. When I'm in the middle of a fight [with a painting], the work always tends to become a little heavy in one direction or another. But I recognize that sooner or later.

Oko: Can you be a bit more specific about this hindsight? Are there particular works that you have done in the past that come to mind?

Danby: Well, for instance, no matter what medium I'm looking at — lithography, serigraphy, watercolour, or tempera — if I look for a very early piece in that medium versus a much more recent piece, I can more readily accept the newer piece.

Oko: Even a print like *Butterbowl*, which I think is a tremendously successful piece in its handling of light? Do you feel that it is inferior in comparison, say, to your significant work in watercolour that was exhibited at Gallery Moos recently?

Danby: Here we are looking at two different approaches. The point is, the way I use the medium of serigraphy is definitely in line with egg tempera painting. Watercolour is a transparent medium, and doesn't offer me quite the versatility in terms of stretching the luminosity of light, by controlling the degree of both absorption and reflection. Watercolour works best in dealing with reflection of light, not absorption. Certainly with the more recent watercolours, I pursued this in a different manner than I would have with tempera, because I'm not using whites to the same extent. For its time, I think *Butterbowl* was one of the better prints. There is a luminosity there. But I wouldn't compare it to the watercolour approach. They are just two different, quite divergent, routes.

Oko: I would like to pursue the relationship between serigraphy and egg tempera in your work. I was very interested in reading your statement describing the serigraphy process. It was very clear in terms of relating the process, but what I found more difficult to understand was its relationship to the stages of egg tempera painting. Maybe you could go backward and relate tempera painting to this serigraphy process.

Danby: I don't want to sidestep the question — I'll come back to it. If you look at the progression proofs for the print *Early Autumn*, which will be in the exhibition, you'll see a staging that is synonymous to egg tempera painting. So, what I'm saying is that I follow the procedure of egg tempera painting — a procedure that attempts to achieve the maximum effects from that medium. Now I'll relate that for you. First, I deal with the control of light, and its degree of absorption and reflection within the panel. Now, you can do this far more readily with the brilliance of a gessoed panel, than with a piece of paper, but the principle remains the same. First of all, I set up a black and white situation on the paper, as I would on the gessoed panel. On the panel, I do it with India ink, and where I paint black, light will be absorbed. Where I leave it white, light will be reflected. Where I make grey tones, through cross hatching or whatever, light will be partially absorbed and reflected according to the density of the tone. In other words, I am controlling the degrees of intensity

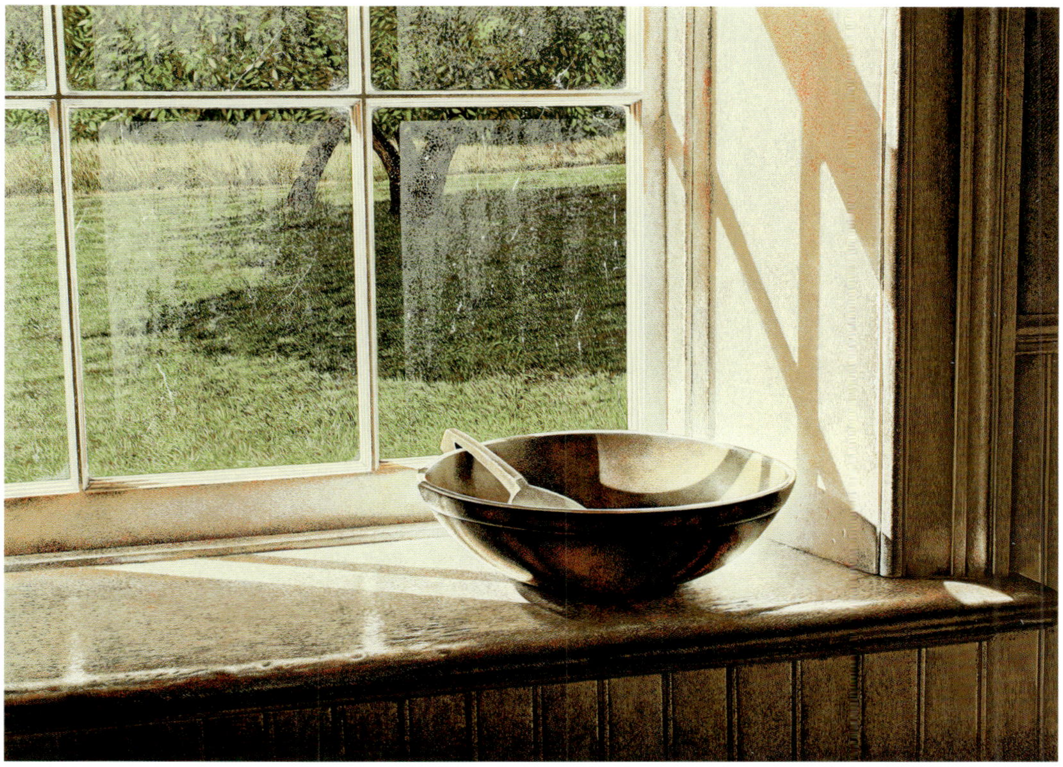

in which light is reflected or absorbed with that initial setting. It also structures the work compositionally. I don't place something here and change it there or turn it upside down. I attempt to anticipate what may happen within that painting, with watercolour studies, etc., prior to attacking tempera itself, because you can't have a willy-nilly approach to painting in tempera. By following certain procedures, it can offer far more than any other medium.

So then I lay down that black, and, in the case of a serigraph, create a stencil to lay down that black in all the proofs that I'm going to utilize in creating that print. They're all printed, exactly the same with the black. Then I take an arbitrary approach to the selection of the colour. Probably a dominant colour, but a local colour in any case. And tonally, I'm aiming for a middle ground.

Oko: Would that be the colour right next to the highlight?

Danby: No. I meant the middle grade of tone. On a scale from one to ten, I aim for a tonal gradation of five. However, there are other concerns as well. I aim for a middle range of opacity, so that the black works for me underneath. I don't want to obliterate it. Neither do I want the black to show so much that I let my colour become too transparent. So, I control the opacity. It's the translucency of that colour that I'm

Butterbowl, 1970

after. And of course, I want to find an appropriate hue. So, I tune the green of the grass, or the brown of the tree, or whatever it is, to the approximate intensity of hue, degree of translucency, and value of tonality required.

Oko: Just relating it back to tempera painting, after you've made the initial black and white drawing.

Danby: You lay in local colour, bang, bang, bang.

Oko: And covering over the black areas in tempera would give you the same effect?

Danby: Except in tempera, my monochromatic is done with India ink, and not the opaque ink used on the stencil. In egg tempera I'm mixing, or tempering, colour pigment with egg and distilled water. But with both media, I'm still just laying in translucent bodies of local colour. But of course, the big difference is that in egg tempera you achieve it rather quickly with brush strokes. Since the graphic process is a more mechanical one, you have to create a stage. However, you can try to be as thorough as possible with that stage. Put the browns where all the browns want to go, and the reds where all the reds want to go and so on. What results at this stage, in both media, is that the pieces of the jigsaw puzzle are now together, completely subduing the black drawing underneath. But the black is still working.

Oko: As darkness?

Danby: As tonality and definition under the local colour. I can look through the flesh colour and still see the face. But I may have to look hard for it. I want to subdue it to that extent. That's when I have to start controlling tints and tones. Since I have the basic local colours down, I want to stretch them now in terms of lights and darks, or tints and tones. That I do with applications of soft blacks and soft whites, and at times including some of the colour of a particular area, if desired. In tempera I can do that fairly quickly, compared to what is required in the graphic process. In order to create a stencil, a drawing in opaque ink is required. The difficulty arises when one must imagine the subtlety of colour intended while creating each drawing. But one learns to work with these things. I work to a point where tonally the work is stretched as far as I feel it needs to be stretched, given its context.

And now, the colour is diminished. Initially, the tonality was diminished by the colour. Now the colour has been diminished by the stretching of tonality and tints.

However, the colour is also still working under there. It now remains for me to restore it. This I do by using a less opaque, more transparent, colour, which reinforces and compliments the local colours applied earlier, without overly interfering with the tints and tones. However, in the end, tones and highlights are reinforced with black and white.

The procedure I've related is very basic for gaining the luminosity and depth of egg tempera. I just redirect it into a graphic medium. The secret, if there is a secret, is to be willing to do it. What I'm doing, in actual fact, is creating a print by following a painting procedure in serigraphy.

Oko: Does this process relate to handling lights and darks in traditional oil painting?

Danby: All media use basically the same technique. The difference for egg tempera is in the procedure, if you want to take advantage of the medium itself. Only egg tempera can offer you the degree of luminosity from within. Let me define egg tempera in another way. Oil painting is, on the one hand, an opaque medium. Watercolour, on the other, is a transparent one. There is only one medium that serves the vast break in between. That is egg tempera, because it has the capabilities of being as opaque [as oil], and certainly the potential of being as transparent [as watercolours]. It actually allows a control of both, and serves the whole middle range of translucency as well. No other medium can offer that.

I really taught myself how to paint in egg tempera. One of the books that I've used over the years is a translation of a very old manuscript written in the fifteenth century by Cennino d'Andrea Cennini, *The Craftsman's Handbook,* translated by Daniel V. Thompson. The language, in its concern for detail — as I first thought, being impatient — was a little overdone. It took me seven years in tempera to realize that everything has its purpose in that reference book. I would go back to it. Now I understand that I had to test, push, and define in order to come to the final realization that what was said and proven over the centuries was fact. There is a reason for it. There is no shortcut if you want to gain the richness that is possible. If you want to take advantage of the real life that only egg tempera can offer, you must follow this procedure. For instance, in my earlier paintings, I was omitting a lot of the advantages

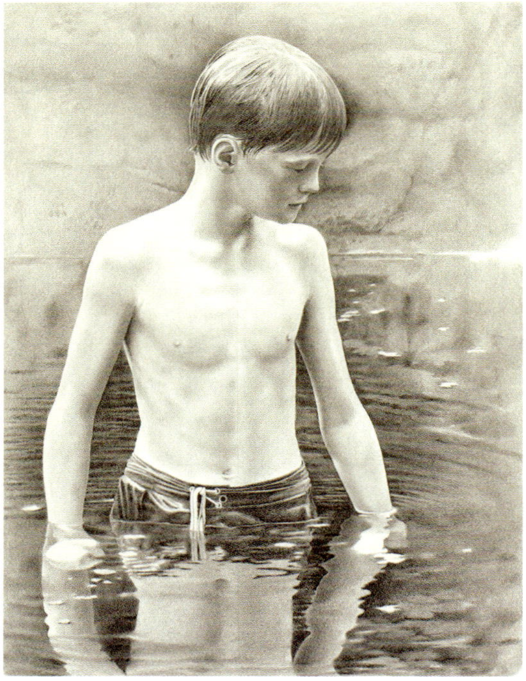

of the ink monochrome drawing, and in many ways was leaning more toward the watercolour approach.

The tonal drawing greatly influences the degree of absorption and reflection of light, and I was neglecting it. So, I simply learned by trial and error. Finally, after seven years in 1970, I started to feel that I was beginning to understand what tempera really had to offer. It rather scared me. Because its potential is that vast.

Oko: What were some of the works that marked that transition point in egg tempera?

Danby: The first one that I really explored fully in this way was *Reflections,* the depiction of the young boy standing in the river by the rocks. I don't know why I explored it further. I suppose because I was apprehensive about the drawing initially. So I just got carried away with an ink rendering first, and then as the painting grew for me, I began to more fully understand the various stages and that there was a metamorphosis that was very necessary.

Oko: Did you take a preliminary course in egg tempera?

Danby: I took about an afternoon a week for several weeks while at the Ontario College of Art. Tempera has had a bit of a revival more recently. But in '58, '59, it was touched on as one of those esoteric media. To my way of thinking, it has such a major role in art, that it is rather sad that it's been overlooked.

Oko: When you mentioned the painting *Reflections*, I immediately related it to the lithograph that utilizes the same subject.

Danby: Which is called *The Swimmer.*

Oko: What interests me there, is that in the several preliminary drawings which you do for every subject, where does a lithograph fit in? Would that have been done before the painting, after the painting? Is there a general rule that applies here?

Danby: There isn't really. It can be the result of either a preliminary exploration of my subject prior to a painting, or my continued enthusiasm for it following a painting. On the other hand, it need not relate to a painting at all.

Oko: In the process of drawing a subject that interests you, if you came across one that you felt was exceptional, would you then consider it for a lithographic format?

The Swimmer, 1970

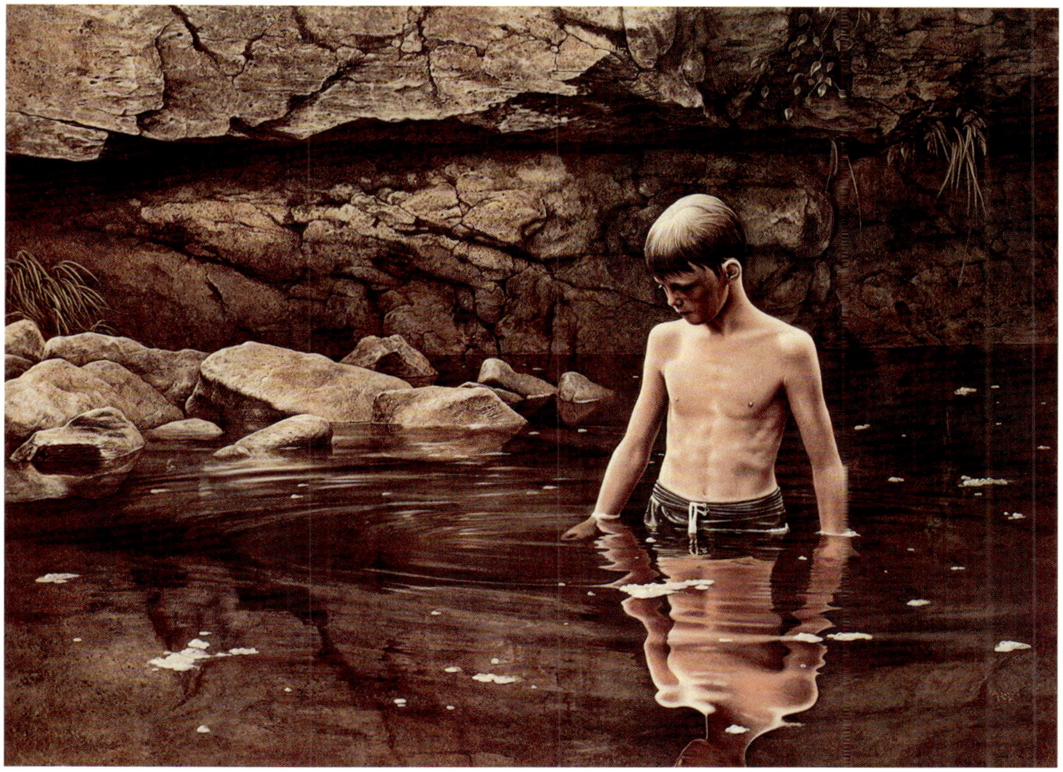

Danby: No, because if it really works exceptionally well as a drawing, I would leave it as a drawing. I wouldn't try to translate a good drawing into a lithograph. Each work is created solely for itself. If there was a good drawing, I would only be trying to repeat some of the excitement that I found in it as a drawing. And that, to me, is not an exciting occupation or endeavour. I would rather try and create an exciting lithograph, and face its challenges and meet them, rather than say "this is a great drawing, let's make a lithograph out of it." You might as well reproduce the thing.

Oko: I certainly didn't realize the complexities of your serigraphs until I read your statement on serigraphy. One thing that intrigues me is that the process that you came up with is unique in several ways. Now maybe you could summarize or clarify what you think the unique facets of the method are.

Danby: I used the analogy before of painting with it. I suppose that's very much aligned with the way of thinking I began with. I wanted to create something with an intuitive assessment rather than a predetermined staging. So, when I start my print, I lay down my black monochrome, and then I add colours as I arbitrarily choose. I don't preplan. That's so mechanical. I will look at the black and there will obviously be something that will trigger me on to the next colour.

Reflections, 1970

These things will come, and then I'll respond to the next stage as I choose, rather than having a predetermined plan that I'm following. It's an intuitive analysis at any stage. I have no idea what the eighth stage will be until I reach the seventh. I have no idea what the fifteenth colour will be until I've seen the fourteenth, and so on. But certainly, through my familiarity with it, I could, by the fourteenth, anticipate what the next three or four stages may be. But I couldn't possibly tell you how many colours that print is going to have. I don't know for certain until it's finished. So, that's where my process of serigraphy is so much aligned with a painting procedure, because it is a trial and error procedure. That's the key: take it as far as it wants to go, until it works. Don't preplan anymore than necessary, in terms of its staging and content, and in terms of what I'm trying to achieve with it. The uniqueness of it is that it is more of a creative painting procedure, and less of a preplanned printmaking process. The uniqueness is not technical. Normally a printmaker might put a blue on top of a yellow to get a green, and be satisfied with the green. Whereas, I'll make the yellow, and I'll make the blue, and I'll make the green that I want, and still take advantage of everything else that happens. I'm going to go as far as that print wants me to go, to build not only an interesting image, but to formulate structure and three dimensional form.

I'm going to create gradations of tone and colour, and do whatever is necessary. I'm going to splatter ink. I'm going to stipple ink. I'm going to scratch it away. I'm going to do whatever is necessary to achieve the results that I want. What matters is responding, one stage to the previous stage, and allowing for an intuitive response, rather than a predetermined dictation of what will take place.

Oko: I was very curious that the dates on which you began working with serigraphy coincide with that masterful change in egg tempera painting we discussed earlier. *Reflections* of 1970 coincided with your first serigraph. I have been wondering whether that was coincidental, or whether there was a closer union between working in both media?

Danby: It's a question that's never been fully explored. So I'm really delighted to hear it. I began to appreciate the merits of tempera procedure when I was interpreting that procedure in serigraphy. Rather than just attacking a painting, I began to sit back a little bit and try to comprehend what I was doing with the paint. You can only comprehend so much of that through the actual painting in a given period of time. But if you can take the painting stages, and spread them out in front of you, you begin to realize that although it isn't predetermined or absolute, there is a kind of an order where one thing wants to follow another. The more I comprehended the procedure, the more insight I gained into what tempera was able to do, and in turn, reflect that back into what ink was going to do in a serigraph. One works very much hand in glove with the other, the way I use them. I'm attempting to orchestrate and create a maximum result within each medium. Serigraphy has been of great benefit to me. For instance, the concept of translucency didn't mean as much for me when I was only painting. I wasn't in control of it as much as I could have been until I began to appreciate it through my approach to serigraphy.

This is when translucency became far more meaningful for me. I began to appreciate the benefits of tempera far more than I had before, because I had to interpret the procedure in my own mind, and refer it back to a stage of the print. So the silkscreen medium, because it has been an instrument of self-teaching and analysis, has given me tremendous confidence in being able to control tempera. If anything, I've learned that egg tempera is a vast medium, and not a narrow or confined one.

Oko: Perhaps we can introduce a much-discussed concept: realism. Various books and articles will talk about it in different ways. Do you ever ponder the concept speculatively, as to what it might entail or what it might mean, and how it relates to the way you approach things?

Danby: Well, yes — but not so much. You see, I really don't consider myself to be a realist, as many do. I don't say that I'm a magic realist, or superrealist, or hyperrealist, because I find that any or all of those are far too confining. I'm a painter and a printmaker, that's it. I'm saying that you should leave yourself wide open and free, and not confine yourself by saying you're a realist and you're this or that. Yes, I paint in a high-fidelity manner. But that's not all I'm after. I'm excited by colour and texture and light, and all of the elements that go into creating art. None of them bore me. I want to utilize all of those things. But I don't want to dwell on any particular one for its own sake.

Oko: Perhaps my question was unfair, in that I'm relating a critical category to something you do, and that's not what I intended.

Danby: No, not unfair. If one has to categorize me, I will concede to working realistically. Yes. And I don't feel uneasy about that at all. I just don't choose to define myself in that way. I want to include the elements of realism in my work, but not at the expense of the other aspects of creating art that aren't as pertinent to realism per se. When I look at that work by [Antoni] Tàpies over there, I get very excited by it. It doesn't have to represent anything realistically or dimensionally to interest me, but it's not my nature to work in that manner.

Oko: Would you consider yourself to be a rather introspective individual? I'm curious about the process of choosing a particular image — the process of taking the time to notice a particular scene that you would like to elevate into art. What I'm interested in is that point of departure. What do you select from nature?

Danby: I'm not looking for an introspective point of view on a conscious level. What I'm aware of is conveying my impression of a visual experience. So, for instance, the young boy standing in the water is not something that I would consciously respond to at the time, but simply, after a bunch of us playing in the water, and at the end of a very tiring afternoon, being stuck with images.

Oko: So, you don't search for your image.

Danby: No, not at all, although I used to when I was younger. But eventually one gains the confidence to respond intuitively to visual experience. Paintings like *At the Crease* or *Pancho*, and prints like *Butterbowl* or *Early Autumn*, are images that I experienced at given points in time, and then forgot about. But a week later, or the next morning perhaps, an image surfaces from a subconscious absorption into a conscious awareness. When an image reappears, I'll become intrigued with it temporarily, and then dismiss it and submerge it again. But if it keeps popping back, it becomes something I must explore further.

A good example of this is the painting *Pancho*. It was the drama of that moment [on Poncho's porch in 1970 (see page 78) that struck me], which I didn't even know about for months. I didn't rush to my paints or say "hold still." It's just that every time I thought of Pancho afterwards, there was this image that kept coming back to me. Every time I thought of it, there he was in a very dramatic light, dripping wet…, [and] the image gnawed at me. Finally, three years later, I asked him to pose for me.

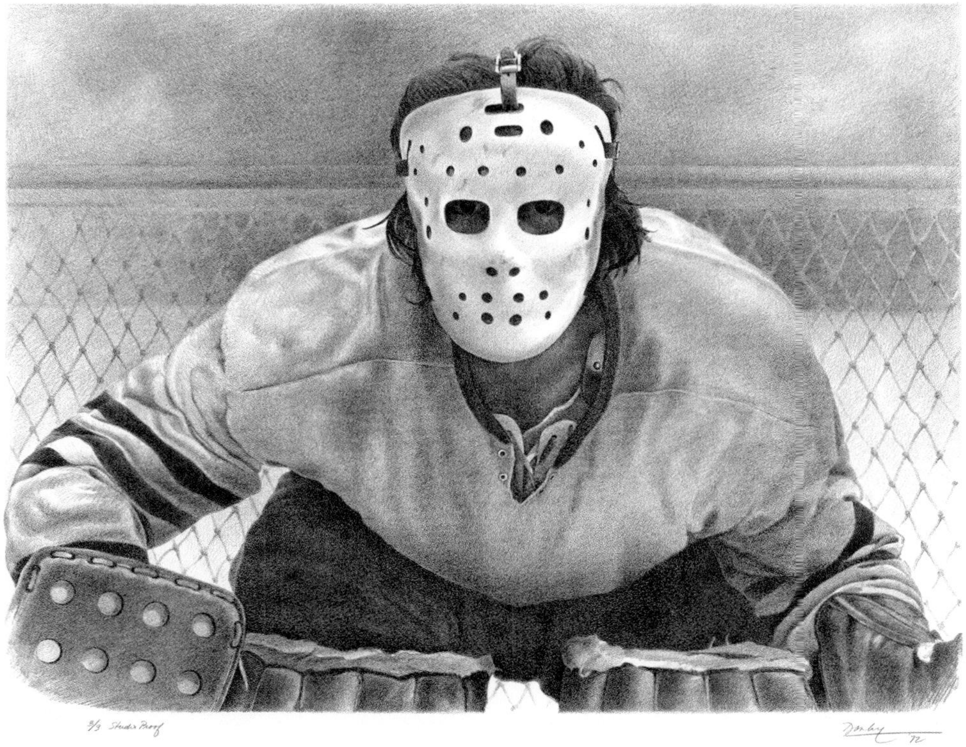

My initial instinct would have been to go back to the porch, but that wasn't feasible. As I worked with him, I weeded those things out. I didn't need the porch. I didn't need the windows. I didn't need anything behind him that I might have seen. It was the image of the man, and it was the water glistening and sparkling in the light. I needed the rain. So I poured buckets of water over him while he posed. But all that happened three years after the initial experience. I wasn't looking for it. But it just appeared and gnawed at me, so I had to work it out.

You know, I played hockey in Sault Ste. Marie as a boy. I didn't play during college, but when I moved out here I started playing at the rink across the road every year. My young neighbour was a goalie, and one day he had his mask on. It was the first time I had ever shot a puck at a goalie who was wearing a mask. For weeks after, the image of this mask kept recurring. So finally, I asked a goalie to pose for me. We set it up on the ice. There was something there. The result was the tempera painting *At the Crease*, a number of studies, and the lithograph called *The Goalie*.

The Goalie, 1972

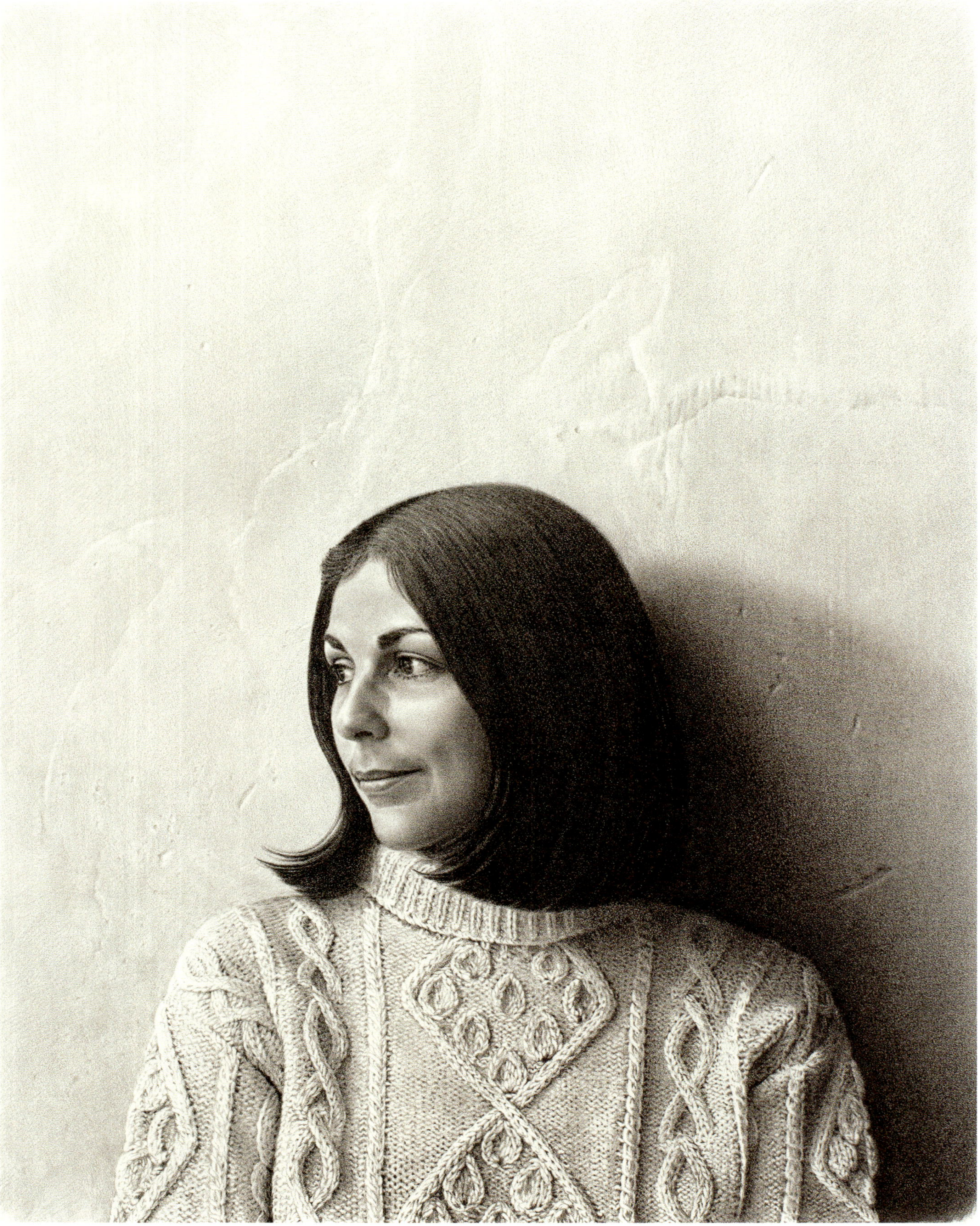

Ken Danby on Printmaking

A serigraph is a fine art term referring to a print created with the use of silkscreen printing. A drawing is made and transferred to a screen stencil, which is then used to apply a coat of ink to paper by pressing the ink through the stencil with a rubber squeegee. While my use of the medium is much more complex, it employs this basic technique. The important principle, however, is that it is employed in the creation of an original image, not a reproductive one. That is, there is no painting or master image that is being reproduced. The serigraph develops through trial and error procedures, much like a painting, engaging as many colour stages and drawings as I feel are required, with no predeterminations. All sheets of paper are printed at each stage, so it actually becomes an original creation, in multiple form.

As my new studio construction advanced through January 1970, I was absorbed with researching techniques in silkscreen printing. My goal was to utilize a graphic medium that would allow me to create original prints. I had already experimented with etching and lithograph media, but hoped to achieve a means of working in full colour, for which I felt they were much less applicable.

I focused on the silkscreen medium as my solution, and developed a rather unique approach to creating original serigraphs as a result, but it was all in my head. Would it work in practice? It remained to be proven. I spoke with various persons in the "trade," including equipment suppliers, who all advised that my ideas were likely impossible to achieve. This didn't dissuade me, and I eventually ordered the necessary equipment, after I'd prepared a room in my new studio for its installation.

The studio building was completed in late February, but it wasn't until the end of March that I was comfortably moved in and able to utilize it properly. It was a huge

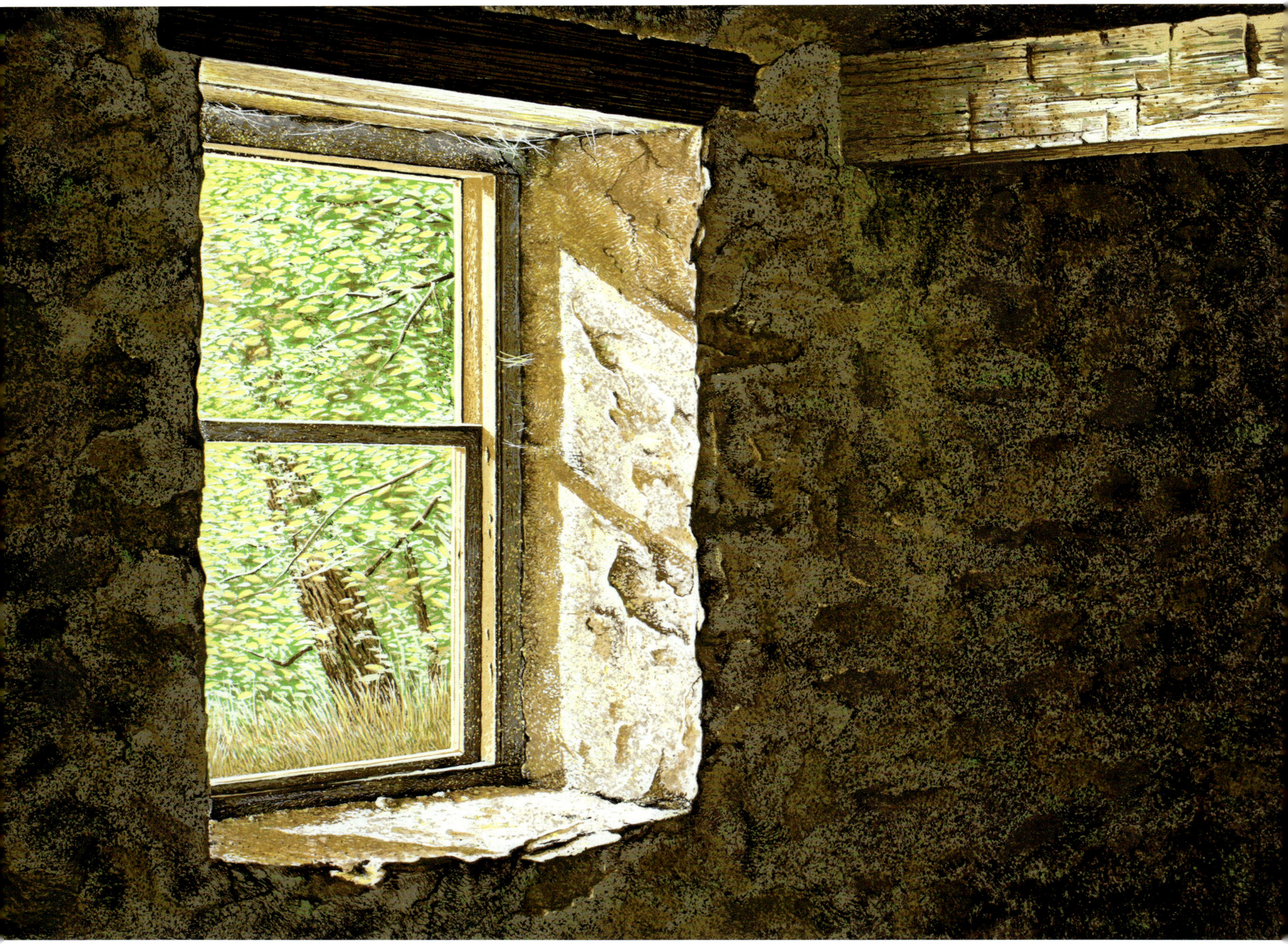

 Mill Window, 1970

improvement for me, and I knew that it would continue to be as time went on. I became acquainted with my recently acquired screen equipment, and began my experimentation. Within a few weeks, I completed my first serigraph, titled *The Wagon*, a thirteen-colour, hand-drawn and hand-pulled print, in an edition of two hundred, and proved my concept to be feasible.

There was a reason for it becoming an edition of two hundred. Walter had advised that if I could accomplish my printmaking goal successfully, his colleague in Germany wished to acquire a complete edition of two hundred for a special portfolio (sight unseen). So that became my quota.

When I delivered the finished edition in April, Walter was very pleased and, later, so was Galerie Springer in Germany, so much so that they requested another seventy-five prints, as if these could simply be readily added! I explained to Walter that this was totally impossible.

So, once that fact was understood, it was agreed that I would create another print, from scratch, in an edition of seventy-five, for their additional needs, which became *Mill Window*. At eleven colours, it was again acquired in total by Galerie Springer.

It was a learning experience by trial and error. Fortunately, my painting experience allowed me to succeed with a minimum of errors, by understanding how I could create the image with successful layers of ink in a creative procedure, rather than through a pre-determined formula. For instance, I wouldn't know what the seventh stage might be, until I'd completed the sixth, and so on. My procedure entailed knowing how to achieve progressive colour stages, while responding to each previous application with an awareness of how it would develop, just as in painting. (Regrettably, however, many assume that there is a painting that is created first, which then employs a type of reproduction process to produce the serigraph. Of course, the reality is that the serigraph is an original creation in itself, albeit produced in a multiple form.) A great advantage of my serigraphs was that they provided the availability of works to be exhibited in various galleries simultaneously, since they were created as original multiples.

While quite successful in its creation, I soon realized my serigraph procedure was very labour-intensive. Much of the preparation and actual printing could be handled by a technician, yet only with my personal supervision. In other words, it was not a procedure that I could "farm out" to others.

Over the course of many months of discussion, my brother Marvin agreed to join me as my office manager and assistant. I felt that he would be the ideal candidate, dependable and trustworthy, with a much-earlier-evidenced affinity for image making. After all, he was my youthful influence. Marvin joined me in Guelph, and together we began to create some significant serigraphs. His office-management skills also provided me with more opportunity to focus on my painting. Marvin and I worked well together, and my productivity benefited. I was able to create a number of serigraph editions, as the months passed, as well as concentrating on my paintings.

The major serigraph presented at my annual exhibition at Walter Moos's gallery in 1970 was *Butterbowl*, a new twenty-one-colour print. Walter decided that he would like to display its complete development, from the first stage to the twenty-first, in the separate room just off the main gallery. The presentation underlined the complexity and considerable effort that went into *Butterbowl*'s creation as an original print, and included a printed explanatory text.

One day, when at the gallery, I inadvertently overheard two individuals referring to it. What I heard was, "Oh look, you can get this picture in different colours." I winced, as I realized that they had completely misinterpreted what they were seeing!

Like so many Canadians, I was mesmerized by the Canada-Russia hockey series in 1972 and watched every game on television. Like many, I was inspired by the tenacious, come-from-behind victories in Moscow, especially after Phil Esposito's pleas for support from the fans after their third disappointing loss in Canada. After the team's second victory there, I felt that I wanted to offer something, to show my appreciation for their marvelous efforts.

I decided to give each player a framed and personally inscribed serigraph of *The Skates*, and informed Walter Moos that we should immediately make this happen. Through Johnny Esaw of CTV, we passed the word to Alan Eagleson in Moscow, and he let the team know. Win or lose the series, it didn't matter, each player would receive an original serigraph, and the announcement of this determination made the evening sports news. Of course, they won, and Canada went crazy! Upon the team's return, they received their prints, and Alan told me later that it was the unconditional gesture that was so appreciated. The entire team membership, numbering thirty-seven in all, each received their framed print, and collectively this represented a substantial value, which then increased considerably as the years passed.

In 1974, I was again working on my large serigraph *Sunning*, which was requiring more than a full year, off and on, to complete. It would be presented in my December show at Gallery Moos. Another serigraph was also on my mind, which had a committed deadline of November that had to be met. This small one was to accompany the special, limited-edition book on my work being written by Paul Duval. But it wasn't until spring before I could realize the ideal subject for it.

The book's publication was announced on February 1, 1974, with an invitation to acquire a copy by advance subscription by a deadline of March 15, with the book becoming available at my December show. It was to be a deluxe edition, numbering only two hundred and fifty copies, hand bound with a gold-embossed leather spine, and including the original serigraph in a separate portfolio and slipcase. By offering it through an early advance subscription, the cost of the project would be covered prior to its costly production. It was an innovative and clever concept by Walter, which in later years has been copied by many other galleries and artists. The book sold out, and the pressure was building for me to create an exceptional accompanying serigraph!

I delivered *Sunning* to Gallery Moos in late summer. I had concluded its creation after twenty-eight separate drawings and progressive colour stages. As usual, the prints were then edited carefully and individually signed and numbered. Walter was most impressed with the edition upon seeing it.

A week or so later, after daily glimpses of a sample print of *Sunning* mounted on the wall of my studio, I began to have second thoughts on its completion. Following a great deal of assessment and analysis, I realized that it would benefit substantially from one more stage. I decided that it needed an additional soft tone application that would greatly add to its dimensional impact. I phoned Walter. "No," he said. "It looks great the way it is, and besides we've already shipped three out to other galleries."

I insisted: "Then let's get them back right away." I was determined to add this additional stage and persisted with my request. Reluctantly, Walter finally agreed, and before long I had all of the prints back in my studio. I set about creating the drawing, and with Marvin's help we succeeded in pulling the prints through one more ink stage. Walter acknowledged that a slight improvement had been made, but didn't feel that the difference had warranted all the extra effort. However, to my eyes, it made all the difference in the world!

In May 1974, I was able to return to the easel and the work-in-progress. I was also developing my concept for my book's serigraph. I'd decided that the subject would be my son, Sean, who posed for me, peering through our kitchen window face-on, with a look of introspection. Not only was he the ideal model, but I thought the concept would be most appropriate for the focus of the book, being a biographic look at his father's life and work to date. The working title was *Boy at Window*, but as it developed, I changed it to *Looking In*.

During the summer and fall of '76, I concluded my focus on Olympic sports with the creation of a special portfolio of original serigraphs, which were featured in my December exhibition at Gallery Moos. They comprised four individual prints representing the sculler, diver, hurdler, and pole-vaulter. While each image represented a unique action relative to its distinctive sport, all four were designed with a geometric relationship so they would visually relate when displayed together. The four prints were available in a linen bound portfolio along with a brief descriptive text, titled *Olympic Serigraphs*.

In 1977 the City of Guelph was celebrating its 150th birthday and in April the city asked me to create a work which in some way would reflect Guelph and would be an appropriate image for this occasion. I said that I'd be happy to consider such a project, if I could feel comfortable with a concept.

At Riverside Park the city had long operated an old carousel or merry-go-round. During visits there with my sons, I'd often envisioned the possibility of responding to it someday in a painting, but I hadn't gotten around to actually pursuing the idea. Perhaps it was time. The more I considered it, the more appropriate it seemed to be. It had an air

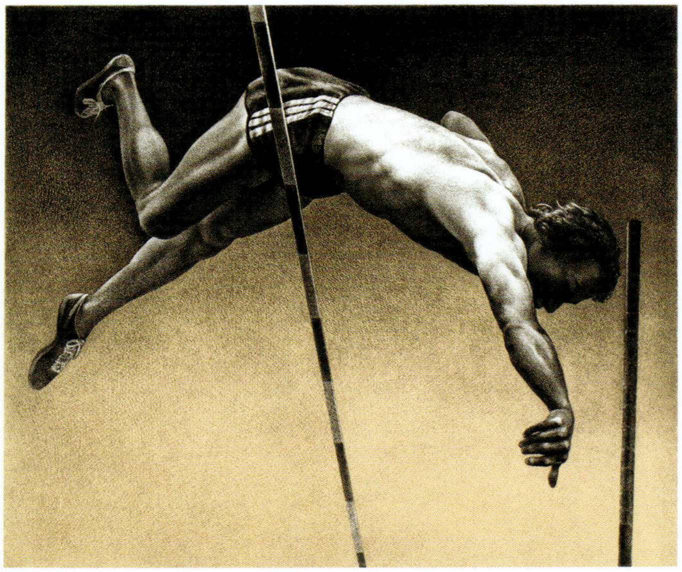

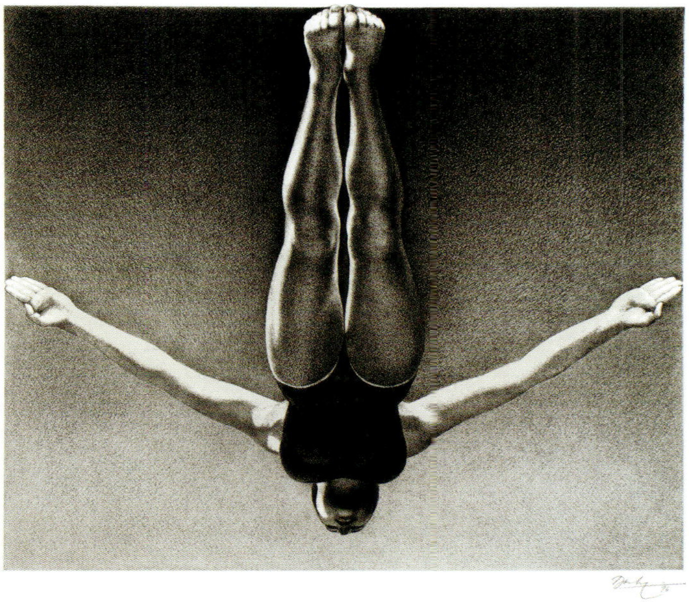

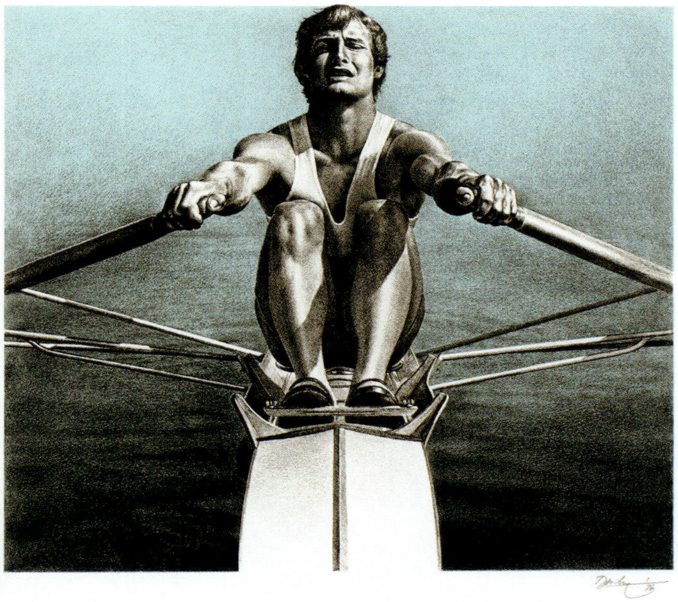

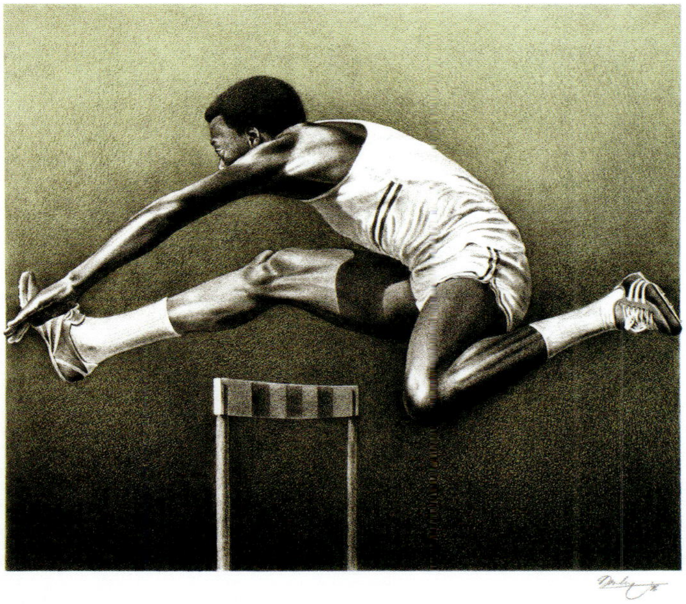

clockwise from top left: **The Vaulter**, 1976
The Diver, 1976
The Hurdler, 1976
The Sculler, 1976

of celebration, with its elaborately decorated horses and canopy, its organ music, and the animals moving up and down with rhythmic regularity on the revolving platform. It certainly conveyed "birthday" to me and, of course, it was in Guelph! Yet I felt strongly that I wanted a youth in the image, as a contrast to the antiquity of the carousel. After a few fruitless visits in hopes of seeing a young volunteer, I decided to volunteer my six-and-a-half-year-old son Ryan to pose for me. On the scheduled day, he decided that he preferred to be elsewhere — in fact, anywhere else. Posing was not on his agenda, even for a few minutes! I had to be firm in order to persuade him and managed to take a few photos before he balked completely. Yet, in spite of his reluctance, I came away with what I was looking for. I could return to the carousel later, I reasoned, as it would still be there and happy to pose.

Weeks later my watercolour painting was completed. I called it simply *Guelph Carousel*. The boy in the picture is Ryan, with a serious look, which I ultimately felt was fitting for the image. The city fathers were equally pleased with my results and it was unveiled in mid-June.

That summer, I received a phone call from Gus Stahlman, the parks and recreation director for the City of Guelph. He asked if I could offer a few ideas for the design of a new parkette to be created in town, at the site of the old Allan's Mill and beside the spot where Guelph was first founded by John Galt in 1827. Within a few weeks, I gave him a design that was used to complete the job. During our discussions, Gus mentioned to me that the carousel at Riverside Park was to be scrapped, as it was in rough shape and too costly for the city to refurbish. I said, "I've always wanted to acquire a carousel horse." He replied, "Well, help yourself to whatever you like — they're in the storage shed, and we certainly owe you." And that's how I soon took possession of two horses, including the one that I had used as a model in my painting *Guelph Carousel*.

Many weeks later, a lawyer friend and neighbour, John Valeriote, called. He and two friends wanted to save the carousel and wondered if I would contribute to the cause. I felt that a public campaign was required, in which I would participate, in order to persuade the city that its citizens were in favour of supporting this goal. But I had two of the horses and said I wasn't in favour of giving them up. John agreed with my proposal and

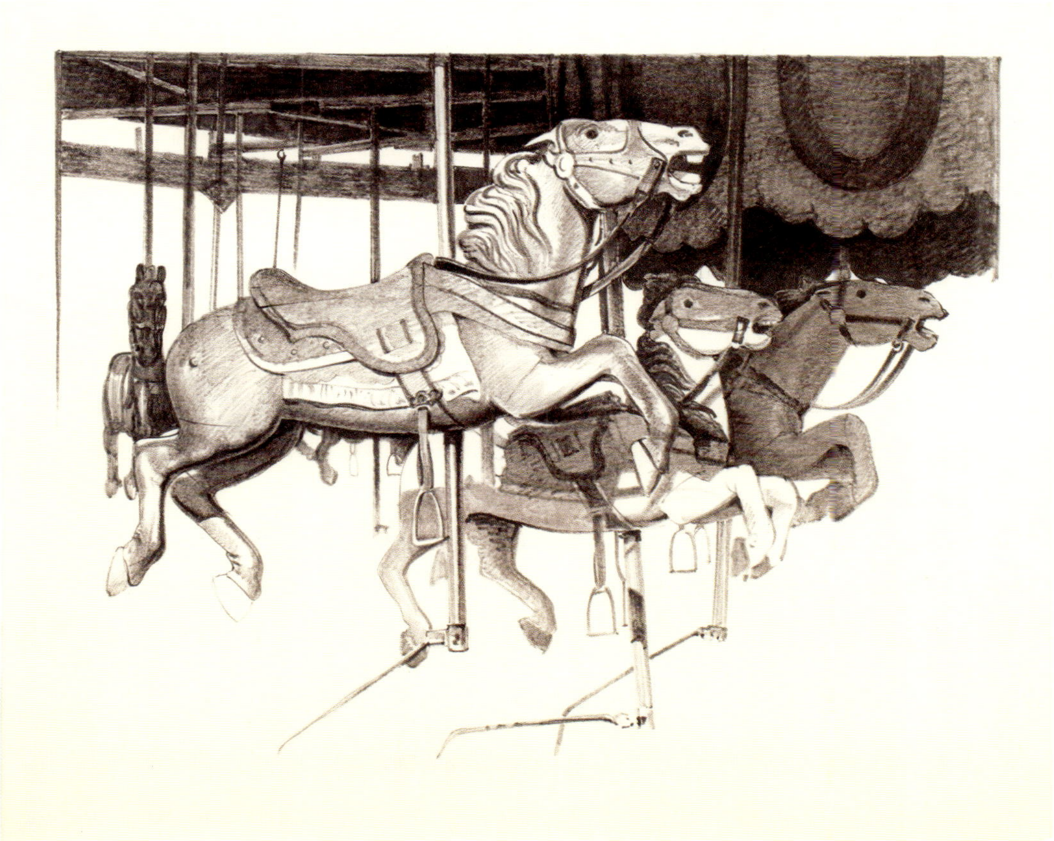

my right to keep the horses that I'd been given. After all, he emphasized, "We'll need to acquire many replacements anyway!"

We set about planning a campaign called "Save the Carousel." I designed and printed a few hundred colourful posters in my studio, which were distributed throughout the city. We had contribution containers placed in all banks, credit unions, various stores, and a few offices. I donated a number of reproductions of my *Guelph Carousel* as prizes in a draw for contributors. We also created a large mounted display of photos, posters, and articles about the carousel, which was displayed in the centre court of a shopping mall.

Within a month, the public's support was confirmed with the collection of over ten thousand dollars in contributions, much of which was received in pennies, nickels,

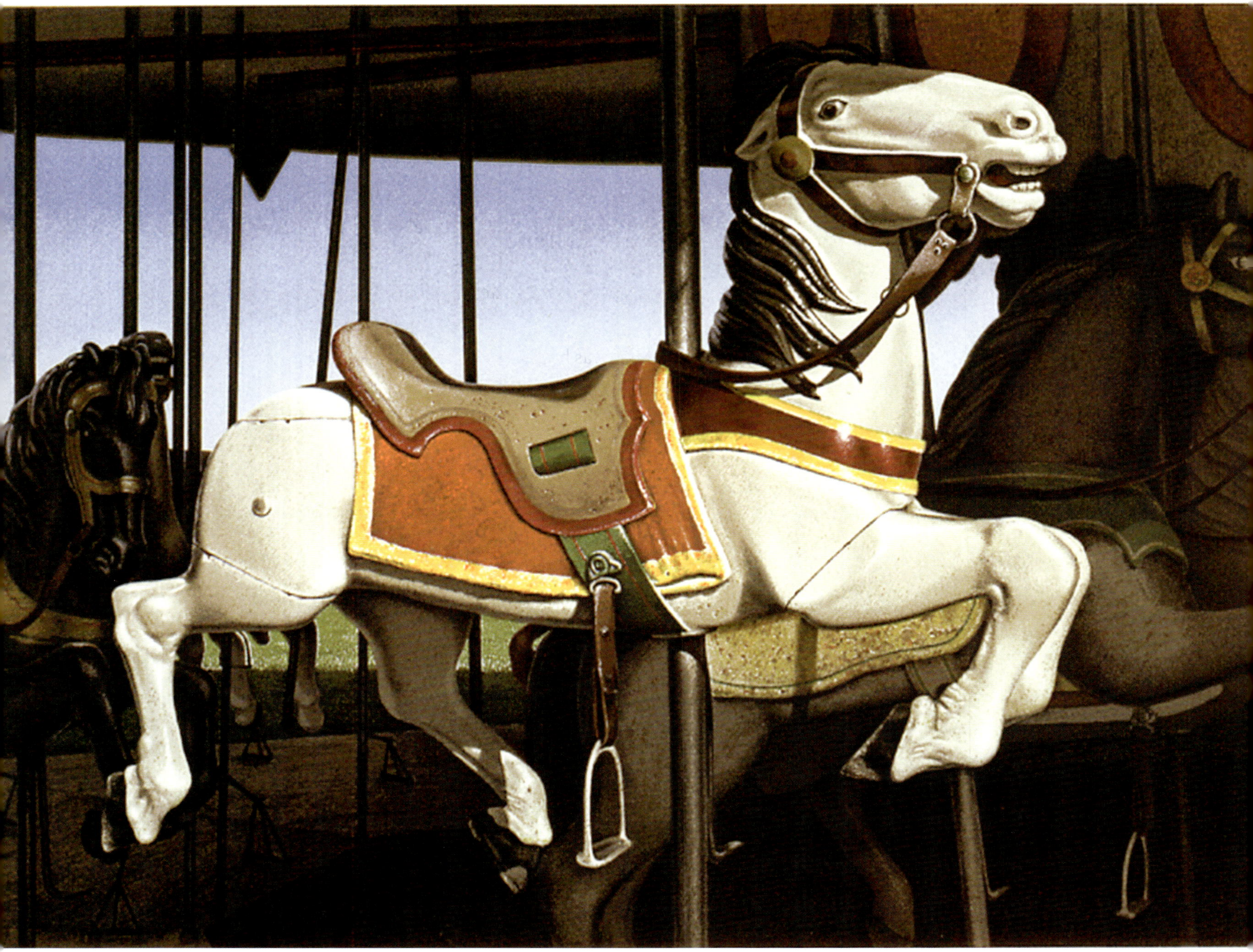

 White Stallion, 1978

and dimes from children and parents. The public had spoken. Consequently, the city announced that the carousel would be saved and refurbished!

The actual work was undertaken during the winter months, by the inmates at the Guelph Correctional Centre. Their carpentry shop was kept busy repairing and restoring salvageable components and animals. New animals were acquired as well. By spring, the need arose for the painting and decorating to be addressed. I was called in to advise and supervise the work where necessary, which took several weeks. I recall my many visits to the shop, having to arrive and leave through the scrutiny of the security guards. My attire of well-worn blue jeans, jacket, and white sneakers was identical to that worn by the resident prisoners.

By mid-summer, the carousel was back at Riverside Park, where it remains as a great attraction for children of all ages. A year later, I designed a building enclosure to protect it from winter, so it wouldn't have to be dismounted and stored every season, and this was then completed, ensuring a long life for Guelph's carousel.

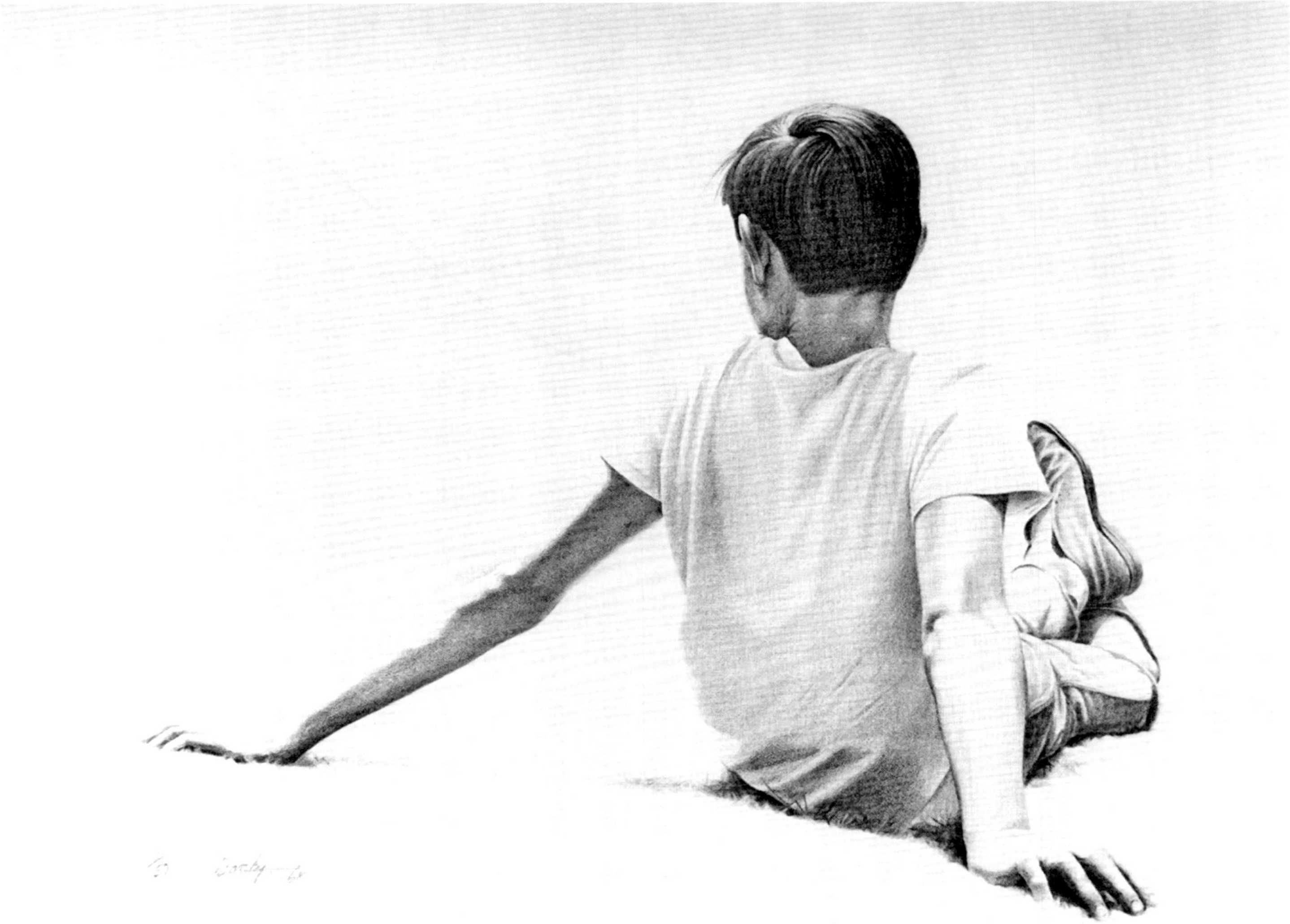

 Looking Off, 1968

facing page: **Looking In**, 1974

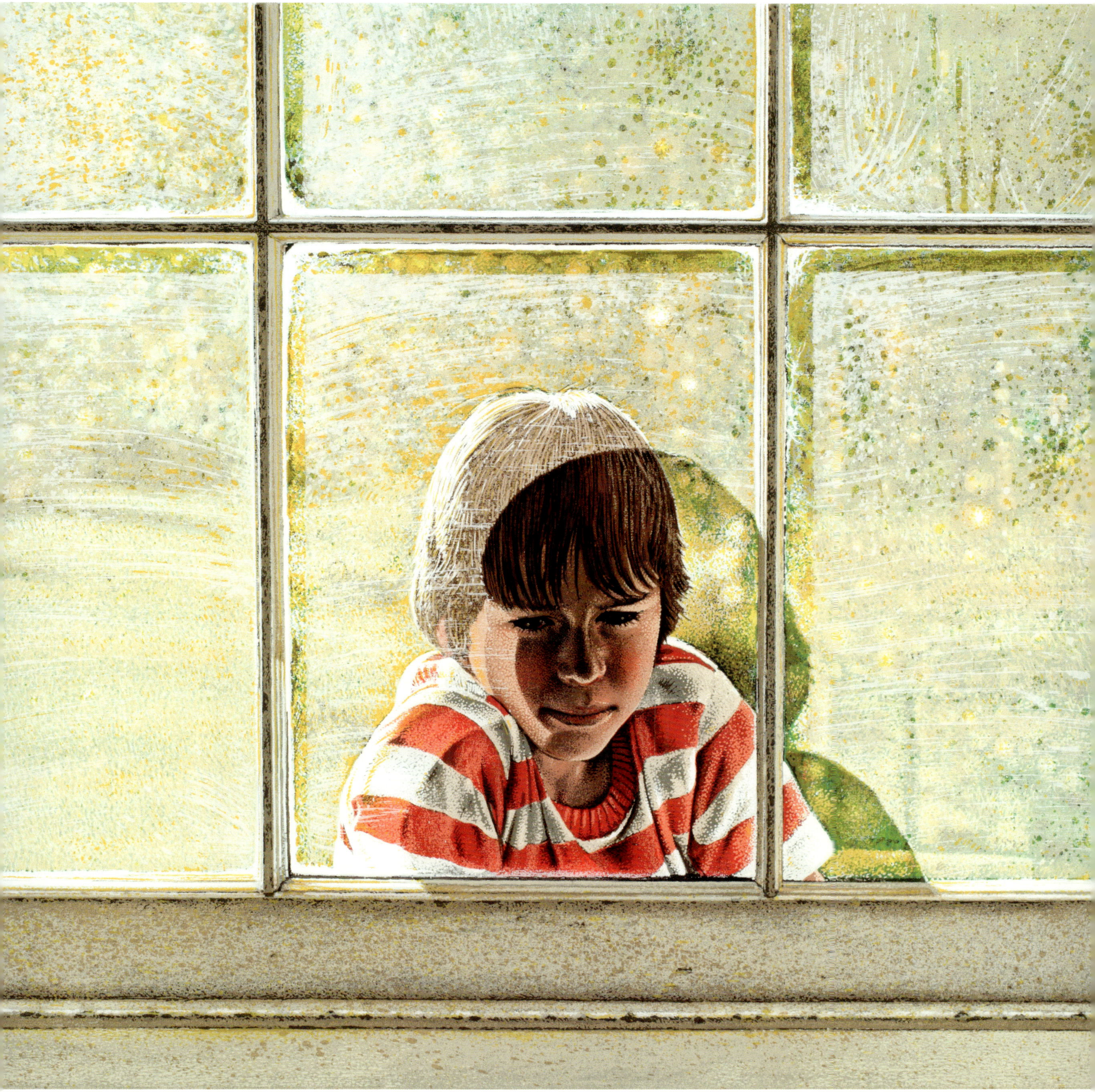

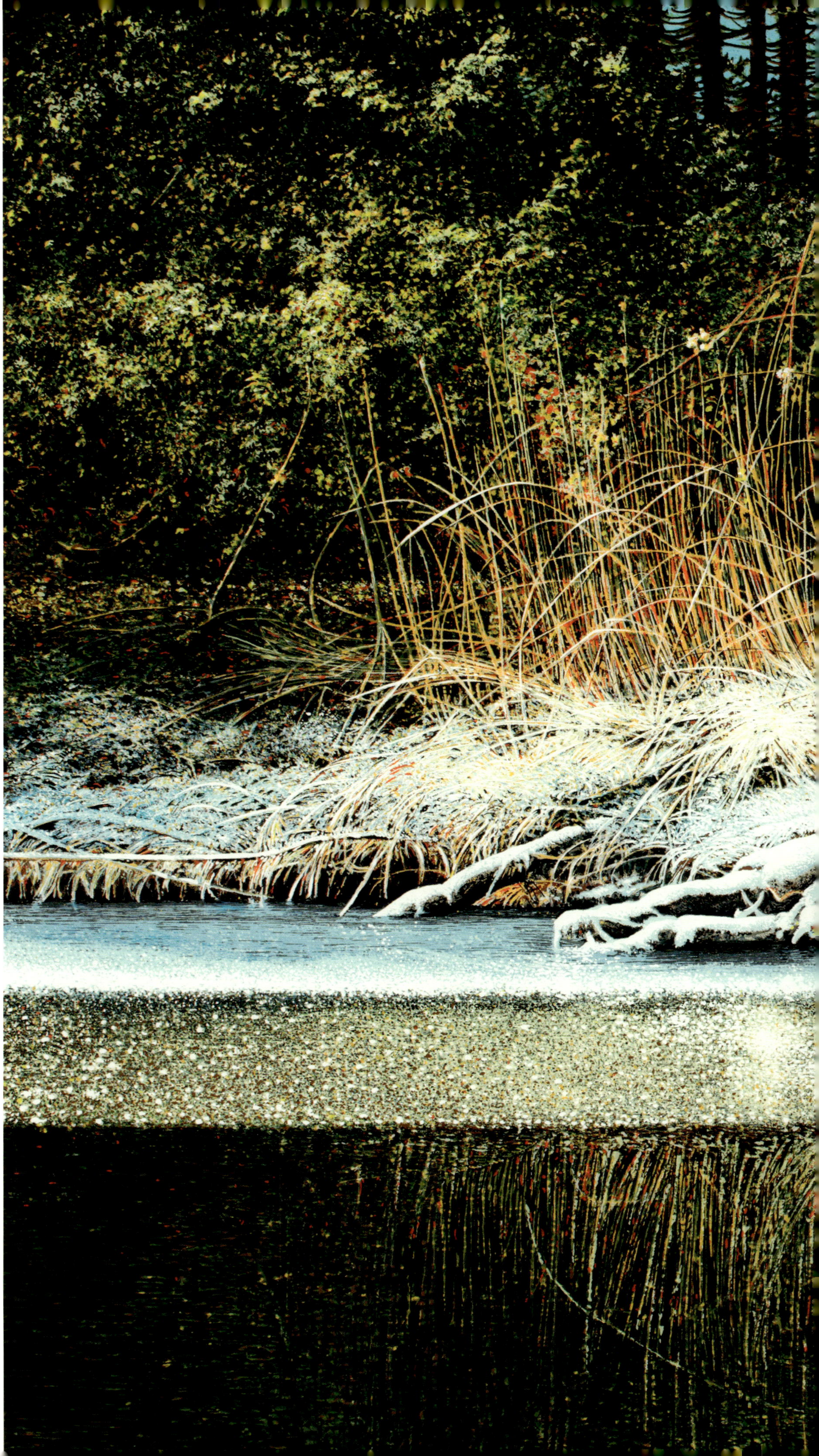

170 **December Morning**, 1981

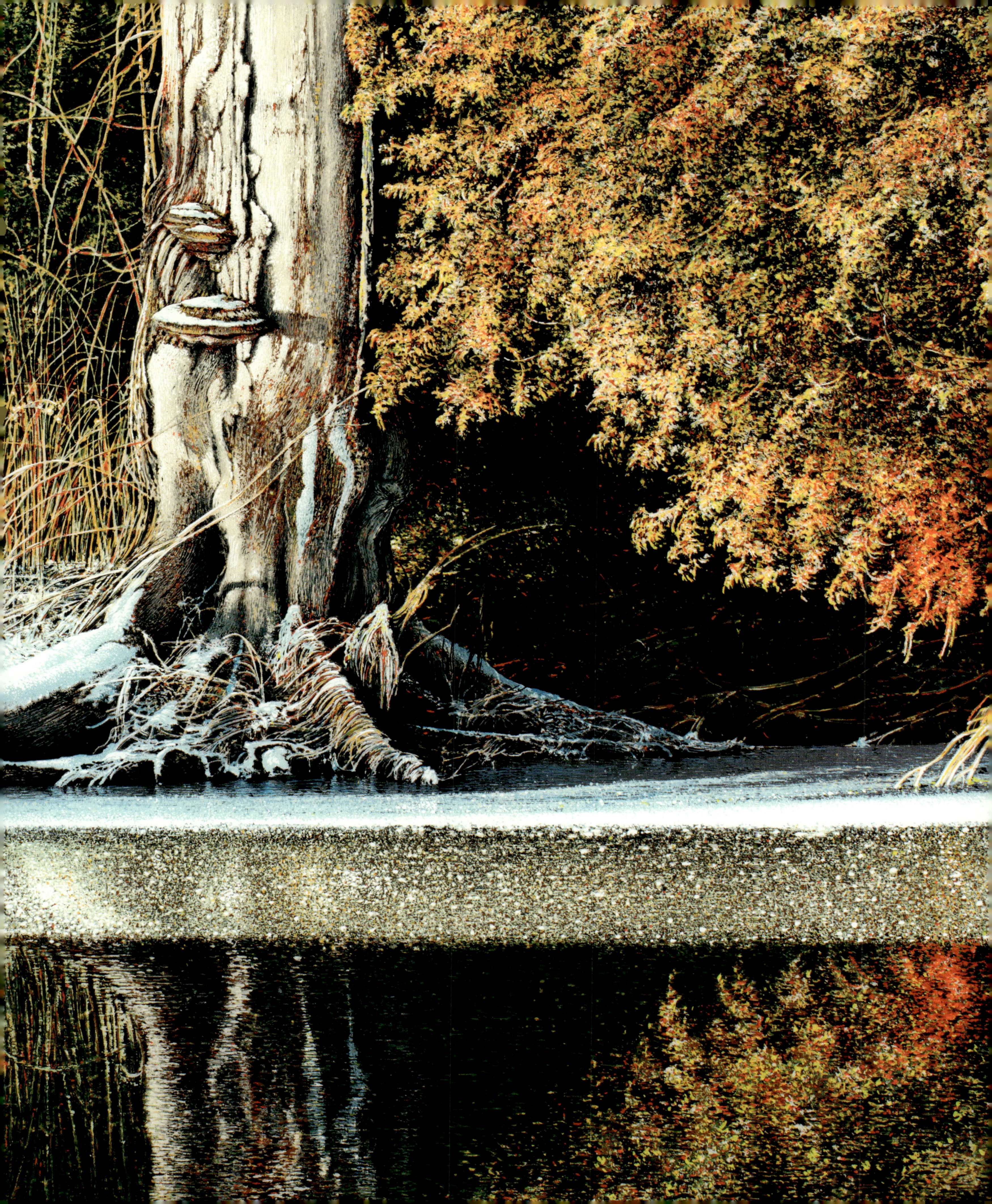

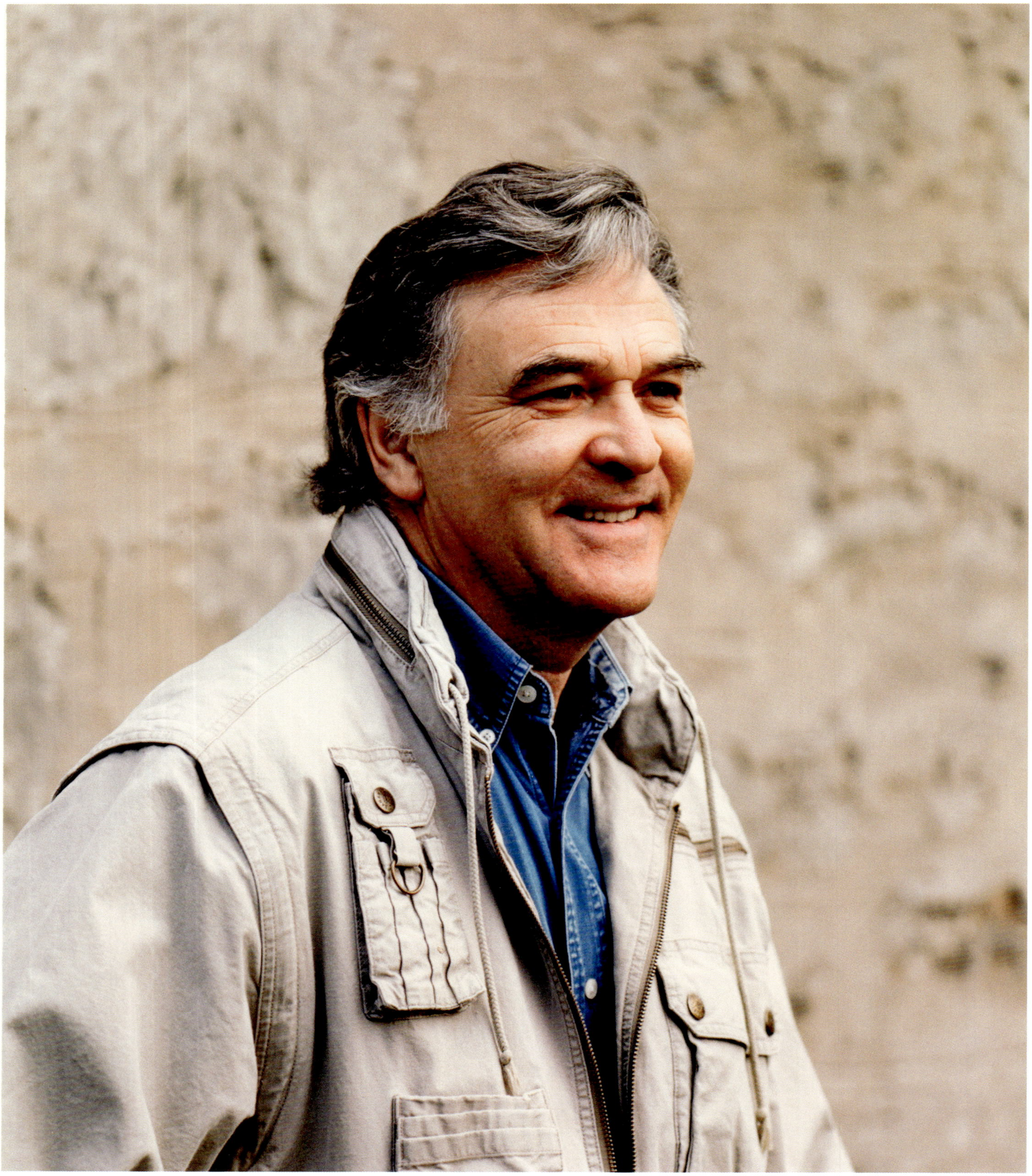

 Ken Danby, 1996
(photo: Lori-Anne McDermid)

Select Chronology

Christine Braun

1940

Kenneth Edison Danby is born in Sault Ste. Marie, Ontario, to Edison Danby and Gertrude Danby (née Buckley). He has a brother Marvin, four years his senior.

1950

Having displayed an early childhood interest and ability in art, ten-year-old Danby wins the prize at Cody Public School's hobby show with a portrait drawing of his father.

1952

Danby graduates grade eight at age twelve and is featured in a local paper with other promising students; he declares that he "will be an artist" (KD:UM, "3/17/08": 1).

1953-1958

Danby attends both Sault Ste. Marie's technical and collegiate high schools with a view to enrol at the Ontario College of Art (OCA), in Toronto, after graduation. He is introduced to the history of art and the work of the Old Masters by teacher Charles Carrington and encouraged to hone his skills in a separate studio room from other students. Considered the "school artist," he creates a large mural for the gymnasium at Sault Tech (KD:UM, "3/17/08": 1).

1958

Danby sells his first work — two small oil paintings to his former grade-seven teacher, Glen McEachern.

1958

Travelling to Toronto to begin first-year studies at OCA, Danby enrols in classes. It is intriguing for him to meet other students and to be introduced to their work. Among the instructors on staff are J.W.G. (Jock) Macdonald, John Alfsen, Fred Hagan, and Eric Freifeld.

1959

Danby returns to OCA for his second year, focusing on drawing and painting. He struggles with the program — given its emphasis on abstraction — while remaining open minded and credits his teachers (especially Macdonald) with instilling in him what author/art historian Paul Duval refers to as "a full appreciation for abstract design and respect for the natural form" (Duval, 1976, 46). While a second-year student he receives a portrait commission, as well as a commission for a wall-relief sculpture for the Wedgewood Lounge in Sault Ste. Marie

1960

April

Danby drops out of OCA at the end of his second year.

Summer

Working at local Sault Ste. Marie television station CJIC as a set designer and painter, Danby is permitted an area to use as an art studio. He is asked to paint a large mural for the space above the Wedgewood Lounge.

November/December

Having returned to live in Toronto in the fall, Danby is employed as a scenic artist for the new CFTO television station in Kleinburg, Ontario, the first colour-television broadcast station in Canada.

1961-63

Throughout this period, Danby is engaged with the local arts and folk music scene and is a regular presence in the Gerrard Street Village, and later Yorkville. "We'd have long philosophical discussions over coffee or playing chess, listen to poetry readings or folk singers, and I could often be found filling my sketchbooks, if on my own" (KD:UM, "3/17/08": 45). He meets Gordon Lightfoot and Ian and Sylvia Tyson, among others, thus beginning what would remain a lifelong interest in music.

1961

March/April

Danby is hired by the Bradshaw packaging company as a designer and artist after having completed a two-week position earlier in the year as a window dresser and designer for women's retailer D'Allairds.

May

Danby begins working as a graphic artist for the *Toronto Telegram*.

November

Danby's first solo exhibition, featuring abstract paintings, is held at the Pollock Gallery in Gerrard Street Village. The show is a success, with half of the works selling.

1962

Danby participates in the second annual Four Seasons Outdoor Art Exhibition (the precursor of the Toronto Outdoor Art Exhibition), and one of his paintings is selected by adjudicator Alan Jarvis (then director of the National Gallery of Canada) to win the purchase prize.

An ardent folk music fan, Danby serves as art director for the Mariposa Folk Festival.

He begins experimenting with a more representative approach to his work. "I knew that this direction was against the grain of what the art world was embracing, but it was a much more comfortable 'fit' for me" (KD:UM "3/17/08": 53).

October

Danby resigns from the *Toronto Telegram* to concentrate on his painting, relying on freelance jobs for income.

November

Returning from a trip to New York City, Danby stops at the Albright-Knox Art Gallery in Buffalo to take in an exhibition devoted to American realist painter Andrew Wyeth. The visit impacts him greatly and bolsters his resolve to continue the creative path he began earlier in the year. "In my mind, he was reinforcing the merits of working realistically and abstractly at the same time" (CM, "3/17/08": 59).

1963

Danby approaches a few commercial galleries with the goal of them exhibiting his work. After a few discouraging attempts, he meets with Walter Moos of Gallery Moos and secures representation. Immediately, Moos purchases a drawing.

Having taught himself how to work with the medium, Danby completes his first egg tempera painting, *Fur and Bricks*.

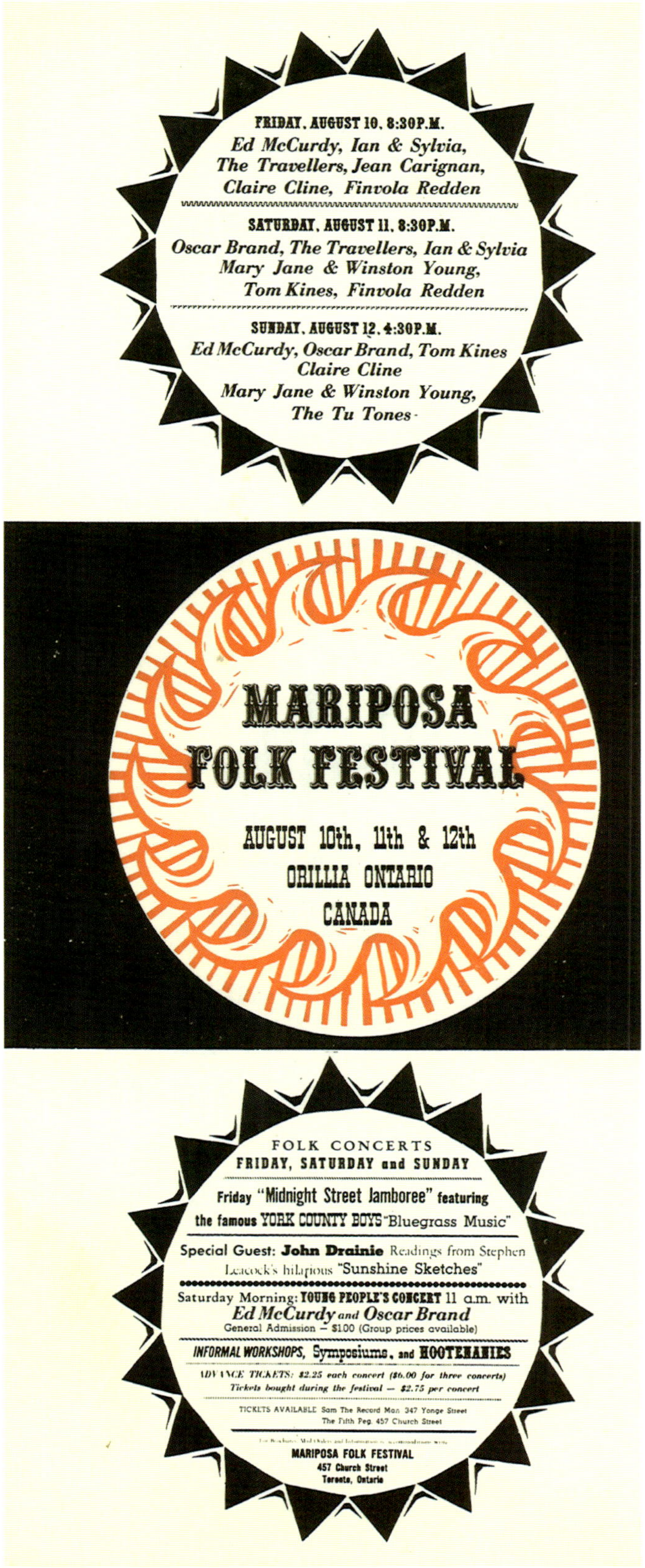

Program pamphlet for the 1962 Mariposa Folk Festival held August 10th, 11th, and 12th in Orillia, Ontario, Canada
(York University Libraries, Clara Thomas Archives and Special Collections, Mariposa Folk Foundation fonds, Accession 2007-009. © Mariposa Folk Foundation)

1964

March

Danby participates in his first exhibition at Gallery Moos — a group show alongside artists Martin Berkovitz and Waltraud Markgraf — to positive reviews.

April/May

Upon seeing *Fur and Bricks*, Moos had submitted it to the Montreal Museum of Fine Arts Annual Spring Show. The work is now chosen by the jury as the best painting in other media and awarded the Jessie Dow Prize (and $250). Along with this honour comes publicity, introducing the artist to a much wider audience. Moos suggests a solo exhibition for Fall 1964.

Summer

Danby travels to St. Joseph Island, near Sault Ste. Marie, and rents a log cabin in which to paint and concentrate on producing work for his upcoming exhibition. Moos supports and funds the endeavour.

November

Danby's solo exhibition at Gallery Moos opens and is very well received, selling out during its brief run.

1965

Grappling with issues around the final application of varnish to his egg tempera works, Danby decides to contact Andrew Wyeth for advice. He travels to the artist's home in Pennsylvania in the hope of meeting him in person. When this is not possible, he has a telephone conversation with Wyeth, who readily provides guidance.

March

Danby marries Judith (Judy) Harcourt on March 20th.

October

Gallery Moos opens the second solo show of Danby's work. It is very well attended and sells out over the course of the exhibition.

December

The Danbys' first son Sean is born on December 15th.

1965-1966

Danby's works are acquired into the permanent collections of both the National Gallery of Canada and the Montreal Museum of Fine Arts.

1966

November

Danby's solo exhibition this year sees half of the inventory sold on the opening evening and the rest sold within days. Included in this show are two paintings that would eventually come to be acquired by the Art Gallery of Hamilton, *The Red Wagon* and *The Rose Bowl*. Danby is featured in *Time* magazine due to the success of the exhibition.

1967

December

Gallery Moos opens what is now Danby's annual solo exhibition. Patrons line up in advance to attend the show, which sells out on opening night.

Danby and his young family move into the Armstrong Mills (built in 1856) near Guelph, a sprawling and picturesque property that he had been interested in for two years. His intent is to renovate the living quarters and construct an ideal studio space for his work.

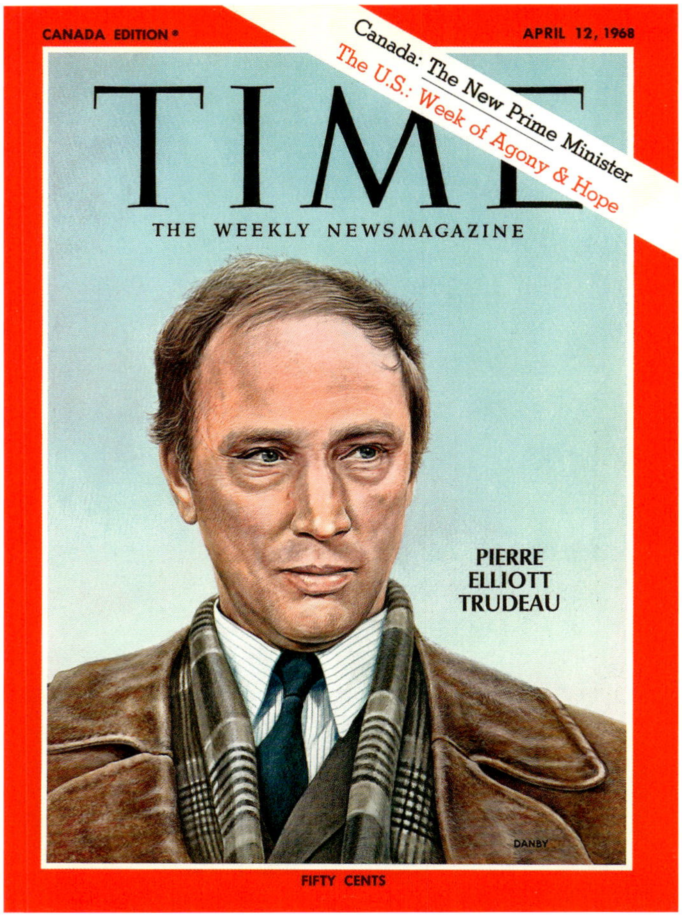

1968

March

Time magazine commissions Danby to create a portrait of Pierre Elliot Trudeau, candidate for prime minister of Canada, for the cover of the April 12 edition of the magazine, in anticipation of Trudeau's election.

July

Danby receives a commission from *Ladies' Home Journal* for four paintings to be used as illustrations.

December

Danby's annual exhibition at Gallery Moos is again popular and the entire inventory sold.

Front cover of the Canadian edition of *Time*, 12 April 1968
(From the pages of TIME. ©1968 Time Inc. Licensed from TIME and published with permission of Time Inc. All rights reserved. TIME and the TIME logo are registered trademarks of Time Inc. used under license.)

1969

December

Danby and Gallery Moos see their most successful collaboration to date with an exhibition that prompts the *Toronto Star* to feature the headline "Lineups like the CNE for Danby Show." The artist recollected that lineups began in the early afternoon (KD:UM, "4/14/08": 95).

1970

Having developed an interest in printmaking, Danby researches different techniques, seeking one that affords him the ability to "create original prints" (KD:UM, "4/14/08": 96). He finds this in serigraphy, or silkscreen printing, and purchases necessary equipment in order to begin his investigations.

March/April

Danby moves into his new studio building on his property. He creates his first thirteen-colour, hand-drawn and -pulled print, *The Wagon,* in an edition of two hundred. The complete edition is sold to Galerie Springer in Germany. They request more, but Danby declares this unfeasible, offering instead to create a new print, *Mill Window,* which is generated in an edition of seventy-five (KD:UM, "4/14/08": 99).

Danby's brother Marvin relocates to the area and becomes his office manager and assistant, thereby allowing Danby to concentrate on his painting.

Rex Bromfield, a filmmaker working with the CBC, shoots the film *The Art of Ken Danby.* The artist proposes music by The Band for the soundtrack (KD:UM, "4/14/08": 101).

December

The annual Gallery Moos exhibition introduces the audience to Danby's serigraphs. Oil, tempera, and watercolour paintings, as well as drawings, are included. The serigraph *Butterbowl* is prominently featured, and Moos displays all twenty-one stages of the print, in order to educate the viewer as to the involved process.

The Danbys' second son Ryan is born on December 12th.

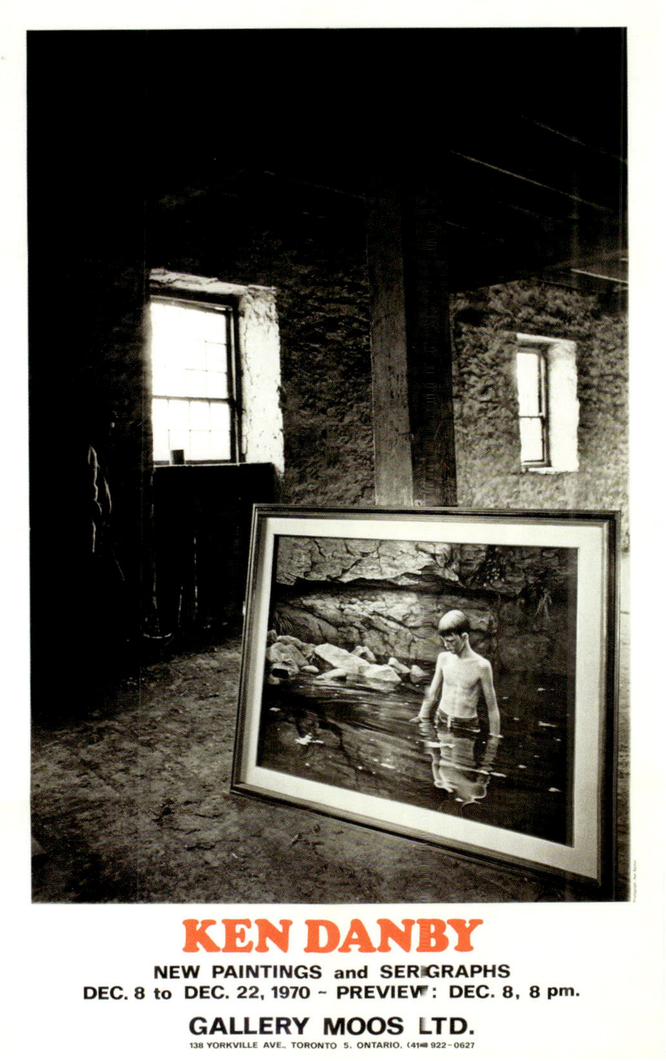

Exhibition poster for the 1970 show at the Gallery Moos
(Art Gallery of Hamilton Archives. © Gallery Moos)

1971

Danby spends a prolific year of great creative output in preparation for his first solo exhibition in New York, planned for early 1972. He is included in the Biennale des Jeunes in Paris, France, and the First International Graphics Mart, in Zurich, Switzerland.

December

The annual Gallery Moos solo exhibition is a success.

1972

The Museum of Modern Art, in New York, adds one of Danby's serigraphs to their permanent collection.

February

Danby's solo exhibition opens at the William Zierler Gallery in New York, the first of his shows in the United States. It features a catalogue with an introduction penned by Mario Amaya, chief curator of the Art Gallery of Ontario, whom Danby had met at the end of 1971. Response, sales, and reviews are positive. Celebrities such as actor Henry Fonda and fashion designer Daniel Hechter are among the purchasers.

March

Danby produces his first work featuring sport as subject, the twenty-two-colour serigraph *The Skates.*

September

An avid hockey fan and player, Danby is enthralled by the famed Canada-Russia hockey series and offers each member of Canada's team a framed and inscribed serigraph of *The Skates* as commemoration. He is adamant that the team receives the gift whether they win or lose (KD:UM, "4/14/08": 111). Thirty-seven prints from the edition of one hundred are gifted.

December

This year's well-attended and sold-out Gallery Moos exhibition features what is arguably Danby's most famous and recognized painting: *At the Crease.* On the day of the opening, a *Globe and Mail* article features an image of the work as the focal point of the exhibition. The painting itself sells to a prominent Toronto collector, even prior to the opening of the exhibition. The overwhelmingly positive response fortifies Danby's position on sport as viable subject matter for art (KD:UM, "4/14/08": 114).

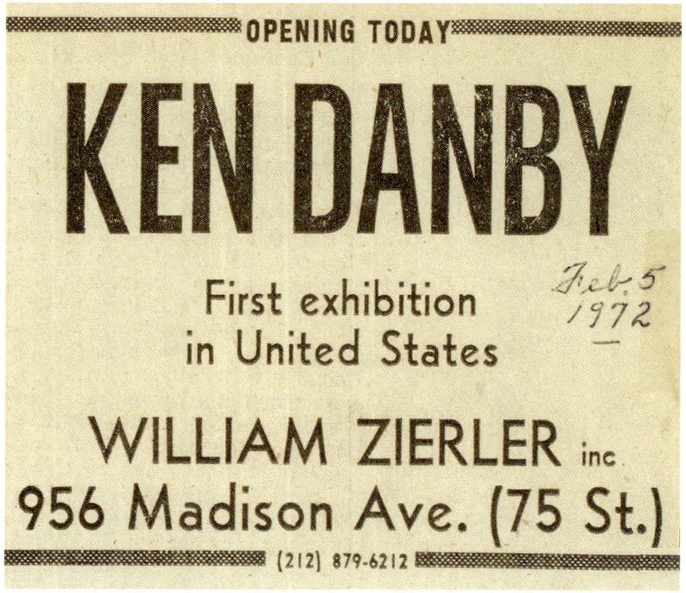

Newspaper advertisement for the opening of the Ken Danby exhibition in New York, 5 February 1972
(Ken Danby Estate)

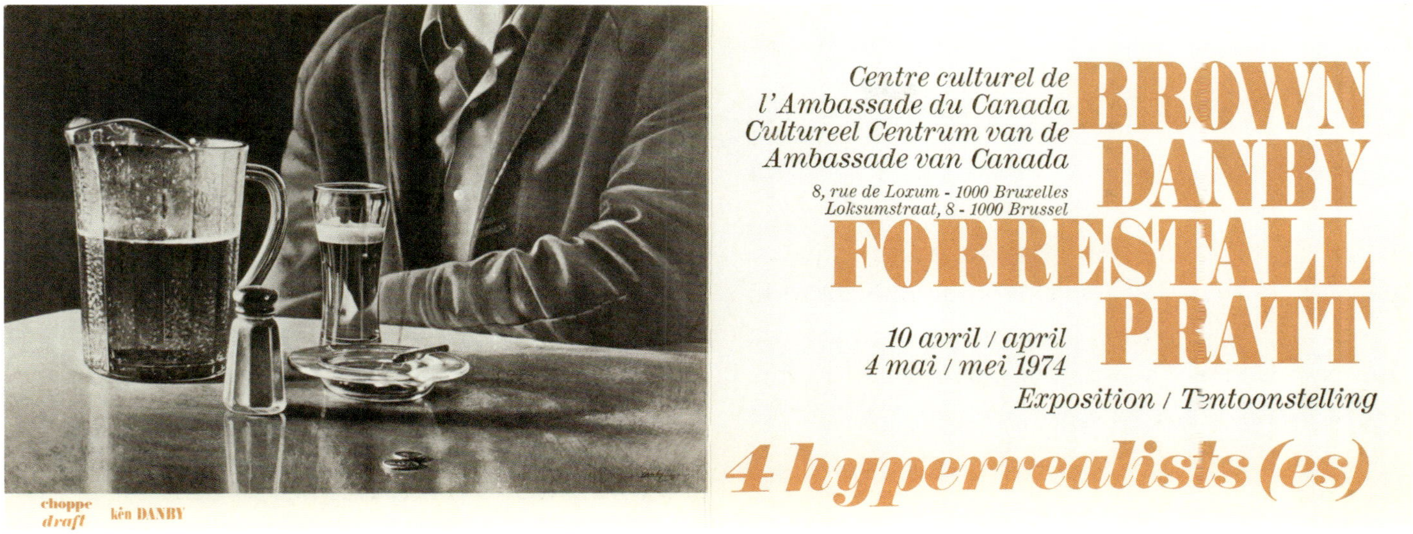

Invitation to the D.P. Brown, Ken Danby, Tom Forrestall, Christopher Pratt exhibition in Brussels, 1974
(Ken Danby Estate)

1973

Spring

Danby is asked to take part in a film produced for West German television, highlighting the careers of Canadian painters Christopher Pratt, Alex Colville, and himself.

December

Danby's second New York solo show takes place at William Zierler Gallery. Due to his commitments for this exhibition, it is the first in many years that he does not hold his annual show at Gallery Moos in Toronto. A highlight is the painting *Pancho*, whose sitter attends the opening to the delight of the attendees (KD:UM, "4/14/08": 121).

1974

Danby is featured in a four-man traveling exhibition, presented by the Department of Canadian Cultural Affairs, on Canadian realism. The show travels to several locations: the Canadian Cultural Centre, Paris; the Canadian Embassy, Brussels; Canada House Gallery, London; the Canadian Consulate, New York. The other artists included are D.P. Brown, Tom Forrestall, and Christopher Pratt.

The Red Wagon is gifted to the permanent collection of the Art Gallery of Hamilton.

April

The Danbys' third son, Noah, is born on April 24th.

October

Danby travels to New York to attend the reception for Paul Duval's publication *High Realism in Canada*, in which Danby is one of the artists showcased.

Larson Industries, manufacturer of the Northland hockey stick, reproduces a watercolour study for *Lacing Up* in an advertising campaign.

December

With the collaboration of Gallery Moos, the Kitchener-Waterloo Art Gallery organizes and opens the traveling exhibition *Ken Danby* (to tour through 1975) that considers the last ten years of the Danby's artistic output. Future venues include Rodman Hall (St. Catharines), the Windsor Art Gallery, and the Art Gallery of Hamilton.

Danby's annual exhibition at Gallery Moos introduces for sale the limited edition of Paul Duval's book *Ken Danby*, which includes an edition of the serigraph *Looking In*. All 250 copies are sold.

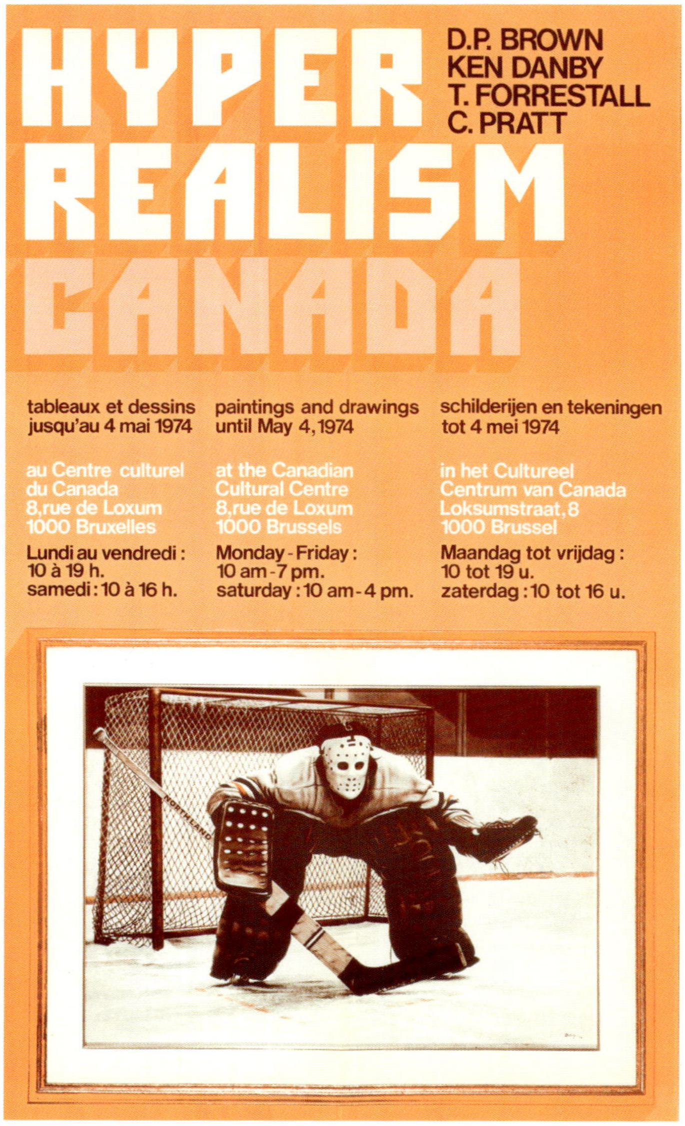

Poster for the D.P. Brown, Ken Danby, Tom Forrestall, Christopher Pratt exhibition in Brussels organised by the Canadian Cultural Centre, Paris, 1974
(Ken Danby Estate)

March

Danby is the inaugural recipient of the R. Tait McKenzie Chair for Sport, an honorary chair sponsored by Labatt Breweries and created by the National Sport and Recreation Centre, in Ottawa.

Spring/Summer

Danby is awarded a commission from the city of Sault Ste. Marie to conceive and execute a painting for its new civic centre. After much research into his subject — a large freighter traveling through the Sault Locks — he completes *Opening the Gates.*

September

Ken Danby, the retrospective exhibition organized by the Kitchener-Waterloo Art Gallery, concludes its tour of southern Ontario in Danby's hometown of Sault Ste. Marie, as part of the Algoma Fall Festival. The recently completed commission is a highlight of the show.

1975

Danby is elected a member of the Royal Canadian Academy of Arts.

January

The *Series III* Olympic coins, for which Danby was awarded the commission, are launched in Toronto in anticipation of the Montreal Summer 1976 Games. His designs for lacrosse and cycling are described on the $10 coins, with rowing and canoeing appearing on the $5 coins.

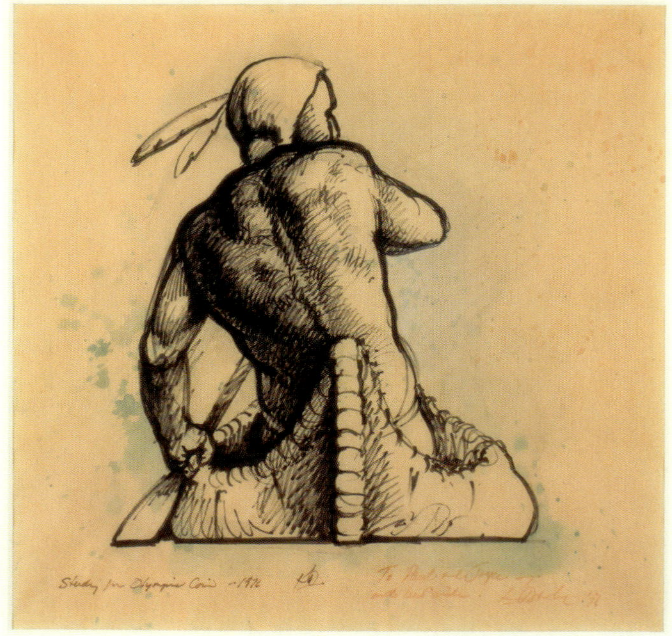

Study for Olympic Coin, 1976

December

Danby's annual Gallery Moos exhibition opens. Due to his exceedingly busy year, only one egg tempera painting is included, alongside many watercolours, drawings, and a lithograph. The response is once again positive (KD:UM, "4/14/08": 147).

1976

March

Gallery Moos previews the six watercolours detailing Olympic sports borne of Danby's association with the National Sport and Recreation Centre. Images depict rowing, diving, cycling, gymnastics, and running.

Spring

Paul Duval's book *Ken Danby* is released to public acclaim, and the artist is occupied with book signings and press events through the remainder of the year, and into the next.

December

This year's Gallery Moos exhibition introduces a set of four limited-edition serigraphs Danby created, inspired by the summer Olympics. The exhibition sells out in two hours (KD:UM, "4/14/08": 164).

1977

Major articles appear on Danby in the *Toronto Sun* and *Maclean's* magazine.

Danby receives the Queen's Silver Jubilee Medal from the governor general of Canada.

Spring

Danby is approached by the Progressive Conservative Party of Ontario to create a portrait of retiring president Alan Eagleson, at the subject's request. This will be Danby's first "multiple portrait," including different views of the same person in an effort to describe the sitter's complexity (Paul Duval, *Ken Danby: The New Decade*, 117).

In honour of its 150th birthday, the City of Guelph enlists Danby to conceive a commemorative work. He uses the historic Guelph carousel as a topic.

Summer

Danby learns that there are plans to demolish the Guelph carousel. He and friends set about campaigning for its safety. Their efforts are successful, and the carousel is refurbished and given a protective enclosure, as designed by Danby (KD:UM, "4/14/08": 172).

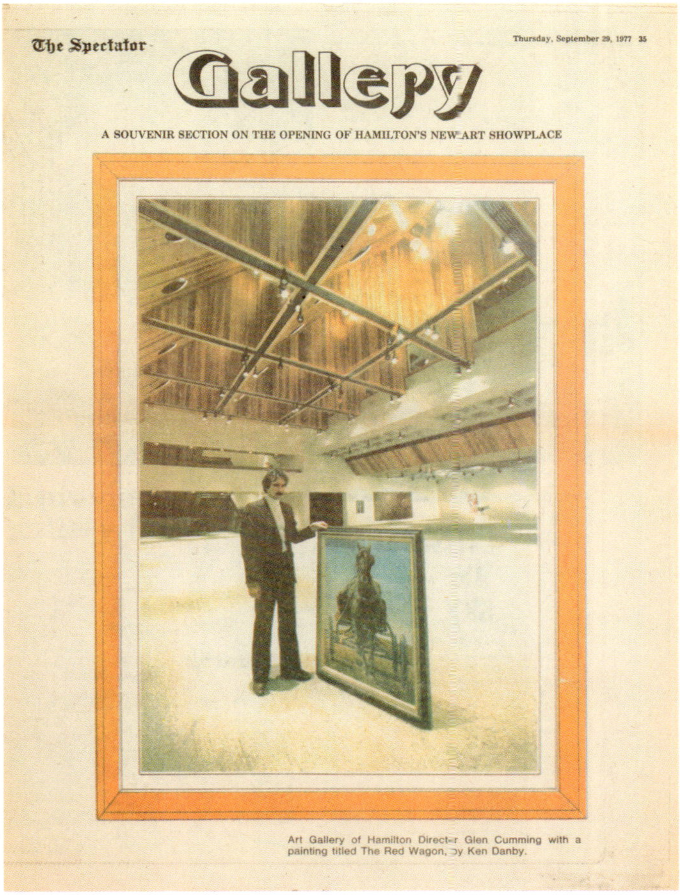
The Spectator
Thursday, September 29, 1977 35
Gallery
A SOUVENIR SECTION ON THE OPENING OF HAMILTON'S NEW ART SHOWPLACE
Art Gallery of Hamilton Director Glen Cumming with a painting titled The Red Wagon, by Ken Danby.

Front cover of the *Hamilton Spectator*'s 1977 special edition commemorating the opening of the new Art Gallery of Hamilton featuring Glen E. Cumming with *The Red Wagon*
(Ken Danby Estate. Reproduced with the permission of the *Hamilton Spectator* and Metroland Media.)

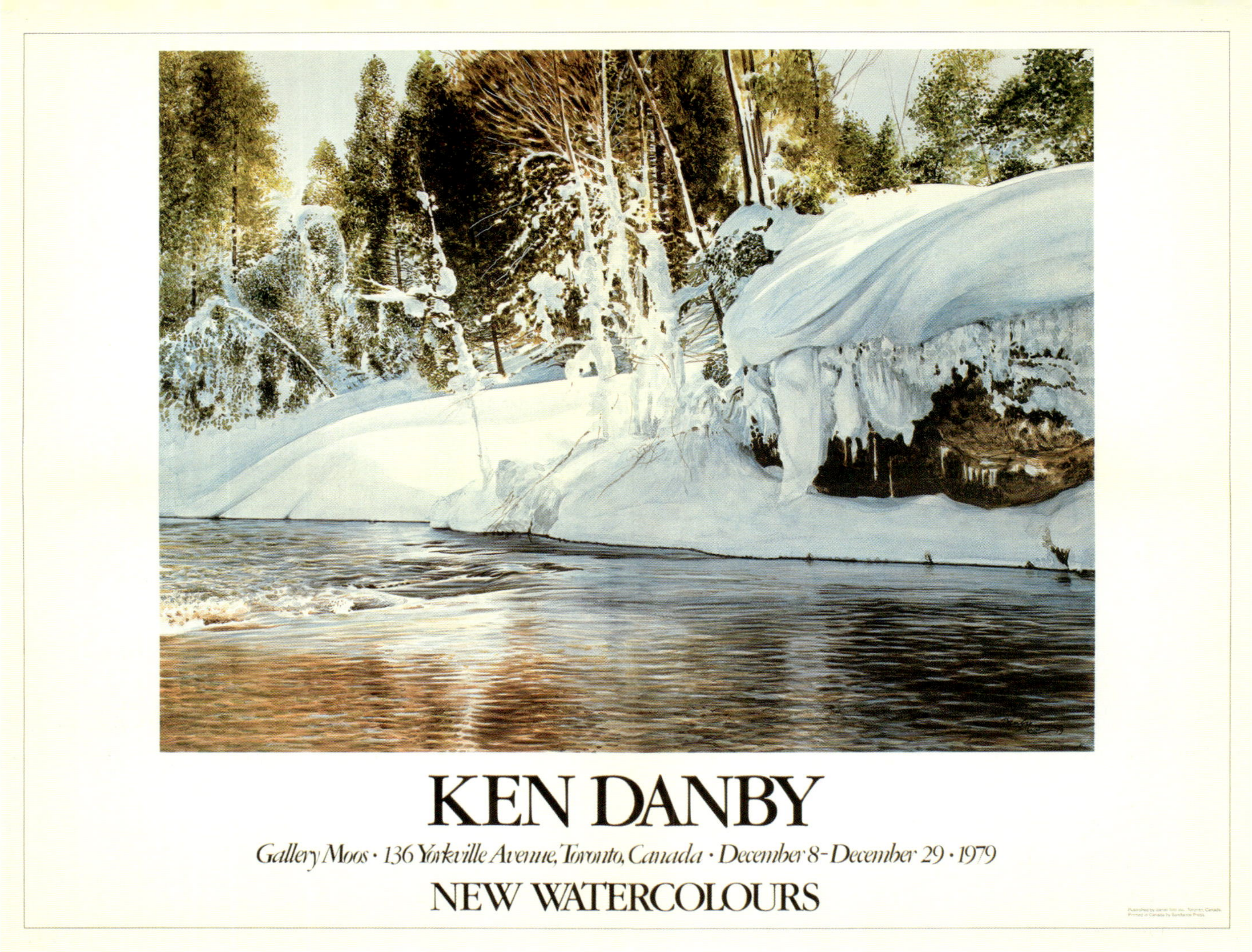

July

Danby is interviewed for the CBC special *Something Ventured*, a portrait of successful Canadians.

September

The Art Gallery of Hamilton features *The Red Wagon*, along with gallery director Glen Cumming, on the cover of a *Hamilton Spectator* supplement, celebrating the opening of the new purpose-built gallery.

October

Danby attends a dinner for "high achievers under 40" in Ottawa with Queen Elizabeth II and Prince Philip, hosted by Prime Minister Trudeau (KD:UM, "4/14/08": 175).

1978

The publication *Danby: Images of Sport* is released, a book accompanied by six prints of the watercolours creating during the artist's time as the R. Tait McKenzie Chair for Sport. The project receives much publicity, and Danby travels to book signings and press events.

December

Danby holds his annual solo exhibition at Gallery Moos.

1979

Danby is commissioned by the Franklin Mint for four colour lithographs. He chooses to depict the four seasons as experienced in Wellington County. These are Danby's first lithographs in colour, and they are released worldwide to public acclaim.

Exhibition poster for the 1979 show of Danby's watercolours at Gallery Moos
(Art Gallery of Hamilton Archives. © Gallery Moos)

Greg McKee is hired as Danby's assistant and studio manager, replacing the artist's brother, Marvin, who had returned to Sault Ste. Marie in 1978.

December

Danby's solo exhibition at Gallery Moos is the first to be comprised of only watercolours, twenty-eight in total.

1980

May

The Art Gallery of Hamilton mounts the exhibition *Ken Danby: The Graphic Work*, a comprehensive show including all of the artist's prints produced to date. It is the first exhibition solely devoted to his printmaking. Included are the progression proofs for the nineteen-colour work *Early Autumn*, with an aim to describe his process. The exhibition travels to seven other venues across Canada.

1981

Danby is commissioned by the National Hockey League to produce a portrait of hockey player Gordie Howe on the occasion of his retirement. He travels to Hartford, Connecticut, to deliver the work and attend the presentation.

The artist paints a multiple portrait of Terry Fox for the permanent collection of Rideau Hall in Ottawa.

Danby is invited to the White House by US president Ronald Reagan.

1982

The Rose Bowl is gifted to the permanent collection of the Art Gallery of Hamilton.

Danby and his wife Judy divorce.

1983

Danby is recruited to create an official portrait of the yacht *Canada 1* from the America's Cup race in Newport, Rhode Island. He travels to Newport to sketch and observe. The final painting is to be reproduced as an official poster as a fundraiser for *Canada 1* and its crew.

He exhibits seventeen watercolour studies at the America's Cup Gallery in Newport.

Danby completes *The Art Dealer*, a portrait of Walter Moos that he began in 1978.

He executes four tempera tondos on the subject of boyhood for Samaco Trading Ltd., producing a set of limited-edition collector plates with the images.

1984

January/February

Danby is enlisted by television network CTV to attend the 1984 Sarajevo Winter Olympics, to create "first hand impressions" of the games (KD:UM, "02/10/02": 3). Danby's first trip to Europe sees him execute fourteen sketches and studies over the twelve-day games, before embarking on personal travel — with an emphasis on gallery visits — to Switzerland, Germany, France, and England.

May

Danby completes a serigraph commission for the Saskatchewan Roughriders, a twenty-four-stage print.

Fall

Paul Duval's second publication devoted to the artist — a follow up to *Ken Danby* — is released. *Ken Danby: The New Decade* sees the artist traveling for book signings and press events.

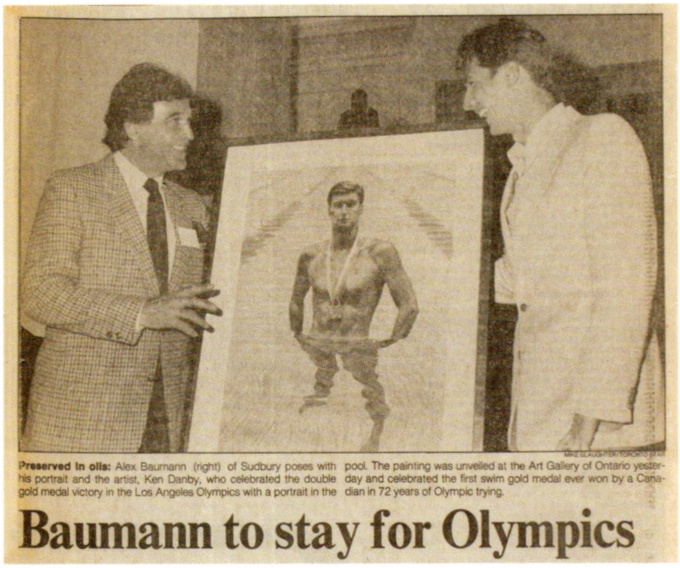

MIKE SLAUGHTER/TORONTO STAR

Preserved in oils: Alex Baumann (right) of Sudbury poses with his portrait and the artist, Ken Danby, who celebrated the double gold medal victory in the Los Angeles Olympics with a portrait in the pool. The painting was unveiled at the Art Gallery of Ontario yesterday and celebrated the first swim gold medal ever won by a Canadian in 72 years of Olympic trying.

Baumann to stay for Olympics

Al Sokol, "Baumann to Stay for Olympics"
Toronto Star, 10 October 1985
(Ken Danby Estate. © 1985 Toronto Star Newspapers Limited. All rights reserved. Used by permission and protected by the Copyright Laws of the United States.)

1985

March

Danby is appointed to the board of directors of the Canada Council for the Arts. He will end up serving two three-year terms.

September

Danby produces a portrait of Canadian swimmer Alex Baumann, as commissioned by the Canadian Egg Marketing Agency and Canadian Amateur Swimming Association, to commemorate the athlete's double gold medal wins from the 1984 Summer Olympics in Los Angeles.

December

Danby's solo exhibition at Gallery Moos features the Baumann portrait.

1986

Danby is commissioned by Barclays Bank to create commemorative medals for the 1988 Winter Olympics. Other commissions this year include work for General Motors and the City of North York, Ontario.

The artist is appointed to the board of directors of the Toronto Arts Awards Foundation.

August

Danby is invited to serve on the board of directors for the new Canadian Centre for Advanced Film Studies by filmmaker Norman Jewison.

The Ian & Sylvia reunion concert takes place at the Kingswood Theatre in Vaughan, with Danby in attendance. The concert includes an appearance by Gordon Lightfoot, which would provide inspiration for later portraits of the musician (CM, "02/20/02": 38).

1987

March

Danby travels to Singapore and Bali and, upon returning home, is inspired to create new work, in particular of Bali (CM, "2/20/02": 40).

April

The Macdonald Stewart Art Centre at the University of Guelph presents a retrospective exhibition of his work, *Ken Danby: A Tribute to 25 years*. This show features work from each year of his output, from 1962 onward.

Spring

Danby designs an inventive easel to assist him in his painting. Adjusting to any size canvas, it telescopes, tilts to various angles, raises, lowers, and affords him the ability to swivel a painting 360 degrees (CM, "02/26/02": 45).

Fall

The artist is commissioned by the Canadian Football League to create a painting in tribute of the seventy-fifth anniversary of the Grey Cup, and attends the championship game.

December

Danby is contacted by Mill Pond Press, a publisher of limited-edition prints and reproductions. He partners with them for four years, producing seven works.

1988

Danby is reappointed to the board of directors of the Canada Council in Ottawa for his second three-year term.

September

Danby marries Gillian Elmitt on September 10th.

1989

After some consideration, Moos and Danby agree to amend their professional relationship. While continuing to represent him, Gallery Moos is no longer the exclusive representative of the artist.

April

Their last collaboration having been in 1985, Moos and Danby open an exhibition of the artist's work at the New York location of Gallery Moos, his third solo New York show.

1990

Danby is commissioned by the Canadian Country Music Hall of Fame for watercolour portraits of select musicians. Among those he depicts are Hank Snow and Ray Griff.

December

Danby is made aware of plans to site a major landfill one mile up the Speed River from his home, at a public information meeting in Fergus, Ontario. Considering the plan a grave danger to the environment, Danby is later prompted to form (with others) the Speed River Preservation Group. Danby devotes much time to the cause; the group's five-year-plus efforts will persuade to Ontario Ministry of the Environment to complete a comprehensive environmental assessment of the proposed site, and ultimately reject it in January of 1996 (CM, "02/25/02": 73).

1991

Danby is selected to serve on the board of trustees of the National Gallery of Canada in Ottawa.

The artist ends his agreement with print publisher Mill Pond Press and signs on with Simon Art Ltd.

1992

Danby is commissioned by the Tim Horton Children's Foundation to create a portrait of Tim Horton. Limited-edition prints and posters are also created to bolster their fundraising efforts.

The artist receives the 125th Anniversary of the Confederation of Canada Medal.

Another commission from the Canadian Diabetes Association results in a watercolour and prints.

1993

Danby receives a number of commissions, producing paintings and prints for Lancaster Financial, Deloitte & Touche, and the Coaching Association of Canada.

He ends his relationship with Simon Art Ltd. and becomes the exclusive publisher of his own works. Moving forward, any images published will be handled by Ken Danby Studios.

1994

Danby is reappointed to the board of trustees of the National Gallery of Canada in Ottawa.

He is commissioned by the CBC to create portraits for the television show *Champions*.

1995

He receives the Award of Merit from his hometown of Sault Ste. Marie.

1996

Having acknowledged the need for a major exhibition of new work, Danby sets about finding a suitable venue for a future show, one over which he would exert complete creative control. He finds this in Toronto's Joseph D. Carrier Art Gallery. Artistically, Danby devotes himself to preparing for this project, scheduled for 1998.

1997

Danby receives an honorary doctorate of fine arts from Algoma University College, Laurentian University.

A retrospective of the artist's watercolours and drawings is held at the Art Gallery of Algoma, in Sault Ste. Marie.

1998

January

Danby is interviewed on the CBC television show *Pamela Wallin Live*.

September

Danby returns to Wallin's show, along with composer Marvin Hamlisch, to discuss the importance of the arts in education.

October

Ken Danby: New Paintings — the artist's first solo exhibition in nine years and first in Canada in thirteen years — opens at the Joseph D. Carrier Art Gallery with ceremony. Some five hundred people attend the ribbon cutting, where Ontario cultural minister Isabel Bassett delivers the opening remarks. Danby sets a sales record for a solo exhibition by a living Canadian artist, and the exhibition is Carrier's most viewed to date, with an audience numbering over ten thousand.

November

The artist is the subject of the CBC series *Life & Times* as *Ken Danby: Behind the Mask* airs.

1999

Danby is the featured artist of the Manitoba Art Expo in Winnipeg. He and Bobby Orr launch a fundraising campaign for the Rainbow Society — a charity for sick children — with limited-edition prints of his portrait of the hockey player.

2000

The Ontario Ministry of Natural Resources enlists Danby as a Champion of the Coast for the Great Lakes Heritage Coast program, dedicated to the protection of the coastline. Among the others involved are astronaut Roberta Bondar and author Pierre Berton. This initiative serves to amplify the artist's interest in the North (CM, "02/26/02": 135).

Danby is nominated for Canada's Walk of Fame in the first ever visual artist category, which would eventually be awarded to Quebec artist Jean-Paul Riopelle.

For the millennium celebration of the Calgary Stampede, Danby is commissioned by Kodak Canada to paint *Trail 2000*. The work is then produced as a limited-edition print for the purpose of fundraising for the Canadian Country Music Hall of Fame.

Danby is commissioned by the CTV television network for a portrait of chairman Douglas Bassett.

Sears Canada commissions Danby to complete a painting to illustrate the cover of its special millennium edition *Wish Book*. He portrays his mill home and family members in *Christmas at the Mill*, and the catalogue is distributed to 4.5 million households.

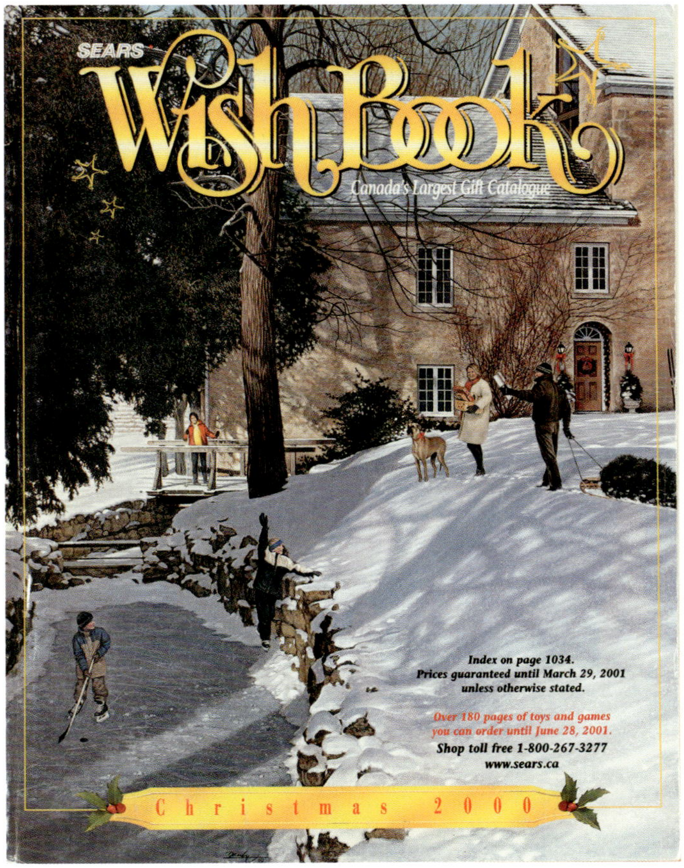

Cover of Sears Christmas 2000 *Wish Book* showing the commissioned painting *Christmas at the Mill*, 2000
(Ken Danby Estate. Used with permission of Sears Canada Inc.)

2001

Danby receives both the Order of Ontario and the Order of Canada, presented to him by the Honourable Hilary M. Weston, lieutenant governor of Ontario, and Her Excellency the Right Honourable Adrienne Clarkson, governor general of Canada, respectively.

May

His portrait of Wayne Gretzky, created in honour of the hockey great's retirement, is unveiled at Gretzky's restaurant in Toronto.

Gallery Moos exhibits the studies for *The Great Farewell* in the exhibition *Ken Danby & 99*.

December

To celebrate its 125th anniversary, the Ontario College of Art and Design hosts an evening with Danby discussing his career with Pamela Wallin.

2002

Danby is awarded the Queen's Golden Jubilee Medal.

October

Danby holds his first New York solo exhibition since 1989 at the Bernarducci Meisel Gallery, titled *Earth, Sky & Water: Recent Landscapes*.

An exhibition held at the Macdonald Stewart Art Centre at the University of Guelph considers the artist's paintings from 1969-2000.

2003

Danby travels to Italy and immerses himself in the work of the Old Masters as well as the countryside.

2004

October

Danby's exhibition *Land, Water & Light: Ken Danby Landscapes* opens at the Joseph D. Carrier Art Gallery in Toronto. It is his largest show to date, contains more than fifty works, and continues his fruitful collaboration with the gallery.

2005

November

Danby opens simultaneous exhibitions in New York at the Bernarducci Meisel Gallery and the Louis K. Meisel Gallery. The collaboration, by way of tandem solo exhibitions, is the first of its kind.

2006

September

The artist's application to trademark his name is approved by the Canadian Intellectual Property Office in the hopes of resolving years of issues related to Internet domain names.

Danby is inducted into the inaugural Sault Ste. Marie Walk of Fame, joining astronaut Roberta Bondar and rock band Treble Charger, among others.

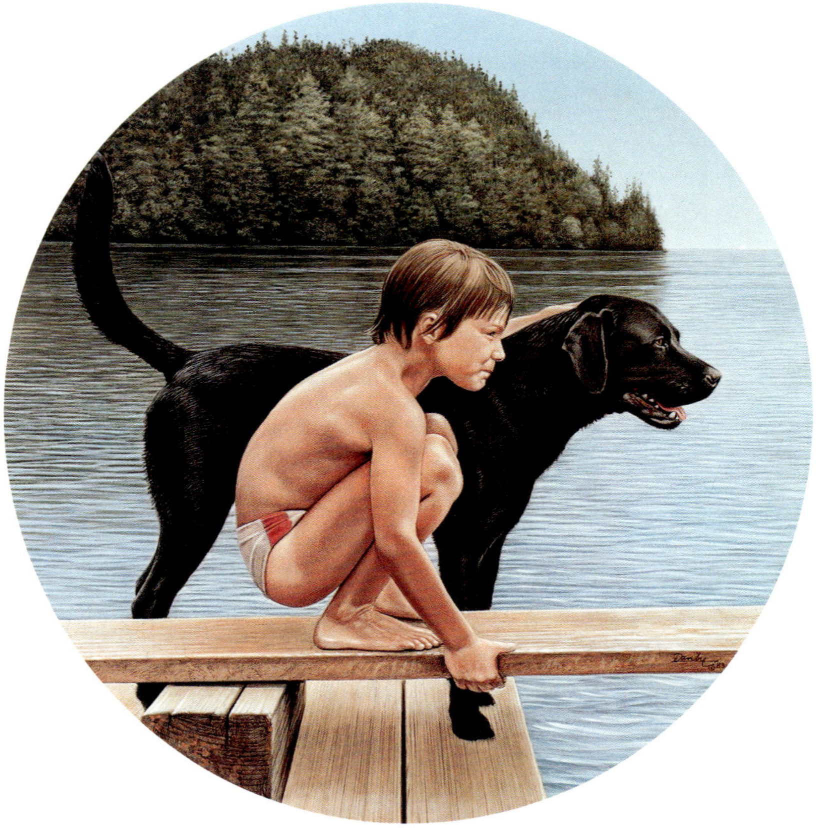

November

Gallery Moos highlights Danby's painting *Free Spirit* at the Toronto International Art Fair. This marks his first appearance at the fair.

2007

July

The Masters Gallery in Calgary holds an exhibition featuring the painting *Stampede*, a work many years in the making, alongside studies for the work.

September

Danby succumbs to a fatal heart attack on September 23rd, having recently departed on a canoe trip with his wife and friends on North Tea Lake, Algonquin Park.

Selected Bibliography

Canadian Cultural Center, Paul Duval, Pierre Boutin, Dan Price Brown, Ken Danby, Thomas Devany Forrestall, and Christopher Pratt. *D.P. Brown, Ken Danby, Tom Forrestall, Christopher Pratt*. Paris: Centre culturel canadien, 1974.

Danby, Ken. Artist File. Art Gallery of Hamilton Archives, Hamilton, Ontario.

Danby, Ken. *Ken Danby: The Graphic Work; Lithographs and Serigraphs*. Hamilton: Art Gallery of Hamilton, 1980.

Danby, Ken. "Ken Danby: Closing the Millennium." Unpublished manuscript, 2002. Danby Estate Archives.

Danby, Ken. Untitled. Unpublished manuscript, 2008. Danby Estate Archives.

Danby, Ken, William Chandler Kirwin, and David Moos. *Ken Danby: New Paintings; October 24-November 24, 1998*. Guelph: Mill Studios Corporation, 1998.

Danby, Ken, William Chandler Kirwin, and Sybille-Karin Moser. *Land, Water & Light: Ken Danby Landscapes*. Guelph: Mill Studios Corporation, 2004.

De Santana, Hubert, and Ken Danby. *Danby, Images of Sport*. Toronto: Amberley House Ltd., 1978.

Duval, Paul. *High Realism in Canada*. Toronto: Clarke, Irwin, 1974.

Duval, Paul. *Ken Danby*. Toronto: Gallery Moos Ltd., 1974.

Duval, Paul. *Ken Danby: The New Decade*. Toronto: Stoddart, 1984.

 The Swimmers, 1983

List of Works

Numbers in bold indicate the page on which works are reproduced

Paintings and Watercolours

6 **Sean**, 1970
watercolour on paper
53.3 x 53.3 cm
Private collection

10-11 **Lake Superior**, 2004
oil on canvas
101.6 x 208.3 cm
Collection of Bruce and Elizabeth Walter

12 **Motel**, 1971
egg tempera on wood
40.6 x 61 cm
Private collection

16 **Study for Pancho**, 1973
watercolour on paper
53.3 x 68.6 cm
Private collection

18 **The Red Wagon**, 1966
egg tempera on panel
106.8 x 81.3 cm
Art Gallery of Hamilton, gift of Frank H. Sherman, in memory of his wife Trixie, 1974

20 **Pulling Out**, 1968
egg tempera on wood
81.3 x 111.8 cm
Location unknown

23 **Leather Hat**, 1975
egg tempera wood
71.1 x 101.6 cm
Private collection

24-25 **From the Summer of '38**, 1966
egg tempera on wood
55.9 x 71.1 cm
Location unknown

26-27 **Charter**, 1978
egg tempera on panel
71 x 106.7 cm
Musée d'art contemporain de Montréal, Lavalin Collection

28 **Untitled (Barbershop)**, 1973
watercolour on paper
52.1 x 67.3 cm
Private collection

43 **The Art Dealer (Walter Moos)**, 1983
egg tempera on board
81.3 x 66 cm
Collection of Martha Moos

44 **Barn Door**, 1967
watercolour and pencil on paper
47 x 66.7 cm
Collection of Dr. Paul and Mrs. Joyce L. Chapnick

45 **Fur and Bricks**, 1963
egg tempera on wood
53.3 x 68.6 cm
Location unknown

46-47 **Early Morning**, 1965
egg tempera on Masonite
55.9 x 91.5 cm
National Gallery of Canada, purchased 1966

49 **Guidepost**, 1965
egg tempera on composite board
50.9 x 60.9 cm
Vancouver Art Gallery, McLean Foundation Fund

50 **Kerosene Lamp**, 1966
egg tempera on composition board
71.2 x 48.4 cm
The Confederation Centre Art Gallery, gift of Aubrey Browne, Moncton, New Brunswick, 1992

51 **The Rose Bowl**, 1966
egg tempera on panel
20 x 28.9 cm
Art Gallery of Hamilton, gift of Mr. and Mrs. Edwin L. Stringer, 1982

51 **The Pickup**, 1967
egg tempera on wood
55.9 x 71.1 cm
Private collection

53 **Untitled (Stone House and Sheds)**, 1967
pencil on paper
46.4 x 89 cm
Collection of Dr. Paul and Mrs. Joyce L. Chapnick

54 **Bleached Yoke**, 1967
egg tempera on wood
35.6 x 50.8 cm
Collection of Dr. Paul and Mrs. Joyce L. Chapnick

54 **The Mill Cat**, 1968
egg tempera on wood
45.5 x 63.5 cm
Location unknown

55 **Towards the Hill**, 1967
egg tempera on wood
61 x 91.4 cm
Location unknown

56 **Pierre Elliot Trudeau**, 1968
(see also page 176)
egg tempera on Masonite
50.8 x 35 cm
National Portrait Gallery, Smithsonian Institution, gift of *Time* magazine

61 **The Armstrong Miller**, 1971
egg tempera on wood
96.5 x 132.1 cm
Private collection

62 **Boom Hook**, 1970
egg tempera on wood
45.7 x 61 cm
Location unknown

64-65 **Blowing Up**, 1971
egg tempera on wood
71.1 x 111.8 cm
Location unknown

66 **Delicious**, 1971
egg tempera on wood
61 x 81.3 cm
Collection of Douglas and Susan Bassett

67 **Study for Snooker**, 1971
pencil on paper
54.7 x 69.8 cm
Ken Danby Estate

67 **Study for Snooker**, 1971
watercolour on paper
46.1 x 69.5 cm
Ken Danby Estate

72 **Study for At the Crease**, 1972
watercolour and pencil on paper
53.3 x 66 cm
Private collection

73 **At the Crease**, 1972
egg tempera on wood
71.1 x 101.6 cm
Private collection

74-75 **Lacing Up**, 1973
egg tempera on wood
55.9 x 81.3 cm
Estate of John F. Bassett

76-77 **Sunbather**, 1972
egg tempera on wood
55.9 x 81.3 cm
Location unknown

79 **Drawing for Pancho**, ca. 1973
felt pen and ink on board
86.4 x 106.7 cm
Collection of Camp Tanamakoon, Algonquin Park

81 **Pancho**, 1973
egg tempera on wood
86. 7 x 106.7 cm
Private collection

84-85 **Opening the Gates**, 1975
egg tempera on wood
71.1 x 97.8 cm
Collection of the City of Sault Ste. Marie

86 **Mannequin**, 1973
egg tempera on wood
66 x 96.5 cm
Rennie Collection

86 **Tethered**, 1976
watercolour on paper
54.3 x 68.6 cm
Collection of Dr. Paul and Mrs. Joyce L. Chapnick

87 **Motorcycle under Stairs**, ca. 1975
felt pen on paper
40.6 x 50.8 cm
Ken Danby Estate

88 **Study for Taxi Window**, 1976
watercolour and pencil on paper
26.7 x 34.3 cm
Collection of Dr. Paul and Mrs. Joyce L. Chapnick

88 **Taxi Window**, 1978
egg tempera on wood
40.6 x 61 cm
Collection of Dr. Paul and Mrs. Joyce L. Chapnick

89 **Great Star**, 1974
egg tempera on wood
54.6 x 80 cm
Private collection

90-91 **Secluded Tailrace**, 1979
watercolour on paper
53.3 x 68.6 cm
Collection of Dr. Paul and Mrs. Joyce L. Chapnick

92 **Trilliums**, 1980
watercolour on paper
35.6 x 50.8 cm
Collection of Douglas and Susan Bassett

93 **Stratford Swans**, 1983
egg tempera on wood
45.7 x 86.4 cm
Collection of Douglas and Susan Bassett

94 **Alex Baumann**, 1985
egg tempera on wood
81.3 x 61 cm
Canada's Sports Hall of Fame

97 **Mask**, 1986-88
oil on linen
101.6 x 152.4 cm
Private collection

99 **Lightfoot: A Study**, 1987
watercolour on paper
68.6 x 53.3 cm
Private collection

100 **Canada 1**, 1983
egg tempera on board
96.5 x 71.1 cm
Private collection

102-3 **Rolling Thunder**, 2002
oil on canvas
81.3 x 167.6 cm
Private collection

106 **Tim Horton**, 1992
oil on canvas
101.6 x 81.3 cm
Collection of Ron Joyce

108-9 **Above Hawkesville**, 1994
oil on canvas
76.2 x 127 cm
Private collection

110 **Completing the Stroke**, 1997
pencil on paper
34.6 x 50.8 cm
Collection of Camp Tanamakoon, Algonquin Park

111 **Cheyne's Walk**, 1996
watercolour on paper
45.7 x 73.7 cm
Collection of John and Velvet Haney

112-13 **Algonquin (in homage to Tom Thomson)**, 1997
oil on canvas
76.2 x 127 cm
Private collection

115 **Face Off**, 1997
egg tempera on canvas
71.1 x 106.7 cm
Location unknown

118 **Gretzky Head Study**, 1999
watercolour and pencil on paper
35.6 x 26.7 cm
Ken Danby Estate

120-21 **Kissing Bridge**, 1996
watercolour on paper
59.1 x 93.3 cm
Ken Danby Estate

123 **Stampede**, 2006
acrylic on canvas
91.4 x 243.8 cm
Ken Danby Estate

126-27 **Trail 2000**, 2000
acryllic on canvas
76.2 x 152.4 cm
Collection of Craig and Patricia Stewart

130-31 **Island Reach**, 2003
oil on canvas
76.2 x 106.7 cm
Collection of Bruce and Elizabeth Walter

132 **Boy on Fence**, 1965
egg tempera on wood
91.4 x 71.1 cm
Location unknown

151 **Reflections**, 1970
egg tempera on wood
96.5 x 132.1 cm
Location unknown

165 **Study for Carousel**, ca. 1975
felt pen on paper
40.6 x 50.8 cm
Ken Danby Estate

180 **Study for Olympic Coin**, 1976
ink and felt pen on paper
35.6 x 35.6 cm
Collection of Dr. Paul and Mrs. Joyce L. Chapnick

188 **The Swimmers**, 1983
egg tempera on panel
40.6 cm diameter
Private collection

Lithographs

17 **The Suncatcher**, 1983
lithograph
58.4 x 45.7 cm
edition of 100

17 **The Cyclist**, 1967
lithograph
58.4 x 45.7 cm
edition of 50

134 **Letting Go (Boy on Fence)**, 1965
lithograph
58.4 x 45.7 cm
edition of 50

144 **The Motorcyclist (Heading Out)**, 1968
lithograph
58.4 x 45.7 cm
edition of 50

144 **The Dreamer**, 1972
lithograph
58.4 x 45.7 cm
edition of 100

150 **The Swimmer**, 1970
lithograph
58.4 x 45.7 cm
edition of 75

155 **The Goalie**, 1972
lithograph
45.7 x 58.4 cm
edition of 100

156 **Aquarius**, 1979
lithograph
58.4 x 45.7 cm
edition of 100

168 **Looking Off**, 1968
lithograph
45.7 x 58.4 cm
edition of 50

Serigraphs

63 **Mill Wheel**, 1971
serigraph
eleven colours
38.1 x 50.8 cm
edition of 100

70 **The Skates**, 1972
serigraph
twenty-two colours
45.7 x 61 cm
edition of 100

136-37 **The Wagon**, 1970
serigraph
thirteen colours
31.8 x 42.4
edition of 180

138 **On the Gate**, 1971
serigraph
seventeen colours
45.7 x 61 cm
edition of 100

138 **Early Autumn**, 1971
serigraph
nineteen colours
45.7 x 61 cm
edition of 100

140-41 **Sunning**, 1974
serigraph
twenty-nine colours
63.5 x 86.4 cm
edition of 100

142 **Under the Arch**, 1972
serigraph
seventeen colours
45.7 x 61 cm
edition of 100

143 **True North**, 1998
serigraph
thirty colours
45.7 x 61 cm
edition of 100

147 **Butterbowl**, 1970
serigraph
twenty-one colours
45.7 x 61 cm
edition of 75

158 **Mill Window**, 1970
serigraph
eleven colours
31.8 x 42.4
edition of 75

163 **The Diver**, 1976
serigraph
five colours
40.6 x 45.7 cm
edition of 150

163 **The Hurdler**, 1976
serigraph
five colours
40.6 x 45.7 cm
edition of 150

163 **The Sculler**, 1976
serigraph
five colours
40.6 x 45.7 cm
edition of 150

163 **The Vaulter**, 1976
serigraph
five colours
40.6 x 45.7 cm
edition of 150

166 **White Stallion**, 1978
serigraph
thirty-two colours
45.7 x 61 cm
edition of 100

169 **Looking In**, 1974
serigraph
twenty colours
29.8 x 29.8 cm
edition of 250

170-71 **December Morning**, 1981
serigraph
twenty-seven colours
45.7 x 61 cm
edition of 100

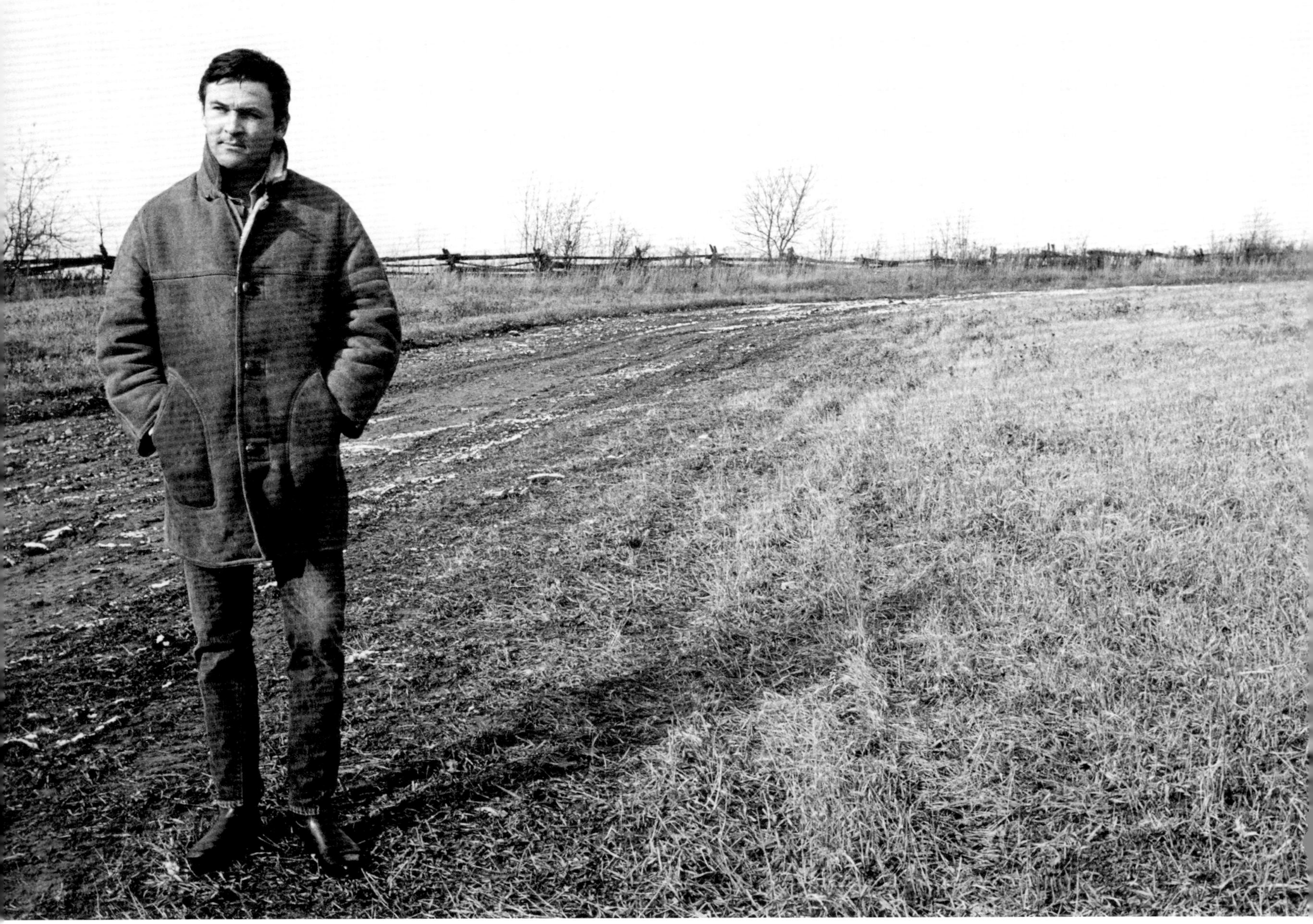

Ken at the mill property, 1968
(photo: John Reeves)

Index

Page numbers in bold indicate reproductions of works

Copyright © 2016 by the Art Gallery of Hamilton.
Art works copyright © 2016 by the Ken Danby Estate.

All rights reserved. No part of this work may be reproduced or used in any form or by any means, electronic or mechanical, including photocopying, recording, or any retrieval system, without the prior written permission of the publishers or a licence from the Canadian Copyright Licensing Agency (Access Copyright). To contact Access Copyright, visit www.accesscopyright.ca or call 1-800-893-5777.

The publishers have made every effort to trace and contact copyright holders of the works reproduced in the book. Errors or omissions that are brought to their attention will be corrected in subsequent editions.

Edited by Catherine van Baren.
Cover and page design by Julie Scriver.
Cover image: Ken Danby, *At the Crease*, 1972, egg tempera on wood, 71.1 x 101.6 cm, Private collection.

Works photographed by Robert McNair, except pp. 18, 97, 73, 99 by Mike Lalich; pp. 26-27 by Richard-Max Tremblay; pp. 46-47 by National Gallery of Canada; p. 49 by Trevor Mills, Vancouver Art Gallery; p. 50 by Paige Matthie; p. 56 by National Portrait Gallery, Smithsonian Institution/Art Resource, NY; pp. 84-85 by Ali Pearson; pp. 94, 112-13, 126-27 by John Dean; p. 118 by Dean Palmer; and pp. 132, 136-37, 144, 166, 168 by Ken Danby Estate.

Printed in Canada.
10 9 8 7 6 5 4 3 2 1

Library and Archives Canada Cataloguing in Publication

Ken Danby : beyond the crease / with essays by Ihor Holubizky and Greg McKee.

Includes index.
Catalogue of an exhibition held at the Art Gallery of Hamilton from October 22, 2016 to January 15, 2017.
Co-published by the Art Gallery of Hamilton.
ISBN 978-0-86492-963-1 (hardback)

1. Danby, Ken, 1940-2007--Exhibitions. I. Holubizky, Ihor, 1952-, writer of added commentary II. McKee, Greg, 1955-, writer of added commentary III. Danby, Ken, 1940-2007. Paintings. Selections. IV. Art Gallery of Hamilton, issuing body V. Title: Beyond the crease.

ND249.D34A4 2016 759.11 C2016-902451-2

The publishers acknowledge the generous support of the Government of Canada, the Canada Council for the Arts, the Ontario Arts Council, the City of Hamilton, and the Government of New Brunswick.

Goose Lane Editions
500 Beaverbrook Court, Suite 330
Fredericton, New Brunswick
CANADA E3B 5X4
www.gooselane.com

Art Gallery of Hamilton
123 King St. W.
Hamilton, Ontario
CANADA L8P 4S8
www.artgalleryofhamilton.com